# Ministry & Mission

## Theological Reflections
## for the Life of the Church

Edited by
Barbara Brown Taylor

Post
Horn
Press
INC.

ATLANTA          GEORGIA

Sale of this book benefits the
James F. Hopewell Scholarship Fund
Candler School of Theology
Emory University

The articles in this book originally
appeared in *Ministry & Mission*, a
quarterly publication of the Candler
School of Theology, Emory University,
and are published here by permission
of the school.

**POST HORN PRESS, INC.**
P.O. Box 98172
Atlanta, Georgia 30359
(404) 633 • 5620

90 89 88 87 86      5 4 3 2 1

ISBN 0-935311-00-9

TO

James Franklin Hopewell

1929-1984

All mankind is of one Author, and is one volume; when one man dies, one chapter is not torne out of the book, but translated into a better language; and every chapter must be so translated; God employs several translators; some pieces are translated by age, some by sickness, some by war, some by justice; but God's hand is in every translation; and his hand shall bind up all our scattered leaves again, for that Library where every book shall lie open to one another.

John Donne
"Meditation XVII"
*Devotions Upon Emergent Occasions*

# Contents

## III. Congregational Life

## V. The Ordained Life

# Foreword

Ten years ago our colleague Jim Hopewell proposed that Candler School of Theology at Emory University inaugurate a new publication—one that would speak thoughtfully to the interests and needs of local pastors and their congregations. Its purpose would not be to advance the parochial interests of the institution, neither school nor church, but to stimulate the renewal and integrity of both.

It is the juxtaposition of reflective teaching and fervent discipleship that has motivated and informed *Ministry & Mission* from its inception. Of course these are never neatly separate realms, and enlightened discipleship and informed teaching characterize both church and seminary. Indeed, it is from the interaction of the two that a clear, reflective consciousness about religion, faith, and discipleship emerges.

Theological faculty are sometimes viewed with a measure of suspicion in the ordinary life of the church. Yet the faculty I have known, and others who write for this publication, are by every measure faithful and articulate proponents of Christian faith. Their creativity presses them to a fresh and relevant expression of what Christian faith means for our time. Their scholarship probes the rich subtleties of the gospel and church life, subtleties which make impossible a simplistic approach to the life of faith that would keep us from savoring the meaning of the gospel.

*Ministry & Mission* has attempted to provide a forum where religious meaning and consciousness would be addressed from new perspectives—and more important, from a base that appreciates rigorous scholarship and attempts to integrate that scholarship into active concerns of church life. Whatever the issue—and we have attempted to address a wide spectrum of issues confronting the church, including some we ourselves have proposed—the effort has been to bring the best of current theological scholarship to the concrete concerns of the church.

Ultimately the church must give voice to its life in mission. Whatever its identity or self-understanding, if it does not find itself in active, intelligent, and articulate advocacy of the gospel it professes, the church has no consequence. Through these articles, and in its continuing publication, *Ministry & Mission* seeks to identify with the activism, the evangelistic passion, the intellectual excitement of a church confidently speaking to a society such as ours.

The future of the church and its ministry is infinitely more complex and ambiguous than at any time in the past. Yet the fruits of scholarship and the industry of those committed to its causes are unstinting. This volume offers a view of that future as well as commentary on the present.

Perhaps at no time since the era of the early Christian communities has the future of faith and its potential impact on the world's people been so urgent or so prospective. May the reflections which follow entice you to that future.

Jim L. Waits, Dean
Candler School of Theology
Emory University

# I
# *Living the Gospel*

## We Have This Ministry

JAMES F. HOPEWELL

Don's voice boomed over the phone early Saturday morning. Don keeps me jumping; he's a salesman and member of the congregation I pastor. "Jim, I want you to have breakfast here with a poor old couple I met up in Tennessee yesterday. They're at the end of their rope; they've lost their home, their savings, and their hopes. We're helping them as best we can, but I need you to tell them how God really loves them, which they doubt."

Our talk the next hour seemed the standard fare we share with despairing people. The couple left Don's home, refreshed by its hospitality but probably not impressed by my words. The significant ministry in this case was that of Don's and his wife's, not mine, but Don had nonetheless looked to me to serve up what many find the main dish of learned ministry: the explanation of suffering and hard times.

When you and I went to seminary we hoped to find that explanation. While not intending to become deep scholars, we nevertheless dug for knowledge that would bare the significance of suffering. We needed to become philosophers of crisis, we felt, because in supplying the explanation for a personal or public disaster we would not only meet a human need but also defend our Christian God.

Meanings, however, proved trite. Do you remember our early panic at having no answer yet having to call on a grieving family? Like peddlers we would offer assorted explanations, even praying some of these to God. But none of our answers cut as deep as did the sorrow they addressed. Through hard ministry we learned that suffering and the gospel were in-

1

dissoluble. Neither dissolved into the other. Suffering did not fade, upon analysis, into good news; it still hurt. Nor did the gospel vanish into sorrow. A gospel ministry, we learned, dealt more with the realities of suffering and redemption than with their explanation.

We now realize that learning did not make us answerers so much as connectors. Our study of the Bible gave us links, not solutions; it gave us the strong ties between present sorrow and the sufferings of Israel in bondage, of Job, Paul, and Jesus Christ. Scriptural insight, moreover, prevents us from being mere announcers of that connection. The manner of ministry in crisis is neither to explain nor to remind, but to comfort. Threading through the writings of the Prophets, Paul, and the Gospels, this masterful concept of comfort—*paraklesis*—dominates what ministers do with sufferers. To comfort means to connect oneself with the sufferer and to strengthen through shared word and act.

To the disconsolate and downtrodden Christ provided himself rather than a secret. A gospel ministry cannot do otherwise.

*November 1976*

# A Small Child's Grief

## A. BOB DIXON

Kirk had answered the phone when the unfamiliar voice of a man had asked to speak to his mother. That look on his mother's face—there had been an accident—dead—that was the word that kept pounding in seven-year-old Kirk's ear—dead—his father was dead.

Now the house was full of people. Some he knew, loved; others were strangers with long faces. Things had been brought, mostly food, and there were flowers. Their sweet smell made him sick. He was hungry, very hungry, because he had not eaten since hearing that word. He wanted to eat but felt that it must be wrong to eat at a time like this.

Kirk wandered from room to room wondering what he was supposed to do. Why didn't someone tell him what he should do instead of just looking at him with sad smiles and patting him on the head, which he hated? Grandma had told him to be brave for his mother. What did that mean?

He slammed the door to his room and fell across the bed. He thought about his dad, and about himself, and about his hurt. He did not want to hurt; it made him angry. Tears came, and pain. His head hurt, everything hurt. Sitting up quickly he cried out "Why?"

Grabbing the pillow he began to hit anything near, but wished there were someone to hit. He hurt. He felt alone. He needed his dad and he could never have him again. He wanted someone, mother, but he had to be brave for her.

Kirk cried not just tears of grief, sorrow, and loneliness for his father, but tears of anger, bitterness, rage, frustration. He secretly hoped that somehow he could hurt those who had not told him what he was supposed to do; he was lost, and all they told him was to "be brave."

In another house in another city, Cindy knew something was happening. It was frightening; their house didn't feel the same. First it was silent, then filled with angry words. Mother and Daddy seemed to hate each other. Cindy's stomach hurt when the house didn't feel right.

So when they told her that Daddy was going to live somewhere else, Cindy thought she knew what it meant, but she wasn't sure. Was that what divorce meant? She heard her mother use the word when talking to Aunt Sue on the phone.

Cindy was sitting at the window, looking for Daddy. Five-thirty; he should be coming home from work, but Mother said he would not be coming except for Saturdays. Saturdays would be the only days that Daddy would see her now because he wasn't living with them. "Why?" thought Cindy. "Why did Daddy leave me? Doesn't he love me anymore? Why did he and Mommy get mad? Did I make them unhappy?"

Kirk and Cindy are both experiencing grief: keen mental suffering over a loss. Children are experienced in losing many things which they value. A playmate moves away, a toy is broken, a pet disappears, they lose mother to the new baby. As soon as children begin to find balance and ways to gratify themselves, they also begin to run into life situations which upset their fragile balance. Loss occurs and thus grief.

Most children seem to handle grief in a natural way: they cry, they yell with pain and suffer without any pretense, for most children are not ashamed of their feelings. But then they begin to confront the platitudes of the adult world, which tells them to be brave, or, by ignoring them, that their feelings are not important. The stress and pain of their loss seems to have no meaning. Many people have accepted the fact that adults cannot live without meaning. But what of the children?

A child's grief is complicated. He feels remorse for the loss that the loved one is dead, that the parents have separated. At the same time he feels sorry for himself because he was chosen for personal hurt. The child faces many problems about which he feels helplessly confused. The adult who can understand that a variety of reactions may occur is well on the way to helping the child towards a positive approach in dealing with loss.

The research of Dr. John Bowlby of Tavistock Clinic in London has shown that children most often experience three phases in a natural grieving process. First, they cannot believe that the person is dead and may attempt to regain him or her. Secondly, they experience pain, despair, and disorganization when they accept that the loved one is really gone. The third phase is one of hope, when the child begins to organize his or her life without the lost person.

To allow these normal phases to develop takes recognition that the child is a human being who does experience loss and who needs to communicate feelings, questions, and sorrow. This requires talking *with* and not *to* children. We must tell them things which are both rational and helpful.

The following statements concerning death are not rational and give children misconceptions and fears:

*Daddy has gone on a long trip.* This is an untruth which must later be unlearned.

*Mother is now up in heaven.* Conflicts with the fact that the child knows mother is buried in the ground.

*Grandaddy died because he was sick.* May produce worry when the child becomes ill.

*God took Timmy away because He needed someone good and sweet like him in heaven.* This reasoning may cause the child to wonder about being good if God rewards such behavior with death.

*Grandmother has gone to sleep, a long sleep.* Unless death and sleep are explained there could develop a fear of bedtime.

*Be brave. Don't cry.* Why not cry? Tears are the most beautiful and natural tribute to pay for a lost one. Unexpressed grief may later find release in a more serious reaction.

*Don't play; we must be sad because Grandmother died.* To force a child to display unfelt sorrow may well block his natural outlets for grief.

It is perhaps easier for adults to respond to a child in times of grief with fiction and half-truths for it makes us appear to know all the answers. We as individuals and as a society have not been able to come to terms with death. But the secure adult is one who has no need to profess infinite wisdom. It may be healthier for a child to share a joint quest for additional wisdom than for immediate hurt or curiosity to be appeased by fantasy that is passed off as fact.

The child may be surprised that there is something parents do not know. Perhaps the most growing experience for a child and an adult would be to admit a mutual lack of understanding of this mysterious area of life.

One of the most beautiful dialogues between an adult and child concerning death is found in the little book *A Taste of Blackberries* by Doris Buchanan Smith (New York: Thomas Y. Crowell). Written for children, the book tells the experience of a boy whose playmate had died from an acute allergic reaction to a bee sting. Feeling all alone and helpless, the boy walks into Mrs. Mullin's garden, the most private place he knows. Mrs. Mullin watches from her kitchen window and after allowing him a time to be alone, she goes to talk with the boy.

> "You know 'bout Jamie?"
> "Yes, I'm so sorry about Jamie. And sorry about you, too, because you were his friend."
> "Why did he have to die?"

"Honey, one of the hardest things we have to learn is that some questions do not have answers."

The boy thought that this made more sense than if she tried to tell him some stuff about God needing angels. "What's it like to be dead? Or is that another of those questions?"

"You just don't know until you find out yourself and apparently you can't come back and tell what you find out."

"Jamie was special."

"I know." Mrs. Mullin stood up and left but the boy knew that she meant for him to stay as long as he wanted.

When an honest and open adult relationship such as this is encountered by a child facing grief, it enables him to move from hurt and pain to meaning. In such a relationship the adult and child may mutually work through many of the questions which come with grief.

One who wishes to help the child who has lost a loved one must understand the youngster's emotional needs. This is accomplished by empathy, understanding, and love. Love contributes to the child's security and gives him the feeling of being valued. Is this not a gift of God?

To be valued is to know that one is a child of God. This knowledge brings meaning to life and death, joy and grief. We reap it from the depth of our understanding and the genuineness of our own love. The child who is understood and loved can give understanding and love now and throughout life.

*September 1977*


# Hospital Calling from a Patient's Perspective

## JOHN ERIK ANDURI

There is no greater opportunity for you who minister to relate meaningfully to your congregation than in your visitation with the ill. In the pulpit, you are speaking to that sea of humanity called a congregation, in which I am one fish among many receiving fleeting glimpses of eye contact with you. In the hospital it is just you and me, both on foreign turf, confronting the reality of my pain.

This brief reflection comes from one who has worn three hats in relation to this discussion: now a doctoral student in the theology and personality program at Emory University, I was for one year coordinator for patient services for the Colorado Division of the American Cancer Society; and, most significantly, I have undergone two major surgeries and months of living around a hospital for radiation therapy and chemotherapy treatments for Hodgkin's disease, cancer of the lymphatic system. Speaking primarily from my own experience of dis-ease, I would like to reflect on what a pastor might offer to a person grappling in a hospital setting with serious illness.

But first, let me share three memories that have guided my remarks.

1) In a divinity school course at the University of Chicago, twelve ministry and theological studies students wrote five-page reflections on a personal experience of suffering and how we dealt with it. Although our traumas varied considerably, as did our responses to them, our professor was astonished to report a striking common denominator in all of our papers: in reaching out for a support system, not one of us mentioned seeking or receiving help from a clergyperson.

2) While planning an American Cancer Society-sponsored program for clergy in Denver, an oncologist mused: "In over twenty years of practice, never once have I had a minister inquire about any of my patients."

3) Late one night I visited a theologian-pastor friend who was recuperating from minor surgery. He was tired, perhaps more from his round of visitors and well-wishers than from the surgery itself. "Today I've been visited by what seemed to be half of the seminary faculty," he reflected somewhat quizzically, "and not one of my colleagues offered to say a prayer with me."

With those incidents by way of introduction, then, let me speak to you from the patient's perspective.

**Bedside Manner.** I don't remember many of your sermons from five years ago, but I'll always appreciate the time you telephoned my hospital room, and when I told you some cranberry juice would sure taste good, you came up that night after your full day and brought three quarts of it. No doubt our cranberry juice jokes ever since have helped keep the memory alive, a pleasant one.

Don't be afraid to touch me, especially if I'm too tired, weak, or uncomfortable to communicate with words. Most people who touch me in the hospital cause some form of inconvenience, discomfort, or pain. Remind me that touch is also an expression of affection and love. It's easy to feel as if I have some form of leprosy. Remind me that I don't. Affirm for me the worth and dignity of my body.

**Ministry of Preparation.** Something like this was never going to happen to me. But now, it has. How have your sermons over the years prepared me for such a life crisis? Especially for me as a young person, can the universe of meaning you have offered me in your sermons withstand the affront of my discovering cancer at age twenty-two? How have all my years in Sunday school laid a groundwork from which my present sense of absurdity can be addressed? What seeds have you been quietly planting that now, at my bedside, we can cultivate? I especially need the resources of Job and the Psalms. Now I need faith without a smile button.

**Minister as Professional.** You, of all the professionals who approach my bed (and you are as vital a part of my health care team as anyone), offer me the fullest context in which to help me fit this intrusive episode in my life. This BIG EVENT for me is another daily routine for the nurses, doctors, and staff who are attending me. A surgeon once told me the most important statement he ever heard in medical school: "Never forget," one of his professors said, "that around every hernia is a person."

You come to my bedside as a representative from my normal, full life. Here where my identity revolves around being a "hernia," I need you to remind me who I fully am. (And, if necessary, to remind those tending me.) Have you taken the time to speak to my physicians or the nurses about my "case"? If they are not willing to help you better understand my present situation, that's something I want to know.

*Support System.* This problem didn't just happen to me; it happened to "us," that is, me and my family. Please let me know you are actively nurturing and supporting them. I once spoke with the exhausted spouse of a patient who expressed the frustration: "Every day the mail brings word of concern for her. The phone rings with friends and people from church wondering how she's doing. I'm glad they do, but I just wish sometime someone would ask about *me.*" By helping strengthen my family's ability to cope, you're helping me to cope.

I am suddenly looking at the world through different eyes. My present state of vulnerability and pain makes for a different "me" from when I saw you last at church. I may want to talk about the Denver Broncos again, but rather than cursing their quarterback, I'm more likely to be amazed at what an odd thing it is to plunk a healthy body down in front of a television set for three hours to watch grown men try to hurt each other. Right now, I'd give anything just to feel strong enough to mow the lawn.

I am experiencing life in its bare essentials right now. What once were unconscious habits and assumed givens are now miracles. The gift and pain of taking a deep breath. The ecstasy of crushed ice on dry, parched lips. The technological marvel of a straw that flexes so I don't spill when I take a sip. The sweet victory of finding just the right position in bed so that I don't hurt in more than two places at once.

Enter into my present reality. Help me interpret my being thrust into such primal helplessness and absolute dependence. Show me that my experience is not merely a sad inconvenience to be numbed by medications, but a profound disclosure of the mystery of being human. And when this interlude has passed, don't let me forget this new experience of how precious life truly is. Help me affirm and nourish my newfound sensitivities. Don't let me discard them because they afford little "cash value" out there in the real world.

You are not in charge of cheering me up, although sometimes that's great. You, perhaps more than any of my medical staff, family, or friends, are in a position to really hear me, to let me speak. Above all, don't make me feel that I have to cheer you up! I've already seen the worry, fear, confusion, and helplessness on the faces of my family and friends, and found myself in the odd position of trying to support *them.*

8

I need you to be willing to feel the brunt of my fears, frustrations, and laments. And please, don't try to talk or pray me out of them; give me the necessary space, in your presence, to wrestle with my demons, and don't feel threatened if I rattle the air with expletives. Reassure me, again and again, that it's okay for me to have feelings, to be angry at any or all of "them"—from the doctors to my healthy friends to God.

Let me speak freely from my depths. Don't try to solve my problems; be present with me in them. Don't hide behind your Bible, but don't deny me its wealth either. Remind me that "thou dost uphold me because of my integrity" (Psalm 41). And remind me that even when I can't pray, God's spirit is ever yet present.

Never underestimate the presence of the child within me, now that the Marlboro Man has been thrown from his horse. You see my mature self lying here. But I'm also the scared six-year-old for whom the hospital will always be the place my parents first left me alone with all those strangers in white; where they put me to sleep and cut out my tonsils and I woke up with a horrible sore throat. Be gentle with that little kid.

And now that I'm out of the hospital, getting back on my feet, please make the church a place I can feel comfortable about attending. As grateful as I am for all the expressions of love and caring the congregation has shown, I feel uneasy about returning to church. I don't want to be the patient other people may see me as. Help me work through this sheepishness, so that I don't resolve the dilemma by staying at home. Help others communicate their concern and support without asking me how I feel. Tell me you're grateful and glad to see me back at church, but please protect me from having to explain myself. The support of the church, and your physical presence during my time of need, mean far more to me now than words could ever express. For that I am thankful. To you, and to God.

*Fall 1980*


# Pastoral Ministry with Critically Ill Children

DALE OWEN

As a chaplain serving in a children's hospital, I have asked many questions about what is involved in ministering to critically ill children, dying children, and to the parents of these children. Some questions I have reflected upon are: 1) What is involved in entering a child's world? 2) What is important to remember about children's needs? 3) What do parents of ill and dying children need in the way of pastoral care and ministry? 4) What does the pastor need in ministering to families with a critically ill or dying child? This article attempts to bring together my reflections and learning over the past two years as a clinical chaplain in a way which will be helpful to pastors who are involved in ministry to parents and their children who are ill or dying.

One psychological fad today is to compartmentalize life into predictable stages or life cycles and to map out a developmental pattern we can rely upon as security over the turbulent waters of anxiety. Perhaps this is the modern person's attempt to harness old anxiety-producing realities with new sophisticated devices. By making our human predicament and journey predictable, our hope seems to be to take another leap away from our finitude and to control our destinies with more accuracy.

Even death has been packaged as "the final stage of growth" (Kubler-Ross). Are we really any different from primitive human beings who sought to allay their fears through the totem, animism, and magic? Perhaps we are only slightly more arrogant in our belief that our gods will prove infallible, for they are based on science, technology, and centuries of learning. But then, the absurd happens: a child dies! Science, technology, and centuries of learning reach their limits and cannot prevent the death of a child.

A children's hospital symbolizes and serves as a judgment upon the Tower of Babel we have built in the twentieth century. In spite of our accumulated knowledge, training, and complicated equipment, children die. This reality, when it happens, does not fit neatly into any scheme of satisfactory logic or developmental time table.

> *Humpty-Dumpty sat on a wall,*
> *Humpty-Dumpty had a great fall.*
> *All the King's horses and all the King's men,*
> *Couldn't put Humpty together again.*

Why Humpty-Dumpty had to fall in the first place seems a natural question to ask, but it only serves to numb us to the reality of what has occurred. Could ever knowing *why*, if in fact there were a reason, aid in putting Humpty back together again?

Medically, it is fairly clear how the disease process works. So in a sense we do know much about why children become ill and why they die. The *why* question is not primarily a scientific question; it is a faith question. It is also a question about the nature of our existence as finite creatures, so it is both a religious and a philosophical question. It is a question for which poets, writers, theologians, and philosophers have sought answers since the beginning of time. And whatever answers they have come up with, we still do not like their explanations.

A child's death confronts us all with the uncertainty inherent in living as human beings. The neat categories fail, and the turbulent waters of anxiety begin to rise to our ankles, our knees, our waists, and our necks. It is enough to make a parent panic and almost drown. The chaos and anguish flood in without respect for logic, science, stages, categories, questions, or answers. There is only loss and grief. And, theologically, our ministry calls us to be there in the midst of the flood with few answers.

Our prepackaged phrases, like our compartmentalized stages of life, seem sterile and cold next to the genuine anguish and grief parents feel when their child dies. We want so much to do something, to say something, to comfort, and to help. We also want to run away, to keep our anxiety controlled, and to distance ourselves from such pain and chaos. Yet, as pastors, we have the special calling to be with people precisely at times like these.

How can we stand in such a place and genuinely minister to bereaved parents? How can we genuinely minister to sick children and parents who are undergoing crisis in their lives? What do pastors need to minister to families with a critically ill or dying child?

***How can we minister to children who are ill or dying?*** The child's world is different from the world of adults. It is of no use to approach children as "little adults." We do so out of our own need for security and for relating in patterns we are used to. They are not "little adults." They are children, human beings with certain capabilities and limitations. Play is their work. They speak important messages through their games. Play with them, and learn their language. Touch is what they understand best, but make it sincere. It must come with time and with trust. A child will jerk away if he or she does not feel you have earned the right to touch.

Unlike adults, children are very attuned to their feelings and will be honest in their responses. They feel no need to put on airs or pretend. They cry when they are hurting, yell when they are mad, laugh when they are happy, and embrace when they need love and warmth. To be with children in a meaningful way means entering their world in a way they can "hear" and understand.

For example, I met Donnie one day in the treatment room. He did not have enough platelets to keep his blood coagulating and was suffering a severe nose bleed. He would not speak to anyone, but lay rigid on the treatment table. His mother had to make several phone calls and asked that I stay with Donnie. Donnie and I had never met. I introduced myself, and spent a good fifteen minutes trying to get Donnie to talk a little. My adult approach wasn't working. Donnie had a cold rag over his nose, which was now all spotted with blood.

Suddenly, he lifted it in the air, as if he were going to throw it at me. I said, "You'd better not, I'll throw it back." With that, he grinned, played like he was going to put it back on his nose, but instead quickly threw it at me. It hit me square in the face. He giggled. Gently, I threw it back and he caught it. Again, he repeated the game. Sometimes I was quick enough to catch it, sometimes he caught me off guard. This went on for some time. I moved closer to look at his nose. He had dried blood caked all over his face. I asked him to let me wipe it off. At first distrustful, Donnie slowly allowed me to wipe off his face. As I did, he began talking: "My name is Donnie. I'm six years old. I have a dog named Pepper." Donnie and I became friends through play and touch, and through approaching each other with respect and honest feelings.

***How can we minister to parents of ill and dying children?*** One way to minister to children who are sick or who are dying is to minister to their parents, so they can fully be with their children. Parents need to be able to talk to someone who can truly hear them, and who can truly be present with them. Parents experience such a wide range of feelings: from anger, anxiety, guilt, depression, and helplessness to hope, tenderness, protectiveness, and love. As pastors, we often make the mistake of assuming we know what another person feels, or ought to feel. We project on them what we think we would feel in a similar situation, or we are open to hearing about some kinds of feelings, but become very defensive and moralistic when we hear other feelings expressed.

People have a way of testing us to see what we as pastors can handle and what we cannot. If we become anxious and defensive, people will sense that and continue to look for someone who is open enough to hear their story, the negative and the positive. It is important to realize, too, that people do not stay in the same place. Feelings change. People do not usually get stuck in one emotion, such as anger, unless they have no outlet for expressing it.

Another mistake we make in trying to be helpful is our misuse of psychological categories and stages. Using these as handles, we sometimes try to identify which stage or category people are in and what they should be feeling accordingly. Then, when they do not conform to our expectations, we become confused. Pastors become abusive when they try to force people to admit to feelings they are not having. Part of our anxiety as pastors comes from our feeling that we have the responsibility to "fix" things and people. We must come to terms with our own human limitations and realize that our greatest gift to others is to let them have their feelings, to share their story and stand with them as they experience what they are going through.

***What does the pastor need in ministering to families with a critically ill or dying child?*** The minister is a broken human being, an inheritor of finitude, a party in the human predicament, and co-sufferer in the realities of human existence. Pastoral authority is based upon our awareness of our common humanity, as well as our awareness of the Divine, however partial our awareness may be.

Warmth, community, and the Word that issues genuinely from these are what is needed in ministering to parents and their children. We can invite people out of isolation and into community. We cannot join them, however, if we have not experienced both of these realities for ourselves, and if we are unwilling to step off the secure stepping stones into the abyss with them. If we must have control, our totems in our hands, our formulated answers in our pockets, and our feet on the stepping stones, we need not bother issuing the invitation to others. But if we can let go of our props and join people, ministry can be an efficacious event, a sacramental moment, and an incarnational reality. God breaks through.

The pastor, as human being, needs warmth, community, and someone to hear his or her story, feelings, and concerns every bit as much as the parishioner. The pastor, so often walled off in a world of isolation, seeks to be bread broken for others without having her or his own soul replenished, renourished, or nurtured. Jesus emptied himself for others, but required time alone to be renewed, time with only his disciples to be nourished by companionship and community, and time to attend to physical needs as well as spiritual needs. If our parishioners need these things, if Jesus needed these, certainly the pastor needs them as well. But how?

Perhaps pastors would better know how to feed the sheep if they themselves were not starving. Therapists must undergo therapy themselves as part of their training. The idea behind this requirement is that the would-be therapist cannot learn to feed others until he or she has had the experience of being fed. But who is to feed the pastor? Perhaps another pastor, who shares the same struggles alone and who could understand. Perhaps a group of such pastors is the solution. Where are you, as a pastor and person, being fed now?

In conclusion, I would like to share what I now believe to be part of the solution for our hungry world. The child as a living symbol of faithfulness, of what it means to be human, confronts our sophisticated simulation games of living. It is not the developmental theorist, but the child, who teaches us most vividly what our human existence is all about. It is not the philosopher or theologian who comes closest to the truth of God, but the child who is not afraid to laugh, to cry, to dance, to play, to run, to show fear, to love, and to ask for what he or she needs and wants. We may all relearn from the child what it means to be human, and how to be fed as well as feed others.

*Fall 1980*

# Deterring the Mission of the Church

JIM L. WAITS

*This article was excerpted from Dean Waits's lecture during the Martin Luther King Symposium held at Candler in the spring of 1980.*

A distinct measure of guilt and sadness indelibly marks those of us who ministered to white churches in the South of the sixties. We make little avowal of courage, for the claims of justice were so enormous and our compromises so numerous, that no ingenious rationalization can now salve our consciences.

I well remember the introduction of Dr. King by the dean of Yale Divinity School in the fall of 1959. He spoke of Dr. King as a modern-day prophet (likening him to those ancient prophets Amos and Jeremiah), and I remember how many of us from the South thought of that acclaim as being a bit overdrawn. Time would prove us wrong. For we had no conception of the enormity of the struggle that was only then beginning to sweep the nation, and of the powerful God-consciousness that informed Dr. King's prophetic acts through his ministry. Our understanding of the true prophetic character of the movement was inhibited, for we were subjects of the same passivity which characterized so much of ministerial perspective and practice and still does today.

What Dr. King and the movement did for us, for some of us, was to quicken our understanding of the radical claims of the gospel against a gradualist, culture-accommodating formulation of religion which would not bestir itself greatly about anything. One of my friends in Mississippi who was in constant trouble for his preaching on the race question was waited upon by a member of his congregation who was critical of his preaching. "Well, what do you want me to preach on?" he said. "Just tell us God loves us and we're doing all right," the member replied.

It was not that there was not an abundance of decent, church-going white churchmen and churchwomen in the South in the fifties and sixties; it was their overwhelming *moderation* that formed the most powerful deterrent to responsible action. Quite apart from their racism, it was their belief that voluntary and gradual means would resolve all ills that kept them from aggressively addressing the conditions of injustice so prevalent in the culture.

Martin Luther King observed that in his *Letter from Birmingham Jail.* "I have almost reached the regrettable conclusion," he wrote, "that the Negro's great stumbling block in his stride toward freedom is not the White Citizen's Council or the Ku Klux Klanner, but the white moderate, who is more devoted to 'order' than to justice; who . . . constantly says: 'I agree with the goal you seek, but I cannot agree with your methods of direct action'; who paternalistically believes he can set the timetable for another man's freedom; who lives by a mythical concept of time; and who constantly advises the Negroes to wait for a 'more convenient season!'"

Frankly, I see little evidence that the appeal of moderation and gradualism is abated in the church and its ministry today. I see all too many clergy who are committed to preserving the status quo, to the maintenance functions of church life, and to the safeguarding of their own careers. Moderation is the luxury of the privileged; it is the source of ever deeper suffering for those who are oppressed. In relation to the gospel, moderation is the chief ingredient of what Bonhoeffer called "cheap grace." Dr. King knew that prophetic acts are not the sum of everybody's consensus.

The main stream that informed his theory of social protest was his belief in the guarantees of the Constitution of the United States and his unalterable association of these guarantees with the natural law of God. This, of course, put him in diametric opposition to segregationists whose own argument fundamentally rested on a natural law justification for the separation and subjugation of blacks.

But far from being an anarchist or even a civil disobedient in the strict sense, Martin Luther King quite consciously appealed to the Constitution and to its guarantees of universal human rights. In that sense he was, in the midst of all the discord and unrest of the sixties, the most obedient of citizens to the authority and true values of his nation. Though not un-critical of the federal government and its policies, King consistently repaired to the Constitution as an expression of moral law for the authori-ty of his protest.

This is the reason the term civil disobedient is seldom appropriately ap-plied to King; in the normal course of protest, he functioned under and assumed the authority of the United States Constitution. It was the local ordinances and discriminatory state statutes that offered occasion for disobedience, with the more powerful aim of bringing to bear the full force of Constitutional authority and moral judgment in behalf of social justice that informed King's strategy. I can find little reference to classic civil disobedience in King's writings (other than his own sense of indebtedness to Ghandi in the Strike Toward Freedom). He seemed to prefer the terms "direct action" or "non-violent direct action."

Responding to the moderate white ministers in Birmingham who chastized him for foregoing the possibility of negotiation in remedying in-justice, King gave this brief definition of his strategy: "Non-violent direct action," he wrote, "seeks to create such a crisis and foster such a tension that a community which has constantly refused to negotiate is forced to confront the issue." In short, the community is forced to confront its moderation over issues that are painfully *immoderate* to those who suffer its conditions.

I speak now to my fellow white ministers: You will be sorely tempted by arguments of gradualism and moderation in your ministry. And many of you will have to function with realism and institutional savvy to be effec-tive witnesses to the gospel. Martin Luther King left these prophetic words for us: "I have travelled the length and breadth of Alabama, Mississippi and all the other southern states. On sweltering summer days and crisp autumn mornings I have looked at the South's beautiful churches with their lofty spires pointing heavenward. I have beheld the impressive outlines of her massive religious education buildings. Over and over I have found myself asking: 'What kind of people worship here? Who is their god?'"

*July 1980*

# Racial Justice and Conversion

## LUTHER E. SMITH, JR.

A new decade always stimulates retrospection that ponders the progress of society. The plight of black Americans has been a special interest of such activity. Comparisons between the 1960s and 70s are often made, delineating social, political, and economic patterns that forecast the future of blacks. While the social scientist's purpose is to describe and predict, those sensitive to black America have a deeper investment in this examination; for they realize that the survival (physical and emotional) of blacks is at stake, and that all analysis must clarify how they are to survive and fulfill their sense of life purpose.

The civil rights struggles of the 60s resulted in major successes that signaled social progress: voting rights, access to public accommodations, the advent of social welfare programs, the election of black public officials, and the affirmation of black identity. In addition, the 60s held promise that new frontiers in social justice would continue to open.

For many the 70s left the promise unfulfilled. Economic policies did not improve the lot of the black masses, court decisions seemed to nullify earlier gains, and social programs were denied funding. A despondent mood prevailed among many social activists. At times the singing of "We Shall Overcome" sounded like nostalgia for the 60s rather than prophecy for the present. Some came to question whether the protests, legislation, sacrifice, and apparent victories made any real difference.

I believe this skepticism is raising two fundamental questions about American society. Is there a commitment to a vision of equal opportunity and social justice? And secondly, is the commitment rooted in (supported by or based upon) *conversion?*

Commitment goes beyond emergency laws and policies that relieve social tension. The nation must be motivated by a passion to correct injustices in the social order, a passion fueled by love rather than fear, a passion guided by the upholding of constitutional ideals and the Christian vision of God's kingdom.

Expressing this commitment requires us to address five issues: *1) Racism.* Racial prejudice is a spiritual illness that infects the institutions and structures of society; discrimination, segregation, brutality, and killing result from distorted racial images. *2) Poverty.* The deplorable conditions and effects of poverty, in this affluent society, witness to the hypocrisy or impotence of commitment. *3) Justice.* Without a fair system of redress that discourages crime by corporations, government, law enforcement officials, as well as individuals, we are left with legalized oppression. *4) Caring.* The spirit of humanity hungers for genuine (those coming from the heart, rather than external authority) expressions of love; the trust that leads to intimacy waits for kindness. *5) Community building.* We need to recognize and act upon the interdependence that characterizes our lives. Rugged individualism, exploitative relationships, competitive and materialistic consumption can stand against life's urge for community. We either live together or die apart.

Commitment to these issues will wane unless empowered by the conviction that it serves an Ultimate Truth. Then, despite the frustration, dangers, and difficulties, the company of the committed will continue because they "can do no other" that will satisfy the Spirit within them. This reflects the difference between cultural change and cultural conversion.   Change can merely be a shift in notions, adjustment to the environment, experimentation with new data, and anticipation of adverse reactions. Conversion is a radical reorganization of life in response to the will of God; a departure from old ways, a rejection of the former order, and a journey toward the promises of God.

Our nation has admitted shame and professed the desire to repent for its history of slavery, Jim Crow-ism, segregation, and discrimination. All the branches of government have put forth laws and policies to correct past errors. We have claimed a national conversion to the founding vision of being one nation under God, with justice and liberty for all.

In light of recent setbacks in social programs and race relations, we must ask if our social commitments grow from and represent our conversion. As civil rights decisions were enacted, many white Americans felt as if they were being pushed into unfamiliar and hostile territory, where they felt insecure and unprepared to cope with new social arrangements. The term "white backlash" came to the fore, describing the reactionary political posture of these persons. Even if the old order was imperfect, perpetuating undue privilege and suffering, at least it was predictable; it lured the people's vision, yet spiritually turned them to pillars of salt.

In the 1980s the church has the awesome opportunity for ministries of reconciliation in race relations. The church is founded upon a truth that reveals our kinship as brothers and sisters. Our proclamation and labors can disclose how interpersonal and systemic expressions of racism destroy the human family. Words are powerful; they nurture a consciousness that transforms behavior. But *experience* yields the certainty of commitment. This suggests that churches might begin by participating in or creating contexts of interracial fellowship, helping people to discover one another while overcoming the anxieties and stereotypes that have grown from years of racial separation and insensitive interaction.

Programs of caring for the victims of social injustice could be outlets for the responsible stewardship of our energies and resources. And faith in the integrity of others' worth is affirmed when we work to give them access to the power structures of society; politics and economics cannot be ignored, because they do not ignore God's people.

Black and white churches have this mission, which is not only for the survival and fulfillment of blacks, but for the total community. Beyond this fact, and most important, this mission exposes us to the peace and joy of pleasing God.                                              *July 1980*

# Serving God and Mammon

LUTHER E. SMITH, JR.

The popular question, "What have you done for me lately?" is also asked of religion. Religious faith lays claim on our lives. It demands something of us. This obligation may take the form of ethical behavior, ritualistic worship, or allegiance to institutional doctrine. But most people are not satisfied with the obligations; they want to know the benefits.

Some Christians find contentment in the belief that their faithfulness assures them a place in heaven. Others require more immediate rewards. The "here and now" is as much a priority as the hereafter. A major response to this concern, being advocated by ministers, stresses that Christianity not only improves one's quality of life, but also improves one's standard of living. This is the gospel of God's desire for Christians to be affluent.

A strong drive to achieve in one's work, friendly relationships with others, health, and skill with resources are considered key elements in realizing affluence. In addition, the prophets of affluence identify "religious" attitudes and practices which guarantee attaining the good life. Their literature, media programs, and sermons profess that this happiness results from such disciplines as positive thinking, possibility thinking, tithing, adherence to dogma, and prayer routines.

There is a measure of truth in this happiness formula. A change of perspective and behavior can alter distressing conditions. Transforming power resides in the various techniques promoted by these clergy. The deficiencies of this approach, however, are numerous.

First, fundamental to the techniques is the assumption that reality can be controlled. If the individuals begin to think and behave "right," the scenario goes, the abundant opportunities of their environment will become evident and available. Absent is a serious acknowledgment of the plight experienced by the poor and the oppressed minorities. They suffer economically because of policies (government, business, education, and social service) which prevent improvement in their condition. Individual initiative will not break the intransigent social forces that perpetuate their poverty. Such social ills require systemic analysis and political activity which transform these forces.

Second, Christianity is portrayed as endorsing capitalism, materialism, and the accumulation of wealth. The injustice and exploitation which accompany affluent societies are not challenged. Economic well-being is equated with God's blessing.

Jesus' message of liberation to the poor is distorted into a blueprint for economic security. He is characterized as a man with a burning ideal who inspires others to excel. While his birth into poverty is mentioned, little is said about his continual state of impoverishment. He would appear to have the social mobility of a middle-class American. This interpretation of Jesus and his message is influenced by the avarice that inhabits our cultural values and dreams. In these testimonies of Christians who adhere to this gospel of wealth, praise is given to God for providing luxury cars, expensive homes, and windfall profits. Considering that over 500 million of the.world's people live under the threat of death by hunger, we must question whether God supports this distribution of resources. Perhaps God is embarrassed by the possessions we claim in God's name.

And third, a perverted understanding of Christian identity emanates from the faith-success-wealth syndrome. Our economic system emphasizes winning over one's competition. The strong overtake the weak. Jesus exemplified sacrificial living. Life is to be lived in caring relationships with others. Domination yields to cooperation. Seeking power to manipulate one's environment in ways that enhance personal prestige is unfaithful to the gospel. Our goal is to be available to God and to serve people. Paul confirms that worldly standards of status have no meaning to God when he writes: ". . . but God chose what is foolish in the world to shame the wise, God chose what is weak in the world to shame the strong, God chose what is low and despised in the world, even things that are not, to bring to nothing things that are" (1 Corinthians 1:27-28). The promise and fulfillment of Christianity is the assurance of God's presence and love. Our beliefs and disciplines may sensitize our spirits to this reality, but they do not create it.

God's presence and love abound in the midst of joy and suffering, wealth and poverty, success and failure. The experience of God is the purpose of religious commitment. Our society is full of people plagued by anxiety about their existence. Memories of hardship, disorder in the social climate, family tensions, and doubts about traditional sources of meaning have driven many to put their faith in mammon. A gospel of affluence addresses the anxiety, only it gives the wrong answer. Our deepest needs are met when we "seek God's kingdom" (Luke 12:31). In this seeking the conditions of our life remain uncertain. The one certainty to which we can submit our existence is God. And for the Christian, this is enough.

*March 1984*

# Is Christianity a "Success Theology"?

## G. MELTON MOBLEY

"Being a Christian, will I succeed in business?" The short answer to this question is: who knows? If the question is rephrased slightly, a more fulsome answer can be given. The version I have heard most often is: "Will being a Christian help me succeed in business?" (Astute lay people cast questions in probabilistic terms, not in absolutes.) Put this way, the answer is: maybe.

I will understand Christian to be what I think it is most often—a social label. Labels have power. And the label "Christian" in our society is one of the most powerful. What does the label "Christian" convey? Do you expect something to be different about yourself, if you call yourself a Christian? Do you expect others who call themselves Christians to be different from non-Christians? If your answer is no, then you are very odd indeed. Most human beings do have different expectations about people according to the label with which we tag them.

Let's take a quick example before we go on. Let's make it a negative example so it will have bite: "atheist." Now that is a label that most of the readers of this article disdain. You are not likely to want it for yourself or for your children, the very high moral character of some atheists notwithstanding. Why would it matter to you to be labelled an atheist, aside from the fact that it is probably not accurate? Perhaps more telling, why would you not want your children to be labelled atheists?

In our society the label "atheist" is likely to have negative consequences. Even Thomas Jefferson, who defended the right of atheists not to believe in God, argued that they could not be sworn before a court of law. Many Americans today say they would be willing to limit the rights of atheists to hold jobs, to speak freely, and to have their books in public libraries. Negative labels can limit opportunities. Limited opportunities can stifle motivation. And the combination can lead to a very difficult life. Who wants that for either themselves or their children?

Positive labels can, on the other hand, lead to expanded opportunities, which tend to enhance motivation and self-confidence. People who identify themselves as religious are in the majority in the United States. Over 95 percent of all Americans say they believe in God. Over 90 percent say they belong to one religion or another. In most elections for public office, a candidate's church affiliation is considered a plus. In 1980 Jimmy Carter's born-again version of the Southern Baptist religion was widely publicized, especially to church groups.

Something lies between the label that is clearly negative or clearly positive, however. And that is the label that appeals to the positive and the negative at the same time. I am going to cut a sharp edge here, one that some readers may take issue with.

Surveying the Atlanta telephone directory for 1983-84, I found more than a dozen businesses with the adjective "Christian" preceding their names—businesses that I judge want to make some capital out of being Christian. Silent alms will not do for Christian Financial Concepts, for example. Or the Christian Construction Corporation, the Christian Chiropractic Center, or even the Christian Counseling Center. We can, I think, absolve the listing for Christian Dior Intimate Apparel from this particular group.

How does the label "Christian" appeal to the negative and positive at the same time in the above instances? On the positive side, people may respond to a clearly named Christian enterprise, expecting to be dealt with in a Christ-like way. The negative implication is that the product of the Jew or Buddhist—or worse, the atheist—should be put lower down the list by the Christian shopper. This is what I understand Carl Jung to have been pointing to in his concept of the shadow—that evil that lurks within us all, but is masked by noble sentiments.

Using the label "Christian" for market appeal, I charge, is clumsy and boorish, if not anti-semitic. Although there are a few Jewish counterparts to the Christian nonprofit organizations, I found no "Jewish Financial Services" and not even a "Jewish Delicatessen." And to put any lingering doubt to rest, I found no entries for "atheist."

"Christian" is a positive label in our society. Judging from the attempts to profit from the use of the label and from the omission of other religious labels from business headings, I think we can infer that Christianity is the most valued American religion. Religion, any religion at all it seems, is preferable to atheism, but our society's first order religion is Christianity.

So, what does the Christian in business do? To hide one's religion out of fear of being prejudicial to other religions would be phobic. One could, however, let the label "Christian" work in the opposite direction—toward oneself.

In 1983 Christmas Day's *New York Times*, the past chairman and chief executive officer of J. C. Penney Company, Donald V. Siebert, argued that this can and does happen, regularly. He said: "During the four decades I have been in business, I have found that the corporate world is filled with businessmen who want to do what is right, not with Scrooges who delight in exploiting orphans and widows." Overly generous to corporate America, perhaps, but telling as a perception of one who has been at the top of the business ladder. Successful businesses, Mr. Siebert suggested, have a corporate credo. The Penney Company has one, he reported, the last element of which reads: "Test our every policy, method, and act in this wise: Does it square with what is right and just?" And what is most important, Mr. Siebert suggested, is that this credo has led to success in business:

> . . . The best business decisions always are totally compatible
> with the high standards of business and human ethics. By logic
> they must be. For the cornerstone of human ethics, which is
> what business ethics are, is the set of laws in the Ten Com-
> mandments—principles that work and have endured.

I will leave to my colleagues the sorting out of the theological implications of that passage, and to others the questions of whether or not corporate America warrants this virtuous rendering of the capitalist soul. What I will note is the putative influence of religion on corporate decisions. The reference in this case is not specified as Christian, but the point holds nonetheless.

Back to the original question. Will being a Christian help you succeed in business? The label Christian may increase your sales, if people shop with the religion of the merchant as a criterion and if the population is primarily Christian—probably a better strategy in Hahira, Georgia, than New York City, for example. To gain these extra sales you will probably appeal to prejudice against other religious groups, and you will probably reinforce negative stereotypes both for yourself and for your customers. If you let the label influence you—take it to heart, some would say—you may have to redefine success. At the very least you would take a long-term view, as Mr. Siebert has suggested, and judge strategy by what is right rather than simply by what sells.

If the Christian would let the faith influence business, we would probably hear fewer references to that shallow cliche, "the bottom line," and more to principles of depth and sensitivity. This would put a very powerful sector of our society, the business world, in the position of reinforcing the attempt to build a society that is right and just. More people than Christians share this dream, at least a few atheists I would wager, and it is this dream that needs visibility more than any particular religion.

*March 1984*

# Mission to Inner Space

## JAMES F. HOPEWELL

Atlanta's dismay over its high homicide rate prompts the question: why are we more alarmed about killings in the city than those committed elsewhere? Not too long ago the safest place in the world was felt to be the city. It was then in the countryside that the dangers lurked; both the banished and the bandits lived out there. By definition outlaws lived in the wilderness because they were there outside the law. It was in the wilderness that Jesus met the Devil, and the witch grabbed Hansel and Gretel in the woods. Evil and chaos became more likely as one travelled away from the structures of values and relationships that constitute the town, and towards the outer space of untamed nature.

Cities were the great achievement of humankind, the mark and assurance of its capacity to wrest from the wild a space in which nature gives way to culture. To be "urbane" or "civil" was to be of the city, and citizens of no mean city, like Saul of Tarsus, identified their persons with their town's title. Indeed civilization itself needed cities for its accomplishment.

From such cities it was possible to view without much alarm the violence of the wilderness. The menace of outer space, the region beyond our cultured life, does not demoralize us; its terror even heightens a sense of human achievement, showing us how far our civilization has come from the brute peril of the cosmos. As mediated through movies and television the horror out beyond is, if anything, entertaining. Snug in our cities we watch killings on the frontier, wars outside the metropolitan world, death rays from outer space, despair on the other side of the globe, tyrants in the tropics. To the more persistent of these remote forms of violence we citizens may send missions, and try to civilize them. But their existence, no matter how terrifying, seldom threatens our local sense of worth and security.

What does threaten that local sense of worth and security is the violence we now find in our inner space. Tolerated in outer space, the killing in the center of our cities slashes our social gut. As long as murder occurs beyond the frontier, it can be viewed without alarm, but its presence within us poses radical questions about our own humanity and human capacity.

Rather than face these questions we and our churches follow the white flight to the countryside, to the wilderness our forebears distrusted. For us civilization takes on a dangerous new form: it tries to contain the evil at its center rather than using the center to link us to each other.

Prisons are a way we contain the evil at our center. We void an inner space in our society, place thick walls around it to envelop the violence, and civilize the areas beyond. Civilization has become a cage for the terrors once felt to inhabit the region beyond it. In a breathtaking switch in religious perception, the Devil is no longer in the wilderness but at the center of society: in the slums, the porno shops, the strange religious movements, the ethnic minorities, the drug dealers. And with this doughnut view of civilization we seek to imprison this menace in the hole at the center.

It was with fervor and zest that the church, when it was an integral part of the city, sent out missionaries to the outer space of the eighteenth and nineteenth centuries. Then the real and imagined terrors of the non-Western world were accepted as part of the risk, and it was indeed in their encounter that Christ was witnessed, and martyrs made. For our times the missionary call directs us to the threat of inner space and to the reconciliation God works there. In this latter call there may be less glamour yet more consequence for civilization.

*October 1979*

# "I Was in Prison. . . ."

## WALTER LOWE

We who have never been in prison must begin by admitting how little we know of it. The prison is for us a world which is unknown and alien. If we think of it at all, it is as something which is regrettable but necessary—a necessary function of the state, carried out beyond our sight. We know the walls from the outside, and they remain forbidding and mute.

But I wonder if there isn't something more. If we are entirely honest, isn't there some corner of our minds which says not only that the prison is alien to us, but that it ought to be alien? Isn't there some voice within us that is proud of the fact that we have never been touched by such a place? We Christians are good people, after all, and good people don't belong in prison. Few of us would put it quite that simply, perhaps. But who of us has not in fact heard the murmur of that voice and felt the vague warmth of its self-congratulations?

That voice is so tempting because it simply removes the prisons from our consciousness, and from our conscience. In fact it assures us that we are good precisely because we are *not* tainted, precisely because we are *not* involved. This, at any rate, is what I want to suggest in this essay: that through this voice we may find within ourselves a clue as to why prisons are the way they are.

The clue leads us back to one of the oldest practices, that of scapegoating. A community which feels itself in the throes of some evil force impugns that evil to a particular creature or person, who is then slain or ceremonially driven out of the community. The aim is that by this act the threatened community may be restored, although at the price of one of its members.

It may be that scapegoating is not only one of the oldest social practices, but also one of the most deeply rooted. It may be that the various separations and barriers which society creates serve to continue the practice of scapegoating in another, more subtle form. A community confirms itself as good by driving other people out, into ghettoes. And when this is not enough, there is a sort of ghetto within the ghetto, which is the prison.

In suggesting this, I am not denying that *some* form of prison is a necessity. But I am saying that whenever we create this sort of division between ourselves and others, we must do so with an uneasy conscience. For the image of the scapegoat is there to remind us that in making such a division we are playing with emotional dynamite. We are risking, in fact, a sort of schizophrenic society: with complacency on the surface and great anger underneath.

The complacency comes from the fact that the tempting voice within us and the community of "good" people around us both serve to soothe our conscience rather than disturb it. And the hidden rancor comes from the fact that the people in prison, once placed there for whatever just and proper reason, have heaped upon them a burden of condemnation, an intensity of rejection, which is measured not by the specific offense committed but by our own fear, frustration, and need for reassurance.

Now I would like to reflect for a moment about the particular *form* of the prison. The prison as we think of it is more exactly the penitentiary, and it is a pretty recent innovation. Significantly, the penitentiary form of prison is an innovation which was prompted in part by our own religious forebears. Before the eighteenth century it was not standard practice to sentence people to long terms of confinement. The normal sentence for a serious crime was rather more direct, including such measures as flogging and mutilation.

Thus the penitentiary, which introduced confinement as the normal sentence, was meant as a more humane alternative. Further, it was thought more likely to lead to rehabilitation. Indeed, in the minds of its religious proponents the penitentiary was conceived as a sort of compulsory retreat. Removed from the pressures of a corrupt and corrupting society, the individual would be given time apart in which to reflect and repent. The commentator Garry Wills has noted that the early penitentiary on Cherry Hill in Philadelphia was "a penal monastery . . . each cell complete with its own little garden" ("The Human Sewer," *New York Review of Books*, 3 April 1975). The penitentiary, as the name suggests, was to be a setting for spontaneous penitence.

This new concept appeared at the same time as the settling of America, and indeed the parallels are remarkable. America, too, was to be a place apart, a land of deliverance from the decadent cities of the Old World. The American wilderness was to be a more natural environment, less crowded, less corrupt: a virtual garden in which a natural human goodness could reemerge. Thus would the new Eden bring forth a new Adam and Eve. And in those isolated cases where this restoration did not in fact take place, the same process would be reenacted more carefully, in miniature, in this new institution, the penitentiary. The garden enshrined in each cell at Cherry Hill was an Eden in miniature, a living symbol of the bond between the early penitentiary and the American religious dream.

It has become too easy of late to speak lightly of this original dream of the penitentiary, just as it has become fashionable to speak lightly of the American religious dream. My intention, on the contrary, is to observe that the two dreams are knit together at their origins, so that if we give up hope for our prisons, we are virtually giving up on ourselves as well.

This, then, is one way in which we are bound to our prisons, despite the appearance of separation. But there is another way which goes deeper still. For on the subject of prisons our Lord was quite explicit. He said that on the last day he will welcome those of whom he can say, "I was in prison and you came to see me." And he knew that those who did visit him would experience him as a stranger.

What is more, our Lord embodied the meaning of these words in his life. His ministry was from first to last a ministry to the outcast. Consistently he strode across the barriers of social pride and separation. And finally he himself was a prisoner, he himself died a scapegoat—and he himself rose to break down all the walls of separation, even the walls of death. This is why we who live in the shadow of the cross must search out the voice of our own complicity. And it is why we who live in the light of the resurrection cannot have an easy conscience about any of the walls which yet, for a moment, stand.

*October 1979*

# Faith from the Underside of History

ROMNEY M. MOSELEY

As a citizen of a "Third World" country, I am encouraged by the various attempts by Americans to expose the American people to the horrendous violations of human rights that occur in nations that use repression and oppression as normative forms of governmental behavior. However, I am also suspicious of attempts to make the United States appear as a paragon of moral rectitude. Denominations which specialize in sending missionaries to the Third World are the very denominations that have been nurtured in the cradle of racism and imperialistic triumphal religion. They selectively use biblical literalism to cast out demons from the illiterate masses while they allow themselves to wallow in self-righteousness and privatized religion.

It is not at all surprising that recent studies have indicated that this segment of the American church is experiencing a significant growth. Like Kierkegaard's deluded innkeeper, "It's the big number that does it"—more television stations, more satellites, more grandiose tabernacles. All this to the glory of God. Human rights and social justice, if mentioned at all, are filtered through the lenses of neurotic anti-communism. To be "born again" is the extent of the prophetic imagination. Like a boomerang, the heart returns to its private chambers wherein dwell only those who hear the same beat.

And so, today, Guatemala remains in the stranglehold of some of the worst violations of human rights in the Western hemisphere whilst its president testifies to his being born again in the Christ preached by swamis of the American Religious Right. Armed with the accoutrements of the electronic church, they pander their pablum to the poor and illiterate masses—ostensibly curing their souls—but fail to address the oppressive economic and political conditions governing their existence. In effect, these missionary zealots offer an antiseptic rendering of the gospel devoid of social praxis and emancipatory critique. Their ethic captures what Max Weber refers to as the "ethics of attitude" (Gesinnungsethik)—all that matters is moral purity, achieved through a total disregard of the conditions and consequences of the political realities governing human existence.

In Barbados, Jamaica, and other territories in the Caribbean and Latin America, these privileged pundits appeal not only to the masses who have not yet developed a critical theology but also to the elite neo-colonialists and plantation aristocrats (the "plantocracy") whose political and economic interests are best served by remaining aloof from the harsh realities of the oppression for which they bear ultimate responsibility.

Given the history of the black church in America, there should be a strong solidarity between the black church and the church in the Third World based upon an "ethics of responsibility" (Verantwortungsethik).

Unfortunately, this has not always been the case. The late Martin Luther King, Jr., and current leaders of the civil rights movement are primarily responsible for placing the struggle for civil rights within an international context of human rights. But, for the most part, black church leaders seem to be addicted to the opium of privatized religion and the seductions of capitalist adventurism. This is underscored by the painful fact noted by historian Lerone Bennett that black America still remains an economic colony of white America.

But let us not be disillusioned by these stark weaknesses. The black church embraces its own dialectics. Beneath the gaudy and sometimes vulgar trappings of storefront temple and tabernacle lies the suffering of people. Here to be found are the foundations of a thoroughly negative dialectic towards the present, an experience of the numinous that is grounded in a powerful eschatological vision. Exodus and Apocalypse are the inseparable Gemini of an authentic black theology. The former recalls the dangerous memories of a tradition of suffering; the latter, a profound eschatological presence. Both elements of this dialectic are recapitulated liturgically through slave songs and spirituals, *chansons de geste*, sung long before they became common discourse.

We in the Caribbean are fellow pilgrims in the tradition and hope of the black church. Our struggle against colonialism, neo-colonialism, and totalitarianism is no less ambiguous in its liberating and distorting elements than that seen in the black church of America. We loathe our dictators, but we are aware that their survival is due not to their dictatorial ingenuity but to our collective parasitic dependence on the hegemony of the superpowers.

The vocation of the church in the Caribbean today is similar to that of the church in other parts of the Third World, i.e., to be a community of faith whose praxis is derived from its theology rooted in the emancipatory values of truth, freedom, and justice. The future of humanity depends upon such values. One of the benefits of being a "developing nation" is that the dialectic of the particular and the universal is acutely sensed. Limited material and technical resources, single-crop production, restrictions in trade, and excessive dependence upon the metropolis heighten our marginality; and, paradoxically, the experience of marginality is our point of entry into the wide collective identity of the Third World.

This is not a completed or closed identity. Rather, it is an emerging global identity united in a common remembrance of suffering. This anamnestic solidarity underscores the active participation of the Third World in history. Not only is this its moral fiber, but also the basis of an openness to a future of freedom from oppression.

Theologian Johannes Baptist Metz reminds us that the church is itself a community of remembrance in which the dangerous but liberating memory of Christ's passion, death, and resurrection radically transforms our present existence and mediates hope for the future. Metz also rightly argues that the gospel's call for the in-breaking of the kingdom of God, with its unnegotiable requirements of righteousness, peace, freedom, and a conventional community of the reconciled, underscores its intrinsically social character.

As the church in the Third World travels along its Emmaus Road with the "less developed," its faith is given new meaning and reinforced by persons who despite their marginality and victimization bear witness to the liberating memory of Christ. It refuses to have its vocation undermined by the lure of consumerist religion and privatized piety. Thus the church in Latin America has given birth to "basic communities"—an unlikely phenomenon in the United States. In the final analysis, congregations in the U.S. have to liberate themselves from privatism and ethnocentrism, and prophetically bear witness to the public and pluralistic character of the body of Christ. Failure to do so encourages specious evangelism by American missionaries and perpetuates the impression that America's forays into the arena of human rights are ultimately untrustworthy and self-serving.

*December 1982*

# The Church and Human Rights: A Mixed Record

## THEODORE R. WEBER

Discussion of the role of religion in the struggle for human rights can lead either to minimizing the role, if one is a secularist, or to celebrating it, if one is a supporter of traditional Western religion. Each conclusion would have some justification, but not nearly as much as its proponents suppose. Certainly religion has been a powerful influence in the long history of the development of human rights as concept and social reality, and its influence is no less evident at the present time. Iran, Northern Ireland, South Africa, and Poland are some of the most visible contexts of human rights conflict, and in each of them religion is a prominent if not dominating factor. Although the processes of secularization may change the particular terms of the relationship between religion and human rights in various cultures and societies, they do not eliminate religion *per se* as a fundamental and powerful factor in social redefinition of claims and limits, duties and responsibilities.

However, to confirm the major role of religion in this process is not to establish a cause for self-congratulation and celebration. Religion has been at least as influential in the retardation and suppression of human rights as in their advancement. Perhaps it is the negative side of this ambiguity that the secularist has in mind when minimizing the importance of religion in the historical development of human rights. Because the editorial concerns that encourage this particular inquiry are those of ministry and mission, we would be remiss if we did not pay special attention to the ambiguities of the record of religion in this development.

In the realm of ideas, religion assists the cause of human rights by pointing to transcendent realities that relativize the powers and principalities of this age. If God is the final authority, kings, dictators, and parliaments are not. If there is a human community of which all human beings are members, essentially and proleptically if not sociologically, no particular community defines and claims our identity with any finality. The way then is open to the emergence of notions of the human and the universal. On the other hand, religions at times claim to possess special revelations which reject appeals to reason and humanity and require the restriction of human rights to the provisions of that revelation alone. The resurgence of Islamic fundamentalism illustrates the formidable capabilities of religion for limiting rights by defining them in terms of special revelation (the *Koran*), as does the emergence of a politicized Christian fundamentalism in the United States. Moreover, wherever human rights of particular groups have been denied and an order of power and privilege established, there always have been religious voices—some of them emanating from the loftiest positions and councils of the churches—ready to justify the maldistribution of power and goods as a mandate of God. The histories of slavery and racial segregation are indisputable cases in point.

Institutionally, the same pattern of ambiguity and contradiction has been present. Religion has provided organizational foci and power for fighting slavery, sexual and racial domination—also for confirming, supporting, and enforcing them. And churches have used their own institutional power and that of the state to discipline or destroy offenders against their orthodoxy, as the history of inquisitions, witch hunts, and pogroms shows.

The point of this contrast is that religion is not necessarily a good thing so far as the struggle of human rights is concerned. As and to the extent that the Christian churches decide to share in this conflict, they should not be surprised and offended if the critics of established order and abuses of power require them to review their records, declare themselves unambiguously, divest themselves of accumulated privileges, and stand vulnerable before the same powers they heretofore confirmed and from which they received protection and support. In particular, the churches must be open to challenges to their cherished orthodoxies from discoveries of the meanings of humanity that emerge in the struggle itself. Nothing less would be authentic to their own prophetic heritage, and to the confession that the truly human is disclosed in our experience through living encounter with Jesus Christ.

*December 1982*

# Trustees of the Gifts of Creation

ROY C. CLARK

Most often in meetings I attend stewardship is treated as a problem because money is a problem. "If we could just get our people to practice good stewardship we would have plenty of money to do what we need to do" goes the familiar litany. So we design yet another "new" program in stewardship cultivation. But the problem persists.

Perhaps the problem is more fundamental than we usually acknowledge. Edmund Steimle, I believe it was, said that when we use the word steward Americans think of being pampered 30,000 feet up in the sky by one of those flight attendants. Aside from that usage and in the conversation of an old-time Methodist who still thinks we have a Board of Stewards, you hardly ever hear the word steward except when we attach "ship" to it and expect it to have dynamic motivating power.

Most churchgoers I know find the word very dull. They sigh when it is mentioned and batten down the hatches for a "money sermon," as they unflatteringly dub the genre. We have weakened the word steward by linking it so tightly to money-raising. Often, however, the proposed cure is as bad as the disease. We are told that stewardship is bigger than money: it includes time, talent, influence—in fact, everything involved in living the Christian life. Stewardship is interpreted so broadly that it no longer claims anything specific of us. All this is too bad because the truth behind the word, in its root biblical dimensions, is the essence of a faithful life. Can we reclaim it?

Perhaps we can, if we concentrate on the essential components contained in the word steward. A steward holds and manages something which belongs to someone else for the benefit of the owner. (Trustee is our culture's word for this relationship.) Stewards have freedom to decide what is to be done with that which is entrusted to them. Because they are free to make decisions, they are therefore responsible and are held accountable for what they do with what is entrusted to them (Matthew 25:14-30).

Holding a trust, awesome freedom to make decisions, and responsibility for which we give accounting are the components of stewardship. What is it, biblically considered, that we hold in trust for which we are responsible and accountable? Along with the whole human family, we are trustees of the gifts of creation. We are placed in this good earth "to cultivate it and to take care of it" (Genesis 2:15, Jerusalem Bible). In possessing life and in using every aspect of the created world, all of us are dealing with that which does not originate with us and does not finally belong to us.

Not all of us, removed as we so often are from the elemental realities of the earth and nature, are either aware of or willing to accept our trusteeship of creation. But Christians, rooted in biblical faith, cannot consider themselves other than managers of God's possession in all their dealings with this created world. Our primal obligation to love God and the neighbor translates, then, into a sense of reverence for God's world in all its material aspects and for its use in ways which serve not only our interests but those of the neighbor as well, considered in the widest possible range of that term, both as to space and time.

Secondly, Christians are uniquely stewards of the gospel of God. "This is how one should regard us, as servants of Christ and stewards of the mysteries of God. Moreover, it is required of stewards that they be found trustworthy" (1 Corinthians 4:1-2). Before money to support church programs there must be acceptance of identity as those who have a unique treasure in earthen vessels—the treasure of the gospel. The "talent" entrusted to every Christian and to the church is the gospel.

There is hunger among us to be related to the transcendent—to do something under God and for God. Campaigns and programs, projects and needs can work their limited fruits, but they suffer the short half-life of all human novelty. More abiding and fulfilling is the awakened sense that Christ has entrusted his gospel to us and the issue is not whether we will raise enough money to pay the bills, but whether we are faithful or unfaithful in fulfilling our responsibility for the gospel.

Disciplined giving to the support of the church's ministry on behalf of the gospel is surely an essential part of any genuine commitment to Jesus Christ. But this giving is not just something the Christian does "for the church" or "because the church needs money." A Christian's disciplined support of the church's ministry is one essential expression of his or her own inescapable personal responsibility to God for the gospel ministry in the world.

When stewardship is seen in its full context of trust, freedom, responsibility, and accountability for the gifts of creation and the gospel given in Jesus Christ, it does indeed encompass all of our lives and the full range of our relationships. But it has a definiteness and a focus that enable us to see the specific claims it makes upon us in daily life. It challenges the best imagination we have to make the truth behind the word stewardship vivid in understanding and experience and to give that truth its full range of influence in our lives.

*July 1979*

# II
# *The Spiritual Life*

## This Strenuous Identification

JAMES T. LANEY

We all like to be identified with important people. It's flattering to hear our names in association with well-known persons, to be "chosen" to belong to certain associations or clubs, or to feel a kinship with significant people. Whom we identify with—and why—says as much about our true religion as our formal relation to the church. In fact one could interpret the biblical notion of righteousness, not as adherence to a moral code, but rather as the identity we seek to establish, largely through our association with others.

Thus Paul's interpretation of righteousness came from a realization that his importance did not derive from his being born into the tribe of Benjamin, being a Pharisee, or having been educated by Gamaliel, but rather came through his identification with Christ. *That* identification—not his status through very significant achievements and birth—became his "righteousness" (cf. Philippians).

Jesus himself refused to take on the identity of the Pharisees (their righteousness), and instead associated with the poor, the lowly, the outcast. This was an unforgivable offense: his rejection of their claims to importance on their own terms—in short, their identity—and his identification instead with those who made no claims either to status identity or to righteousness. His mercy and kindness conferred on them new worth, and they in turn responded warmly to their new sense of dignity in his eyes.

It is important for us in the church to appreciate how seldom doctrine or beliefs *per se* become the basis for identity association, and how much we rely on social standing and economic and institutional power to confer importance. When we understand righteousness as having to do with status and identity, and how we obtain it, we realize afresh the distinction between the righteousness of this world and the righteousness of God. In light of this we can sense how crucial it is for us as a church actively to identify with those whom we might otherwise ignore or avoid. This strenuous identification is the essence of discipleship and issues from our primary identification with Jesus Christ.

*February 1977*

# The Continuing Favor of God

## JAMES T. LANEY

We seldom use the term "favor of God" today. We tend to prefer words like grace, mercy, or forgiveness. Yet favor recurs frequently in Scripture: both Samuel and Jesus are described as increasing in favor with God and man; the outpouring of the psalmist speaks of finding favor with God; at his baptism Jesus is pronounced pleasurable—well pleasing—favorable—to God. Indeed the very creation itself, by being pronounced "good," connotes God's favor upon it.

In an impersonal world our religion increasingly assumes general and abstract expression. Even such a rich concept as grace has come more and more to be understood independently of any specific reference to God. Favor, on the other hand, is intrinsically personal; it always has reference to a subject. The decline in its use stems in part from that very fact—its personal reference seems to imply arbitrariness, capriciousness. But there is a more profound reason for our avoidance of its use. To speak more personally requires from us a definite stance.

In the scriptural context, favor conveys warm endorsement, personal affirmation, and support. To speak of God's favor as a primary disposition toward humanity is to suggest God's "consent to being" (Jonathan Edwards), God's delight and joy in creation. It implies that our primary relation to God is not so much moral, based on approval and evaluation, but, as Jesus taught, more like the relation of a child to a parent. The child's security is not sacrificed by behavior, however delinquent. Rather, the fundamental relation of favor makes possible the child's continuing restoration and growth over time (the Prodigal Son).

Theologically this suggests, too, that Jesus came not only to save us from sin, but to restore us to confidence in the continuing favor of God. Such a message speaks to the condition of alienation in our time, where so many have lost any essential relationship to God within a continuing religious community. While it may be that from our standpoint within ministry God's mercy and forgiveness loom paramount, it is the dawning appreciation that God can look upon one with favor which constitutes the true miracle to an outsider. And is not that the joy of the gospel?

*November 1976*

# To Will

JAMES T. LANEY

When we consider Paul's admonition not to be conformed to this world, we usually associate such conformity with unacceptable forms of conduct or thought. Paul may have had something like that in mind—there are actions and modes of behavior which are clearly destructive in any age. Yet it is more likely Paul was referring to the dominant mood or "mind" of his time in his warning against conformity. Christians are not to be suffused with the same coloration and the same values as others.

One such unquestioned assumption, or prevailing mood, in our own time is the identification of a *significant* life with one which is busy and accomplishes a great deal. There is a tendency to identify personal effectiveness in terms of power or control: building, organizing, directing, running something. The success motif of modern society permeates our thinking.

This leads us to think that our will—our capacity to order and direct and intend—is primarily an agency of domination or shaping. In the Scriptures, however, the emphasis is less on the will seen in these forms than on the will understood as our capacity to be attentive, to direct our attention, to listen. Hence the recurrence in the Psalms of "waiting" upon the Lord. The posture here is not passive, but is inwardly alert. We are told that they who wait upon the Lord in this sense will renew their strength.

Maybe some of our exhaustion in the church derives from our confusing these two meanings of will—one the active ordering and directing of others and things, and the other an active ordering and directing of our own attention. Only the latter enables us to be receptive and to be nurtured. It alone finally determines the quality of our lives. The classical term for this kind of activity of the will is prayer.

*Summer 1976*

# Transformation

JAMES T. LANEY

For a number of weeks our covenant group struggled together over the meaning and significance of Romans 12 for our ministry. One of the things which struck us, upon reflection, was the difficulty we had in giving content to the term "be transformed." And this difficulty appears to have been more than intellectual, for we seemed more comfortable talking about adjustment than about transformation.

Whence this difference? It may reflect a desirable reluctance to avoid being prescriptive about the Christian life. To have a pattern in mind that is too pat, too clear, invites a new kind of conformity, and surely partakes of the being "conformed to this world" which Paul cautions us against. It's all too easy to conform to anything. And all of us are aware how readily self-styled authorities come forward with a new conformity model, whether in religion or in the emotional life.

It appears Paul's contrast of conformity and transformation does not refer simply to different images of the Christian life. It refers to different ways of being Christian altogether: any conformity in the strict sense is a denial of the spiritual transformation he invites. That's why all patterned life tends to be stultified. It is for that reason that all adjustment ethics, born of contemporary psychological fads, tend to fall into the same trap. The transformation suggested in Romans 12 is into a new and generous openness of spirit. Such a spirit leads irresistably to an appreciation of the plurality of gifts in the church, and to an acknowledgment of the variety of life in the spirit. The capacity to affirm others in their integrity, even though they are different, is a sure index of a love which knits the body together.

In looking back over our consideration of this, it seems that our uneasiness with "transformation" is justified insofar as we interpret it as a new, idealized conformity. But such uneasiness is a premature closure on the creative possibilities of Christ's spirit. To be genuinely open to that invading power as it enlarges and affirms us is to be transformed, and its results ("fruits") are its justification.

*April 1976*


# Christian Presence

JIM L. WAITS

The idea of *Christian presence* has a long tradition in the community of faith. It has variously represented claims to individual Christian piety and personal religious commitment, as well as the prophetic tradition and at times also the pain of martyrdom. Christians have debated about "real presence" and "symbolic presence" in the sacrament of our Lord's Supper. More recently the church has manifested a Christian presence in countless situations where people suffered deprivation, racial injustice, war, and other social ills.

Particularly in this Christmas season we speak about *presence*. For this is the time of Immanuel: God with us, God present, God incarnate in the human events and conditions of life. Jesus comes, not in ideology or abstraction, but in the embodiment of God's nature and intention in the world. Ministry is itself *presence*, and in an important respect this is its most thoroughgoing characteristic. Not the presence of an idle or impotent observer, nor the presence required by obligation. Not a crassly "professional" presence, either. Such notions betray both the legacy of Christian presence in the world and the fulfillment of Jesus' own ministry.

The character of ministry as presence takes its definition from an incarnate Lord, One present with intention, willingly, and with conscious purpose. Such presence makes a difference in the situation of ministry because the person of the minister is made fully available for God's intentions. On one occasion to be present may mean quiet companionship, on another unswerving proclamation. At times presence may find us about unfamiliar tasks and on strange terrain. But what excitement accompanies the surety that presence has ultimate meaning in the range of God's purpose.

*December 1975*

# Self-Defense

## JAMES F. HOPEWELL

Larry seemed too radiant for a man whose marriage was falling apart. "Just had my second TM session," he explained. "That meditation gives me the only peace I get in this lousy life." While glad that Larry had found port in a storm, I was uneasy about his landing on the edge of the mind-expansion movements. My caution was like that of most ministers. We may not understand the workings of transcendental meditation, Arica, est, and the like, but we sense that these movements challenge the sufficiency that we claim in Christ, and that for a number of people, they may deliver a joy and tranquility never found in a congregation. The continuing growth of these new ventures into human consciousness seems to reproach an inept and unfeeling church, and we are wary about further consequences.

It is with some relish, then, that we read about the shortcomings of these movements: reports from their dropouts, scenes of silliness, and the more probing conclusions of those who try to analyze their prominence in current culture. One of the latter is Peter Marin's "The New Narcissism," which appears in a 1975 issue of *Harper's*. As Marin's title implies, the movements serve to exalt the individual, providing the follower with an awareness of personal power and control through entry into an interior, radically different state of consciousness.

Such self-enlightenment is felt to be so significant that through it individuals can determine their own destinies. Beholden to no one, and believing that everyone, like themselves, wills his or her own fate, followers feel freed from responsibility for the world's misfortunes. Marin finds in the movements a "growing solipsism and desperation of a beleaguered class, the world emerging among us centered solely on the self with individual survival as its sole good." Hooked on this new consciousness, the follower can forget his or her own conscience. Babies can starve, people can be degraded, wars can explode without direct concern of the person inhabiting a deeper private realm of consciousness. A troubled world reality is swapped for a cozier inner reality.

Before we ministers cast the stone that Marin's critique provides, however, we had better see how accurately it might be aimed at our own congregations. It may hit narcissistic leanings there as well. Try the following check list:

1) In our insistence upon personal encounter with the saving power of Christ, have we implied that redemption is uniquely an inner reality without equal consequence to the world at large?

2) Do our words about Christian life emphasize a private, almost isolated quest in which one is tested and benefited by things rather than people?

3) Do our bulletins speak more about the joy and satisfaction of our congregation than they do about its overflowing love?

4) Are we selective in the way we cultivate our experience of God, concentrating upon God's power more than upon divine justice?

If these leanings are present, our congregation may owe its dynamic more to the new narcissism than to the old biblical message.

*June 1977*

# Worship and Spirituality

## DON E. SALIERS

Recent years have brought a remarkable awakening of interest in prayer and the recovery of "spirituality" among laity and clergy alike. There are many reasons for this awakening. For many of us, our talk about faith and personal piety has been without honesty and spiritual discernment. Conventional morality, often middle-class manners, is more often the basis of church life than is dying and rising with Christ. Many laypersons admit that organized church life is not reaching deeply into their lives to touch, heal, empower, and redeem. Pastors of local churches are pushed and pulled in so many different directions that their own sense of spiritual identity in Christ is forgotten or lost in the activity of "managing" the church. So we are *all* raising some fundamental questions about our basic Christian spirituality.

Where are the persons and communities that can be our guides in prayer, simplicity of life, engagement with the world's crying needs, and places of fellowship, joy, and human maturity? These are the basic questions we are asking of the church and of the seminary. At the heart of all our other concerns for ministry is this one primary aim: *We are called to be living reminders of Jesus Christ and the mystery of the church's life before God in this world. Unless our ministry and life flow from the essence of what we are called to be and do, all theological learning, professional competence, and "churchly activity" will be temporary and illusory.* This is true of all baptized Christians and of all communities of worship and mission.

We cannot divorce the question of spiritual formation in seminary education from the larger issues of the kind and quality of spiritual life in the churches. With respect to our vocation in baptism, and our call to sanctity, there are no first- and second-class members: there is one journey for all, with a variety of gifts and ministries to be received and expressed in the church's mission and worship. A Christian seminary is a community of learning and preparation whose task it is to shape the leadership of those gifts and ministries. Spiritual formation must be integrated with the intellectual and personal training of the special tasks of ordained ministry: proclaiming the gospel, celebrating the mysteries of Christ's death and resurrection, teaching, and building the church in love and service.

This is why the recovery of authentic spirituality in our tradition is dependent upon the renewal of corporate worship. Worship is the primary occasion for the church to remember and proclaim its faith, to enact and to receive again its identity as the people of God. Worship itself continually shapes and expresses the fundamental reality of the Christian life. But if our worship is impoverished, so is our continual formation and growth in Christ impoverished. Conventional worship forms conventional Christians!

Where preaching is biblically illiterate, where corporate prayer is narrow and full of pious cliches, where there is no genuine and sustained thanksgiving, where there is no sense of connection between worship and the realities of daily life, where the sacraments are regarded as mere "ceremonial" outward forms—there the faith is not being received and celebrated. In fact, in such circumstances Christian faith is being *deformed*, and the gospel is not coming to its fullest expression. Unfortunately, too many churches are in this situation. In part this has resulted from the poor formation which preachers and pastors have received.

Within our United Methodist tradition, as well as in others, we inherit a legacy of the separation between liturgy and personal faith. Generations of ministers and laypersons have been brought up to understand common worship as "external and outward forms" belonging to the public rituals of the church, while *real* faith is something private and highly individual. Any approach to spiritual formation and growth (whether in the seminary or in the church) must address this attitude at its root. The genuine recovery of mature Christian spirituality in our ministries must overcome the dichotomy between liturgy and the life of vital piety.

This means that we must grow together in centering our lives upon a renewed liturgy of both word and sacrament. This was, of course, the intent of the Wesleys. Spiritual life centered upon the recovery of biblical preaching, authentic congregational song and prayer, and the sacraments of baptism and the Lord's Supper is at the heart of the ordained ministry.

*What* we do as the gathered community in worship, and the power and grace of *how* we proclaim and celebrate are essential to *who* we are in the world. Personal faith cannot be sustained without being part of the community's active remembrance and participation in the gospel mystery and the "Gospel feast"—to use Wesley's phrase for the Lord's Supper. What is true of the spirituality of the laity is also true of the spirituality of the ordained ministry.

What are the essentials? The word of God in Scripture (adequately read, sung, and proclaimed); communion with the mystery of Christ's life, passion, death, and resurrection in the sacraments; authentic prayer (both corporate and individual); and the practice of hospitality among the saints (honest and graced fellowship). All of these are part of the exercise of the gifts of ministry which should mark our self-giving to the world. This is our pattern given in the love of Christ. Growth into fullness of God in Christ means a deepening participation in all these things.

In this sense, spiritual formation is continuous growth in grace generated by virtue of our common baptism. Every "churchgoer" must encounter this; every "church" fails to be Christ's Body when its worship and mission are not rooted and grounded in the liturgy and likeness of Christ.

*December 1978*

# Worship's Hidden Tongues

## DON E. SALIERS

Questions about why and how we worship have begun to get to us. How we preach and pray and celebrate our faith, many of us have discovered, are expressions and exposures of what we believe about God and the world, and what we are prepared to live and die for. This is why conventional patterns of worship often no longer satisfy people looking for depth of encounter, a more sustaining memory and hope, and a deeper sense of beauty and mystery in the Christian life. At the same time, present Western culture has, despite our technological surfaces, developed a new sense for symbol, myth, ritual, and the visual. This is why Christian worship which is merely verbal, with little or no sense of the deeper languages of symbol, gesture, and space, may in the long run fail to satisfy our deeper hungers for God and our modes of cultural communication.

In Protestant circles, worship is often regarded primarily as a background setting for the main verbal act: preaching. Indeed we still hear people in our churches speak of the congregational hymns, prayers, creeds, the readings, and psalms as the *preliminaries*. This clearly expresses the idea that the main event of the community gathered to worship God is the sermon, or that the primary kind of worship we have in mind is the preaching service. In fact, the standard test for the success or failure of worship is "Was the preacher any good?" A small child remarked in my hearing: "Worship is boring because we never *do* anything. Just the man in the black robe talking to us."

There is, however, something quite misleading in these customary ways of regarding worship, whether on the Lord's Day or otherwise. For even if we were to grant that preaching is the chief worship experience within most local churches, a view which is increasingly challenged by the recovery of the classical balance of word and sacrament, the effectiveness of preaching itself rests upon the vitality of what I call the hidden languages of worship. In other words, the power and range of the Word can never be confined to the words uttered by the preacher.

Christian proclamation has many modes, and it receives life and depth only when a community of faith comes to full, active, and mature participation in the hidden languages of worship. The words of worship depend radically upon the nonverbal dimensions of worship. Preaching in the black tradition, for example, shows this very clearly.

One of the most powerful insights gained in recent years concerning Christian worship has to do with its nonverbal character. This is both a theological and a cultural discovery. All of the reforms of the past fifteen years among Protestants and Roman Catholics alike bring this out for us. We have rediscovered what the biblical witness assumed and the early church took for granted: worship of God is essentially the gathered community in active remembering, proclaiming, and acting out of life lived before God in relation to neighbor. It is response to God. It is *leitourgia,* to use the New Testament word, the activities of God's people gathered to praise, acknowledge, hear, invoke, supplicate, and intercede for the world. Above all, worship enacts the mystery of faith in the signs God has given the community: water, bread, wine, oil, words, the laying on and lifting up of hands, and the graced rhythm of gathering and scattering.

This powerful insight into the symbol and gesture of worship as response to God's self-giving is the key to our understanding of the hidden languages. The words spoken have range and reference and emotional force so far as they grow out of and point back to the fundamental graced activity of worship. Every pastor and leader of worship must become acquainted with the languages of time and space, of sound and sight, and of taste, texture, and bodily postures if we are to grasp the depth and mystery of authentic corporate worship. Our symbols and rituals—and every church has them one way or another—either invite or prevent deeper experiences of faith and common life.

These languages give us experience at an emotional intensity which transforms what we speak in words to something beyond words. The quality of love, care, and hospitality at eucharist or in a foot washing, for example, creates powerful silences and powerful spaces for preaching and praying. Only by discernment and growing participation in these forms of communication lying behind the texts and orders of worship can Christian believers reach beyond conventional faith which is all too comfortably expressed in buttoned-down styles of worship.

*A Theology of Worship.* Suppose we define Christian worship as the ongoing word and prayer-action of Jesus Christ in and through his Body in the world. The chief characteristics of worship become focused by the pattern of life and worship we discern in him: teaching, preaching, touching, healing, reconciling, feeding, suffering, pleading, and obedience even unto death. The whole history of God, with the world and with the people God has called forth to covenant and faith, is brought to symbolic and ritual focus in the "liturgy of Jesus Christ." So far as we recognize and accept ourselves as baptized into his life and death and resurrected presence, we are to become participants in this ongoing word and prayer-action. This is his continuing life in our midst; but it is also to become our own "sacrifice of praise and thanksgiving." Not only are we to "do these things in remembrance of Him," but if we are to worship in spirit and in truth we must learn how to offer ourselves *in union with him.* In this sense, too, worship can never be abstracted from how we live our daily lives. Our prayer and our work are finally to be the continuous web of praise and thanksgiving to God whom Jesus calls Father.

Christian worship is a response to the grace of God found in creation, in time and in history, in prophecy and precept, in care for neighbor and the very created order itself, and supremely as that grace is encountered in the life, teaching, passion, death, and resurrection of Christ. This is always much more than words. It is essentially a corporate action of God's people who are initiated and growing in relation to God and neighbor. It is, in brief, a way of living out the baptismal grace and covenant which authentic conversion, prophetic word, and sacramental life imply.

All of this, of course, opens up awareness of the hidden languages beyond the words we speak and hear. A necessary complement to this theological account might be called "phenomenological." Whatever we call it, we know that Christian worship involves time, place, sound, symbols, and people. These simple words provide the clues we need to discern how the hidden languages are themselves forms of communication which are essential to any worship worth its salt and light.

*Time.* The language of time involves the discipline of the cycles of days, weeks, and seasons. It is essential to remembering who God is and what God has done, and to marking the particularity of what God does and will do in history. The Jewish cycles of time, with feasts and seasons, carried over in a remarkable way into the Christian patterns of the first centuries.

If human beings need to mark birthdays, deathdays, anniversaries, and the like to grasp the significance of life and to celebrate it fully, how much more should Christian worship celebrate the gospel by participating in feasts, fasts, and seasons of particular memories. Looked at from this standpoint, the church year is a christological treasury of our corporate memories of who God in Christ is: Christ's advent and birth; his appearance and ministry; his life and teaching; his passion, suffering, and death; his resurrection, ascension, and giving of his Spirit to the church.

*Place and Space.* The second hidden language concerns place and space. The places in which we gather and the uses of the spaces involved have a profound effect upon the quality and point of our worship. Certain spaces invite a more static and sedentary approach to God—an auditorium for hearing. Other spaces invite movement, freedom of encounter and gesture, and lend themselves to variation in sight and sound.

During a time of building and transition at the Candler School of Theology, we have had the extraordinary experience of moving from a small, temporary, upper-room chapel to the demanding and challenging and beautiful austerity of Cannon Chapel. There are always pluses and minuses in the differences between such rooms. But it is certainly true that a whole new perception of symbolic action, of hearing the Word in song, instrumental music, preaching, and silence has been ours. It will doubtless shape generations of pastors to come.

In the local church, there is the crucial language of history of the building and the interior spaces: where families have gathered for generations; where weddings, funerals, and all their other rites of passage have taken place. This sense of local history of prayer and life is part of the hidden language of place and space which pastors and laypersons must learn to appreciate and to shape so that authentic Christian worship may be encouraged. How we arrange furnishings—pulpit, altar-table, reading desk, font, chairs—determines what is heard and seen. But it also expresses what we believe about the relationship between word and sacrament, prayer and human encounter, faith and action.

*Sound and Silence.* The hidden languages of music and silence must surround the reading and hearing of the church's corporate memories contained in the Scriptures. The art forms of music—congregational, choral, and instrumental—grow naturally out of this fundamental perception. Singing is an extension of speaking; music is the language of the soul becoming audible.

But just as powerful music requires much attention to the spaces between notes, so our worship must learn once again to attend to our need for silence. The spaces surrounding our words must be deep and honest. Here we can learn something from the Quaker tradition. The use of music in worship should never be a mere ornamentation of the Word, but rather its expression. There is a hidden music in how we dance (gather and scatter, stand and sit, move and come to stillness) and how we speak, which music should serve to express.

**Sign and Symbol.** The language of sign and symbol leads us directly to the question of how we celebrate the sacramental actions of the gospel, most especially Baptism and the Lord's Supper. I must confine myself here to one observation: uncovering the depth language of the gestures of taking, blessing, breaking, and sharing is absolutely essential to our Christian life. Likewise, learning to celebrate the mystery of dying and rising with the whole congregation, rather than tacking on a convenient little ceremony with the baby, is of utmost importance to our recovery of both the theology and the powerful beauty of conversion and initiation in faith.

**Community.** The final language of worship is, of course, the human body and its life in community. Jesus' own liturgy finally involved his laying down his life by stretching forth his arms on the cross for us and for all the world. The arts, once related to the redemptive drama of his life, can serve our worship truly, provided we never substitute being "artsy" or merely "aesthetic" for the expression of the gospel mystery in word and in the sign-actions of the church. We must come to know the hidden languages intimately if we are to serve the church's liturgy and our ministry of worship adequately in our culture today.

One more thing must be said. We have been speaking of the meaning and point of corporate worship from a human point of view, attempting to throw some light on the nature of the phenomena and patterns of experience involved. When all such anthropological descriptions are given, we must return to a theological claim: Worship is that continuing occasioning through time of the activity of God. One way to say this is that worship is the ongoing prayer of Christ in his church. The central mystery of Christian life and worship is found here: Christ, through God the Spirit, prays for the world in and through our prayers in his name. Yet the mystery of faith in our worship goes infinitely beyond that as well. For in the themes of death and resurrection, time, history, and the consummation of all things, our worship draws us into the very life of God.

This point cannot be said casually. It is not an ordinary piece of information, nor is it a clever piece of theology. It speaks a mystery hidden from the eyes of the world, even in a "world come of age." It links the activity of worship with the mystery of God's hiddenness from the plain view, from the indifferent and passionless attitude toward existence. Worship is a time and space where language about God shapes and expresses us in such a mystery. It is a way of being and a way of understanding. So we turn again and again, in all times and places, to the ideal of that community lived in praise of God. *September 1982*

# Worship That Comes to Terms with Death

DON E. SALIERS

Christian worship, when authentic and faithful, has a connection with the deepest things in our life. It addresses birth and death, hope and fear, love and guilt, grief and joy, as well as our yearning for happiness. Living worship enacts and lives through those aspects of existence in the name and power of God through Jesus Christ. This is why ritual words and actions in our sacraments as well as in our weddings and funerals can have a powerful effect, for good or for ill, particularly as our fundamental emotions are aroused and addressed in worship.

Grief is one of the most complex of human emotions. Our vocabulary about grief is deceptive, since the words we use are relatively simple, yet the reality of grieving can be extraordinarily involved and lengthy. We speak of grieving over a death, or over leaving friends and home. Yet grief is rarely a matter of simple feeling of sadness, mourning, or regret. Rather, it connects with deep patterns in our common life: our loves, resentments, hopes, fears, angers, and needs for release and healing. Even in the "ordinary" situation of grieving the death of a long-lived grandparent, much is hidden both from those who mourn and from those who seek to minister to the bereaved. Thus there can be no simple correlation between doing a funeral service and honestly dealing with human grief and bereavement.

We are creatures of time *in* time. We continually restructure the past by re-thinking, and re-valuing relationships now lost to the past. This restructuring of the past is often a struggle with guilt, anxiety, and regret. This is how grief is tied up with other emotions.

In any given occasion of grief, we accept varying degrees of responsibility for the loss and, most certainly, for failures in the relationship before its loss. These are to be worked through in the whole process of coming to terms with death and loss through memory. Good liturgy can enable this process by showing, over time, the profound connection between the remembrance (*anamnesis*) of the death and resurrection of Christ and its saving power over our guilt, anxiety, and grief in the face of death and loss.

The church in its funeral rites has traditionally done three things: commended the dead to God, witnessed to the future resurrection of the baptized with Christ, and ministered to the bereaved, supporting and sustaining the faithful. It has, of course, often failed to do these things adequately. In many instances we have come to concentrate on other matters, such as the need to repent in the face of death, judgment, and damnation. Funerals too often become occasions for "evangelistic" fervor. But the most singular failure on the part of most church funeral customs and rituals is the inadequate handling of bereavement and the grieving process itself.

Our basic problem stems from an abuse of the heart of the gospel; namely, the death and resurrection of Jesus Christ. In twentieth-century American culture, we have inherited death-denying attitudes which are easily supported by a quick appeal to "God will take care of everything." Appeals to general immortality or to a resurrection without honest realization of the cross and death of Christ can often reduce our funerals to exercises in avoidance and sentimentality. Instead, Christian ritual ought always to express the mystery of death and resurrection so that the human process of grieving is addressed with honesty and healing power.

The language of the psalms which have been part of the funeral rites since earliest times helps us to clarify the reality of our life. Death is real, and loss is very present. God is our refuge and help, not by providing illusions and false comfort, but precisely by identifying with our pain and suffering and grief. There is room in the psalms for expressing some of the negative feelings which are part of loss. Powerful and sometimes conflicting feelings and attitudes need to be acknowledged.

In individual grief, we need to work through both the genuine love and the possible idolatry of such relationships. The good and the bad need to be symbolized in the process of finding how to live without the person. But corporate worship goes beyond the individual process involved to reorder and restructure one's life in the community of care and belonging. Death is faced in the context of "in Adam we all die; so in Christ we all are made alive" (1 Corinthians 15:22).

Christian ministers cannot expect the funeral liturgy itself, no matter how powerful, to be a sufficient occasion for dealing fully with grief. In many cases, a pastorally sensitive funeral service may be only the beginning point for what must take time and continuing communal experience of healing. Since grieving is itself a long-term, temporal process, we cannot expect one event to provide release. On the other hand, creating the illusion of escape from the reality of death may seriously impair the healing process, no matter how pious or sincere the faith of the minister or the family may be.

The continuing communal context of gathering for prayer, Scripture, the Word, and sacraments is essential. Here the quality of honesty in the fellowship is very important. Reincorporation into the liturgical life of the church community is a distinctive aspect of ritualizing the process of grief; for only by the common reality of the paschal mystery in a living community of the faithful can the deeper healing and release take place.

Pastoral experience teaches us that many people who grieve over the death of a close family member find it difficult to "return to church" and, more often, to participate in the sacrament of the Lord's Supper. This is a natural reaction to the pain of returning without the loved one to such a significant place of human gathering. Yet if our funeral liturgies are to express the mystery of death and resurrection with Christ more adequately, we cannot shy away from dealing honestly with death and loss in the ongoing worship of the community. Every baptism and Holy Communion should speak Christian reality with freshness and vigor. This means we must not fail to preach the great themes of death and resurrection, of facing our guilt and grief and hope even when we are not immediately in the face of death. In other words, preaching the great baptismal themes and a more adequate sacramental theology is essential to the church's ministry to the whole process of bereavement and grief.

Pastoral counseling is crucial in all of this, but the communal celebration addresses aspects of grief and the need for relatedness to others which individual counseling and meditation cannot. But being more pastorally aware of the complexities of human grief must also inform the manner in which we design and lead the funeral rituals. The prayers, actions, and other texts need to have integrity. The whole ritual process—the vigil in the house with the family (or in the "funeral home"), to the church service, and to the cemetery or other committal rite—requires both faithfulness to the whole theological range of the gospel and a keen insight into the nature of this particular grieving family's situation.

The meaning and function of Christian rites of death and resurrection are to express and enact the gospel in a manner which enables human persons to begin the work of mourning and grief and to grow into the wholeness of life together in Christ. There are many variations among persons and communities, but the ritual must always be "strong, loving, and wise."

The process of grieving and mourning will go on, and will become especially intense for many on anniversaries and holidays. The church's corporate worship over time must provide continuing occasion for the acknowledgement of such intense memories and feelings and seek ways to remember and to make honest connections with the reality of "in the midst of life there is death."

Many United Methodist congregations are recovering the powerful significance of an annual "communion of saints" celebrated on All Saints' Day (November 1 or the first Sunday in November) in which the names of all who have died in the past year are read. This way our own experiences of bereavement are recalled and joined with the ongoing proclamation of the church's faith in which the central reality is the death and resurrection of Jesus Christ our Lord, "whose death we proclaim until he comes again."

*September 1977*

# Israel's Ancient Cry

## JOHN H. HAYES

In the Book of Psalms, one finds psalms expressive of the gamut of human emotions. Some ring with the exuberant thrill of praise; others reverberate with the throes of human desperation. The heights and the depths of human life resound through its poetry.

In the Psalter, one finds the two basic modes of addressing the deity: petition and praise. Petition is expressed in the psalms of distress or laments. Praise is found in the hymns and the psalms of thanksgiving. In psalms of distress or laments, the individual gives expression to his grief, gives verbal form to his difficulties, and petitions God for assistance. Psalms of this class comprise the largest group in the Psalter. Over fifty of the 150 psalms belong to this type.

Psalms of lament belong to the crisis situations of life. They are the products of the crucible of grief and distress. In the ordinary course of life, people encounter conditions which threaten their well-being, even their very existence, and which challenge their faith and trust. The worship of ancient Israel—as any authentic worship should—sought to deal with such situations, to offer the worshipers means for overcoming the grief and distress, and to provide the means for contact with the divine. Such means for encountering and dealing with grief and distress were prayer and sacrifice.

When sickness and disease, personal calamity, sin, and adversity struck, the worshiper could present the situation to God and, in psalm and sacrifice, could appeal to the divine. The laments of the psalms were no doubt elements in a complex of ritual. One should, in a fashion, read the Book of Leviticus, with its rituals for sacrifice, and the Book of Psalms, with its prayers, in parallel columns. Psalm and sacrifice, ritual and spoken word go together.

Psalms of distress reflect many of the grief-burdened situations of life: sickness and disease (Psalms 6, 13, 31, 38, 88, 102), being falsely accused (Psalms 3, 13, 35, 52, 56), and the guilt of sin (Psalms 25, 51). The Christian notices immediately that no place is given to the grief produced by the experience of death. The reason for this is that in ancient Israel funerals and death rituals played no role in the cultic services. Death and funerals were handled outside the arena of worship. The dead and things associated with death were in the arena of the unclean. A priest could not officiate in the temple for days after any contact with the dead.

A number of elements in the psalms of lament are worthy of note: 1) The psalms are shot through with a sense of confidence, with a firm belief that God could redeem and remove the cause of grief.

2) The psalms allowed the worshiper to give full expression to the sense of grief. All laments contain a description of the distress, often in strong and formulaic language (see Psalm 22:6-18).

3) The laments frequently allowed the worshiper to depict God as the enemy and the cause of his trouble, and thus to issue a complaint against the deity (see Psalms 13:1-2 and 44:9-10, 17).

4) The worshiper was allowed to bargain with the divine, to remind God that if he was allowed to die he could no longer offer praise (Psalm 6:5), and to make promises that were to be kept if the prayer was granted (Psalms 7:17, 22:22, 35:28).

5) The lament allowed the ones praying to face openly and honestly their predicaments and to express their genuine hostility toward that predicament and its cause (see Psalm 109 where a vitriolic form occurs).

Finally, the laments frequently already embody praise and thanksgiving. Thanksgiving psalms (such as 30, 32, 34, 73, 103, 111, 116) looked back upon the past distress and offered thanksgiving and praise for redemption in the context of offering the fulfillment of vows.

However, a number of the laments are characterized by a shift from lament to praise, from anguish to celebration, from mourning to joy. One of the clearest examples of this shift within a lament is Psalm 6. The first seven verses of this psalm lament the condition of the worshiper, describe his distress, and appeal to God for help. Suddenly, the tone of the psalm shifts to a note of assurance and certainty. Verses 8-10 no longer lament; these verses bombastically scold the workers of inequity and display an assured arrogance.

These psalms show the worshiper turning from grief to joy. What may have been the cause for such a shift? For one thing, we know that Israelite priests, unlike modern Protestant preachers, were willing to declare the worshiper as forgiven, as righteous, and as one whom God has heard (see Psalm 6:8-9). Secondly, the worshiper was allowed to give expression to the depth of the grief and to the hostility experienced—in itself therapeutic. Thirdly, the offering of psalm and sacrifice was itself an act of assurance, a participation in the ordained means for experiencing and contacting the divine.

The laments give vivid embodiment to Israel's belief that when grief was expressed in psalm and sacrifice, life could be transformed and restored, enemies overcome, and the troubled soul consoled.

*September 1977*

# Praying Ecumenically

## DON E. SALIERS

The renewal of worship and the recovery of spirituality go hand in hand. Among various Christian traditions we find an increasing recognition of this interrelation. Prayer is essential to all Christian ministries, and corporate worship is the heartbeat of the church's continuing dialogue with God. When our public liturgy and personal prayer are trivialized, made rootless, or become one-sided, our lives before God and our vision of ministry are impoverished. Spirituality, which may be defined as our embodied relationship to God and neighbor in response to God's gracious offer of salvation, is thus not an option for those who are interested, but essential to converted lives and to the renewal of the church.

Recent years have witnessed increasing interest and concern with prayer and worship among Christians of widely different traditions. The very term "spirituality," which once seemed the special province of monastic communities and mystics, is now becoming part of our common vocabulary—though some are still mystified or embarrassed by this. At the same time every major denomination has undertaken during the years since Vatican II the reform of public worship, from the rites of Christian initiation (baptism, confirmation, and renewal), daily prayer, and the church year/lectionary, to the sacrament of the Lord's Supper.

Reforming how we worship is part of the larger ecumenical and liturgical movements of the twentieth century. However, producing new texts is one thing, and the authentic renewal of the church's prayer is another. Renewal certainly requires reform, especially when our general practices have lost contact with deeper historical, theological, and existential roots. But renewal of living prayer requires a faithful community formed in the Word and animated by God the Holy Spirit in commitment to serve the world.

Many of us in ministry who must also be leaders of worship and teachers of prayer sense the lack of sustaining spirituality in our own lives. We are concerned that the church not just *talk* piety and recite the language of Zion, but that it experience genuine discernment and depth in worship and ethics beyond cliches of piety and conventional morality. To our surprise the deepest reforms in worship have also been the points of challenge to personal spirituality, often at the point of congregational struggle and resistance. This is in large measure a result of recognizing authentic Christian prayer and life across denominational lines. Yet this aspect of reform and renewal also creates a special problem. How can we learn to pray and worship ecumenically without giving up our sense of belonging to a particular tradition, whether Methodist, Lutheran, Roman Catholic, or Baptist?

The process of deepening our spirituality and searching for more adequate public worship does require the pain of change and growth. With the liturgical reforms of sacramental services and the renewal of preaching, prayer, and song, we encounter new forms and often a shift in "style" in the deepest sense of that word. This is evident in the Supplemental Worship Resources of the United Methodist Church. Celebrating the Easter Vigil or Ash Wednesday or the baptismal covenant renewal takes us in new directions. To many sincere persons in the United Methodist Church—or in any other church body—these very forms may seem *not* part of "our tradition." Ironically, we encounter in local churches people who resist more frequent celebration of Holy Communion or a more joyous resurrection-oriented tone because they have been formed in a pattern of infrequent, highly penitential style of the sacrament (heavily dependent upon an uncritical acceptance of the modified 1662 Anglican Prayer Book). Or, people may resist a more informal evangelical style of congregational prayer, or the recovery of singing the psalms because these appear "un-Methodist."

Yet it is precisely in such elements that we may begin to sense our belonging to a much larger Christian tradition which may liberate us to discover our own specific tradition anew. For United Methodists this includes a marvelous combination of sacramental life, a rhythm and constancy in prayer, a deeper understanding of the Word of God in Scripture, the practices of fasting and a disciplined life, and the vital link between prayer and good works. The convergence of catholic substance in worship with a prophetic word and evangelical witness in personal and communal-ethical life: this is where reform and renewal can lead us.

Shifts in the language and style of prayer and worship cannot be undertaken lightly. Resistance to such growth and change often result because the clergy themselves have not done an adequate job of teaching and preparing the whole congregation, including the enabling of good teaching by the laity. In my own pastoral experience I have seen churches which first disliked the idea of becoming more intentional and reflective concerning liturgy and devotional prayer ("Don't give me Nouwen or Merton when we have the Daily Blessing!") suddenly bloom like flowers in the spring when they were given historically grounded and theologically sound teaching on the richness of the Christian liturgical and spiritual traditions. A broader and deeper vision of prayer and worship is appreciated. Our problem at this point may not be the use of cross-tradition, patristical and ecumenically shared forms, but the lack of trained persons who understand the necessity of sustained pastoral teaching and encouragement. More deeply still, it may be that we are not perceived to be men and women of prayer. In this latter case our own spiritual growth and further formation may be the one thing most needed.

So we must understand that the call to be more ecumenically alive in our worship and prayer is not *away* from identity, but more deeply *toward* true identity in Christ. This idea is painful because it requires that we assess our practice and theology right at our most vulnerable point: how we pray and worship. We must discern whether we have domesticated the mystery of life before God.

It seems appropriate therefore that we examine with honesty and humility the question of how ecumenical our prayer and worship are, not because we wish to forfeit our identity as United Methodists or Baptists or Episcopalians, but precisely because we are called in our time to a more profound unity in Jesus Christ which transcends our parochial and limited understandings of the gospel as simply "what our kind of folks pray and do." This deeper unity, thank God, is already given in our common baptism, and it is the work of God the Holy Spirit in our age which has caused us to recognize again in Christ that "one faith, one baptism, one God and Father of us all" which constitutes our deepest unity.

Once we see this connection and are grasped by its reality and power, we cannot go home again to our sectarian and defensive ideas of worship and life; but neither can we settle for a mere "paper church" or simply structural uniformity which would supress the rich variety of ways in which Christians pray and worship. So whites must learn from the black traditions, and Roman Catholics from evangelicals, and Protestants from Anglicans and Orthodox. This richness of ways is also a plentitude of gifts given by the Holy Spirit from the beginning of the churches which, in our time, we have been called to gather in our search for deeper spirituality.

Pray ecumenically? Yes. "Lord, teach us to pray." And in the midst of recovery of the ancient, and the surprising discovery of the authentic forms in the present, we will count it joy to become a more faithful church and sign of God's kingdom which is and is to come.

*February 1982*

# Early Worship around the Supper Table

## CHARLES D. HACKETT

To talk about "worship" in the early church is anachronistic because such talk implies the image of people who are in this time or this place "worshiping" while in another time or another place "not worshiping." The dichotomy suggests our modern consciousness of a split between the sacred and the profane, the spiritual and the worldly. Our brothers and sisters of the early church apparently did not experience reality split in such a manner. Rather, the tension they knew was the tension between this present world and the new and glorious world which was about to come. The question was not whether or not one was worshiping, but whether one was a citizen of this present world or of the world to come. It was the matter of this citizenship which described one's activity.

In this world the powers of sin ruled so that every human endeavor, even the most evidently religious, was doomed to frustration. In the world to come God's will would prevail so that every activity, even the most mundane, would be a glorious articulation of creative love and harmony. Put most simply, in this world worship was impossible; in the world to come everything was to be worship. The Christian was a person who, through association with the person, death, and resurrection of Jesus lived paradoxically in both worlds.

A Christian thus continued the necessary activities of existence in this world but experienced himself or herself to be proleptically participating in the world to come. The context for this proleptic participation was the community of the church which, in its fellowship together, experienced a foretaste of the world to come insofar as in that fellowship there existed love and spirit of a quality (and perhaps quantity) different from elsewhere. This love, this spirit, they thought, was God's "down payment" to them on the kingdom to come in which they had citizenship.

Thus, the earliest Christians did very little different from others. Rather, they continued to do much that they had always done (though surely with a greatly elevated moral discernment), but they invested the ordinary with proleptic meaning. Activities which in this world were means to transitory ends became, for the Christian, vehicles of participation in the perfect world to come (cf. 1 Corinthians 10, 2 Corinthians 4-6:11, Romans 8).

An important center for everyday activities in "this world" for most first-century people was the supper table. It constituted for Gentile and Jew alike the center of primary community—family or closest associates who ate together in important places such as homes. It represented the result of most human effort. People worked to get food to eat. Fortunate people had enough or more to eat, unfortunate people did not. In our culture of technology, prepared foods, and relative abundance we forget how a culture such as that of the first century was oriented around eating: first, getting enough to eat and second, elevating the quality of the eating experience as a center of meaning in life. The infamous Roman "orgy" was not primarily sexual; it was an effort to raise the experience of dining and socializing to such a level that life itself would take on meaning (Paul's reference to those whose "God is in their belly...." [Philippians 3:19] is to be understood in this light). In effect, eating was a religious endeavor.

For the Jew, the supper table was doubly important for it was in the meal (the Passover) that Jewish identity was manifest and renewed. It was in the Passover that the Jewish history was recalled, and it was in that same meal that the Jewish expectation of the fulfillment of God's promise to Israel was renewed. For the Jew every meal was to some degree a reflection of the Passover; every gathering for table fellowship was worship.

The important tradition of the "last supper" witnesses to the centrality of the meal in early Christian life. The picture Paul draws of the life of the early church (cf. especially 1 Corinthians 11:17ff.) suggests that the supper was the central focus of the life of the church. The early church gathered naturally around the supper table. There they would eat, socialize, and in so doing, participate in some reality. The question was: *What* reality? Was it to be *this* world, the world to *come*, or, perhaps (the genius of St. Paul!), a dialectical coincidence of both at once?

Depending on how he or she understood that meal of meeting, the early Christian tended to understand all other activities in the same way. If the meal was only of "this world," there would be no hope of salvation. If the meal was somehow only of "the world to come," there would issue a gnosticism which pretended that the hard realities of sin no longer existed. So Paul argued for the eschatological tension of both cross and resurrection, of this world and the world to come. Only in holding to this tension could one worship properly—or, indeed, worship at all—for only in this tension could one manage human life. Only in this tension could one enjoy and do what was good and true, and abhor and stand against what was evil and ugly, while at the same time experiencing them as relativized and made bearable by the reality of the coming kingdom of God.

Worship was, then, nothing less than the whole of life lived in and understood from the dialectic of eschatology. The paradigmatic center of this worship life was the supper table of the church where the ordinary and necessary eating and drinking and socializing became infused with the presence of that Life and Death and Resurrection which promised the World to Come.

*December 1978*

# Gluttony and a Deeper Hunger

RODNEY J. HUNTER

The traditional image of the glutton—a sort of Henry VIII figure two-fisting his way through a heap of food—is not what we generally encounter as gluttony today. At least our gluttony usually has a more civil appearance. Nevertheless, most Americans eat too much and, as any day on the beach will reveal, are moderately if not grotesquely overweight.

Yet we fool ourselves if we think that the problem is simply one of eating too much, or if we suppose that the solution lies in imposing dietary asceticisms: 1,500-calorie limits, no sweets or french fries, exercising daily, and the like. Food carries deep and powerful psychological significance. From infancy it is associated in the most intimate ways with love, care, and protection. Eating together is still one of the primary symbols of social acceptance, and food soothes the soul even as it eases the pangs of hunger. Not surprisingly, therefore, anxiety and conflict in human relationships readily find expression in patterns of eating and drinking.

American life in particular seems to generate an almost continuous charge of tension, anxiety, and felt conflict, deriving from our institutionalized patterns of competition for daily bread and daily care. Caught in the tensions of often superficial, hurried relationships and meaningless work, who is not tempted to plunge impulsively into the succulent sugars, fats, and carbohydrates that our fast-food technology offers us in almost limitless quantity?

Food fills a void in the physical sense, but for many its deeper significance lies in its deceptive spiritual promise, insofar as it tempts us with immediate gratification of the longings of our souls for just and loving relationships and meaningful, valuable work. But when we accede to its temptation the inner corruptions and contradictions of our lives are made evident. We fill our bellies over and over without being able to fill our souls. And the rapacious gusto with which we bite into our food, consume and destroy it, reveals the frustrations of the competitive pressure and lifestyle we have made for ourselves in America, with its technological values of dominance and control.

Because the problem is rooted so deeply in our culture and hence in our very personalities, the answer cannot lie entirely in simple attempts to reassert moral ascetic controls. My own frustrated history of broken diets and forsaken regimens of daily exercise has convinced me that we deceive ourselves if we believe that acts of moral self-discipline and will, apart from a more searching, personal judgment and healing of our souls, will save us. Even Weight Watchers and health spas cannot finally deliver us. For whatever their immediate achievements, which apparently derive from their social and authority dynamics, all such solutions pit self against self or against others for the sake of achieving personal and moral self-control. Solutions based on this sort of conflict, however unconscious or invisible, are bound to be unstable in the long run. Instead, control must be rooted in faith and trust and express an integrated selfhood, if it is to be durable and true.

Thus the answer lies in the direction of personal, social, and spiritual renewal, which requires that we undertake the honest and painful task of acknowledging the many ways, in ordinary living, through which our own values, commitments, and capacities are perverse and backward. I refer primarily to the ways in which our loving is unjust and domineering, and our work meaningless, trivial, and uncommitted to large pursuits of inherent worth beyond ourselves. For the everyday gluttony of our lifestyle reveals the deeper contradictions of our hearts and spirits.

Only by coming to terms with these basic perversions of our social and individual living, in repentance and faith, can the outward disorder of our lives, the gluttony of our bodies, hope to be transformed into the image of him who alone gives us our daily bread, the Bread of Life.

*December 1977*

# Gluttony and Gospel

## ARTHUR WAINWRIGHT

Since gluttony is one of the seven deadly sins, it might be expected to receive special treatment in the Gospels. It does not. No equivalent of the word "gluttony" occurs anywhere in the New Testament. There are words translated "riotous living," "profligacy," and "drunkenness," but no specific word meaning "gluttony." On one occasion Jesus is falsely accused of being "a glutton and a drunkard" (Matthew 11:19, Luke 7:43), and in the letter to Titus there is a reference to gluttons in a quotation from the Greek poet Epimenides (Titus 1:12). But neither in the Gospels nor elsewhere in the New Testament is there any specific teaching on the subject of overeating.

Silence about this theme does not imply approval of the practice of overeating. It does indicate, however, that gluttony is a vice which cannot adequately be considered in isolation from the rest of conduct. If attention is paid to the Gospels, instructions about appropriate limits to eating are not to be found there. But there is teaching about attitudes connected with eating.

Anxiety about food and drink is the theme of a warning uttered by Jesus (Matthew 6:25ff., Luke 12:22ff.). Anxiety does not mean a responsible concern for obtaining a livelihood. It is a persistent worry about material things that takes control of the mind. It is likely to be found where people are obsessed with a desire for the acquisition of goods and property. Matthew's Gospel puts Jesus' teaching on the theme immediately after the assertion, "You cannot serve God and mammon," and Luke's Gospel puts it after the parable of the rich farmer whose life was dominated by the desire to provide a large stock of goods for his future.

Eating is viewed adversely in the Gospels when it is the result of covetousness. The parable of the rich farmer (Luke 12:13-21) depicts a man who, having accumulated a large amount of wealth, said to himself, "You have ample goods laid up for many years; take your ease, eat, drink, be merry!" According to Luke's Gospel the rich man, eager for the pleasures of the dinner table, was an example of covetousness. "Beware of all covetousness," says Jesus before he tells the parable. It is not just eating of which Jesus speaks, but preoccupation with material wealth, of which food and drink are only a part.

The Greek word for "covetousness" means literally "having too much," and refers to the selfish desire to obtain too much at the expense of other people. When individuals or whole classes of society are able to indulge in lavish and luxurious living, it is because other people are being deprived of things that should rightfully be theirs. Sometimes covetousness takes the form of unreflecting neglect, when people are so obsessed with their own ambitions that they have no concern for the welfare of others. Sometimes it takes the form of a deliberate appropriation of wealth that belongs to others. It is this kind of covetousness which is condemned when the letter of James says, "Behold, the wages of the laborers who mowed your fields, which you kept back by fraud; and the cries of the harvesters have reached the ears of the Lord of hosts. You have lived on the earth in luxury and pleasure" (James 5:4-5).

The Gospels also speak adversely of eating when it proceeds from a neglect of God. The parable of the rich farmer is followed by the statement, "So is he who lays up treasure for himself, and is not rich toward God." Once again eating and drinking are seen as an example of a more deep-seated malady than mere gluttony. The farmer loved himself so much that he failed to love God. The desire to acquire material goods leads to the worship of wealth ("mammon," Matthew 6:24) and therefore to worship of the self.

Today the physician's warnings about overweight and the fear of shortening our span of life are the main inducements to self-discipline in eating. But the Gospels show that there are other factors to consider. When we are totally preoccupied with anxieties about food and other material things, when eating is the product of covetousness, and when it leads to the neglect of God, we need to review our priorities. It is not just a matter of achieving self-discipline in our eating habits. It is a matter of our relationship to other people and to God.

The message of the Gospels in this respect is not all warnings and condemnation. In the parable of the prodigal son (Luke 15:11-32) Jesus tells of a man who, having squandered his goods in riotous living, repented of his behavior and was received by his father. There is mercy for those who turn to God. Jesus also gives positive advice. His teaching does not concentrate, however, on the discipline of fasting. Although he himself practiced it and recognized its validity (Matthew 4:2, 6:16-18), he did not live as ascetic a life as John the Baptist and his disciples (Mark 2:18, Matthew 9:14ff.). Jesus' advice about eating makes other emphases. Concern for food and drink should be subordinated to concern for God: "Seek first his kingdom, and these things shall be yours as well" (Luke 12:31).

As for feasting, Jesus, who participated in festive meals himself, says "When you give a feast, invite the poor, the maimed, the lame, the blind, and you will be blessed, because they cannot repay you. You will be repaid at the resurrection of the just" (Luke 14:13-14). There is nothing wrong with feasting when food is shared with those who need it most. It is the motive that counts: love and compassion instead of covetousness; not the craving for treasure for the self, but richness toward God.

*December 1977*

# From Holy Meals to TV Dinners

JAMES F. HOPEWELL

Food is going to hell. Not only has it grown more tasteless, it has also grown less religious. Throughout most of human history what one ate had extraordinary ties with how one prayed, but now, except for the grace sometimes cast in front of a meal, the connection between food and faith has largely disappeared, deadening both our prayers and our palates.

Most peoples in the past would not understand how eating and piety could be so divorced. For most the supply of food was so precarious that it required a prolonged and precise rhythm of community action to produce it, as well as an imaginative attitude of the partaker to value it. This rhythm would mark the holiest of community rituals, and this imagery was the stuff of sacred myths. Gods were found in grain; sacrifice involved the preparation of food; communion required its eating. Daily bread became hard and holy.

Ordinary families knew this. Both their day and calendar were charged with food-getting, -preparing, and -eating activities which also presented the nature and rules of their deity. "You are what you eat" would carry for these folks a primarily spiritual meaning. By what they ate, and did not eat, they showed what was holy and what was their personal relationship to that holiness. The possibility of showing the holy through how and what one ate, however, also carried such a misplaced focus of correct behavior and such an illusion of mystic control that Jesus Christ and his first followers deliberately severed many of the connections between food and piety.

"Not what goes into the mouth" has sacred significance, Christ proclaims, "but what comes out of the mouth." This revolutionary freedom in Christ allowed the early church to cancel the dietary laws that other religions commended. For Christians, however, there remained some basic and striking bonds between food and God. The central act of worship for most Christians is still the eucharistic meal. Holy days of the church were feast-days, and devotion to Christ was marked by the fasts that acknowledged his sacrifice. Lenten and Friday fasts communicated God's passion, as holy days did his bounty.

The supply of food in present Western society has grown less precarious for most of us. God now seems much less significant to its supply, and food curiously responds to the nature and rules of its new provisioner: technology. We even call our foods according to the holy names of technology: TV dinners, fortified bread, instant breakfast. Food even senses these connotations: it seldom tastes heavenly; it often tastes like television.

Now that food has such minor consequence either to our souls or to our tastebuds, one bite tastes like any other. Freed from the sanctions of taste and piety, our appetite becomes mechanical. If our pocketbook is thick, then we eat a lot. If our belt grows too small, then we eat a little. Belts and pocketbooks have become the puny governors of an activity once dependent upon God.

Eating has become a lonely affair as well: cut off from farming and the preparation of food, severed from God, increasingly undertaken in solitude, and controlled solely by the size of our personal waists and pocketbooks. What is the role of ministry in such an era of fast foods? We ministers could give more constructive attention to this question than we have, but here are some suggestions heard around Candler's Institute for Church Ministries:

*Regaining a sense of the precariousness of food.* A gospel ministry must expose the delusion of our communities that food automatically and abundantly appears on supermarket shelves. This is bad ethics in the light of the physical hunger of the world at large, and is bad theology in light of the spiritual hunger of our neighborhoods.

*Reinstating feasts.* At a time when McDonald's is pushing its totally individualized "McFeast" concealed in a private package and consumable without reference to anyone else, a gospel ministry should renew the celebrative and communal aspects of feasts. Feasts, especially when the Eucharist is prominent within them, may be antidotes to lonely and godless eating. Perhaps that is why a feast would occur about once a month.

*Observing fasts.* The counterpart of feasting, fasting is equally essential for a gospel ministry.

*December 1977*

# The Practice of Fasting or Abstinence

## THEODORE H. RUNYON

"Will you recommend fasting or abstinence, both by precept and example?" ("Historic Examination for Admission into Full Connection," *United Methodist Book of Discipline*)

Standing before the Annual Conference, I answered that question when the bishop asked it in the same way that many of you did: as a historic question, one preserved with "Are you going on to perfection?" because of its association with Methodism's founder. Now we are suddenly discovering that the question is not the quaint anachronism we thought it was but a searching, searing intervention that threatens our fat, comfortable lifestyle and points the way toward responsible Christian stewardship.

The Holy Club at Oxford fasted two days a week, Wednesdays and Fridays, in imitation of early Christianity. Wesley recommended this practice to his preachers, but settled for a weekly fast. The term "abstinence" in the vow, Wesley defined in accordance with the Church of England as a lesser fast, "which may be used when we cannot fast entirely, by reason of sickness or bodily weakness" ("Upon our Lord's Sermon on the Mount," *Discourse VII*).

Methodists were to fast or abstain every Friday. American Methodists were exhorted to continue this pattern, though the *Discipline* in both the northern and southern branches after 1846 made fasting obligatory for members only on the Friday before each quarterly conference. And so it remained until well into the 20th century.

Why this popish practice in Methodist circles? Wesley's motive was not to promote medievalism but to obey the Scriptures, where fasting was clearly enjoined not only by the apostles but by the Son. Higher authorities for the practice he did not need or want. True, he could also argue, as do some health faddists today, that fasting promotes good health. But that is not the proper scriptural ground. Instead, Wesley was convinced that fasting is a means of grace when used as a discipline to "add seriousness and earnestness to our prayers."

Let us beware, he warned, "of fancying we merit anything of God by our fasting." We can in no wise establish our own righteousness thereby. Fasting is a discipline of waiting and trusting, "with our eye singly fixed on him." Loss of this focused and disciplined life is what Wesley feared for his followers. In a late sermon on "The Causes of the Inefficacy of Christianity" (1789), Wesley insists that even proper theology, if it is not accompanied by discipline, cannot result in "that mind in us which was also in Christ Jesus."

The discipline of fasting of which he here speaks is no preoccupation with self but precisely a sensitivity to the needs of the poor. Insensitivity "grieves the Holy Spirit," who refuses to send any blessing on those Methodist assemblies which have become affluent and complacent.

> Many of your brethren, beloved of God, have not food to eat; they have not raiment to put on; they have not a place where to lay their head. And why are they thus distressed? Because you impiously, unjustly, and cruelly detain them from what your Master and theirs lodges in your hands on purpose to supply their wants! See that poor member of Christ, pinched with hunger, shivering with cold, half naked! Meantime you have plenty of this world's goods—of meat, drink, and apparel. In the name of God, what are you doing? Do you neither fear God, nor regard man? Why do you not deal your bread to the hungry and cover the naked with a garment?

Fasting means, therefore, increased sensitivity to God and neighbor. As such, can we afford to neglect it in today's church? Can our "inefficacy" be overcome apart from this kind of discipline, a discipline which challenges our culture at its very socio-economic heart? Be not misled. Fasting is dangerous. It is downright subversive. It sensitizes people to challenge the deep-seated notion in our culture that we have a right to whatever we can afford. Wesley veritably explodes against any such claim.

> You say you can afford it! O be ashamed to take such miserable nonsense into your mouths! Never more utter such stupid cant; such palpable absurdity! Can any steward afford to be an arrant knave? To waste his Lord's good?

So much for one of the dearest notions of the consumer economy. Fasting sensitizes stewardship. Stewardship demands fasting. What could be a more pertinent way to revive inefficacious congregations?

*December 1977*

# On Self-Denial

E. BROOKS HOLIFIELD

*This article was first delivered as a sermon at a Candler School of Theology Honors Convocation.*

I am indeed honored to preach on this occasion. Upon being asked, I began searching immediately for a text that seemed to speak to the situation of seminarians departing (for the most part) to new parishes.

By some perverse accident I first hit on Luke 9:2-5: "And whenever they do not receive you, when you leave that town, shake off the dust from your feet as a testimony against them." One could luxuriate in fantasies about that text. I began even to envision a mass ministerial exodus from recalcitrant parishes. The phrase "sawdust trail" began to take on unheard-of dimensions of meaning. One could even imagine clerical labor unions with such exotic slogans as: "Pure in heart, clean of foot."

The possibilities were mind-boggling—I did not trust myself with that text. But I read further and discovered that in the Lukan narrative the return of the disciples from that "dusty" mission stands in close juxtaposition to Jesus' hard and enigmatic teaching about self-denial. And it seemed that probably no text was more appropriate to a mission into ministry than those words of Jesus: "If any man would come after me, let him deny himself and take up his cross daily and follow me. For whoever would save his life will lose it, and whoever loses his life for my sake, he will save it" (Luke 9:23-24).

A text on self-denial seems appropriate on this occasion for a variety of reasons, some relatively trivial and some cutting to the center of the faith.

I think it is undeniable that a nagging impediment to ministry in our time is the intrusion of a certain kind of self-consciousness. Seminary has presumably been an occasion for asking profound and weighty questions: What is the nature of God? What is ministry? Will I survive the professional assessment? But presumably one unanswered question floating now in the back of your minds is a simpler one: What will my parishioners think of me?

The question is not new. In rummaging around the 19th century recently I came upon a diary by a southern minister named Joseph Cottrell who in 1855 occupied the pulpit of Pensacola, Florida, and agonized about the scrutiny of his parishioners. Cottrell had taught French and mathematics. He was a college graduate. But when he went to Pensacola he became extremely self-conscious.

He began plodding through English and Latin grammars, as he said, "trudging through that which others think I am (accomplished) in," fearing even to send a letter "lest some word has been misspelt." He would arise at daybreak in order to study before breakfast. He studied in the early morning, took a walk, studied throughout mid-morning. His pastoral duties occupied his early afternoon hours—and then more study. He tried to study Latin and history in the morning, theology in the afternoon, and more general topics at night.

Cottrell had high ambitions: he wanted to "be far wiser and better than persons imagine—to surpass the ideal of the vulgar mind, and attain to heights to which they are wholly ignorant." He sometimes bemoaned his efforts to keep up appearances: "One half the labor spent in studying which is thrown away trying to hide ignorance, would make scholars of many." And it was hard for him to escape a sense of inadequacy and failure: "Oh, that I had improved my time regularly, and studied with system. My advancement would have been much greater."

I suspect that we can all sympathize to some degree with Joseph Cottrell's worries about his capacities to meet the expectations of other people. Cottrell struck me as a quite human character. But I also suspect that most of us have begun to realize, intellectually, if not emotionally, that we cannot shape others' perceptions of us. That lies largely beyond our control.

Probably most of you can recall that occasion in a classroom when you began to speak and then realized that your words exposed you to judgment, with the result that you became utterly inarticulate, groping, self-conscious. That, I think, is an accurate emblem of entry into the parish for many ministers: the experience of being gripped by self-consciousness.

Of course this will pass. But perhaps it is well to linger on it for a moment, because like most trivial issues it points to larger ones. Let me suggest that one of the pressing issues of human life in our time and place is the attempt to transcend self-consciousness.

Now I am beginning to speak of self-consciousness in a slightly different and more profound way. I am referring to our consciousness of ourselves as finite, fallible, creaturely beings, our consciousness of ourselves as beings who make mistakes (tragic mistakes), who die, who hurt other people for reasons that we fail even to understand.

On that level self-consciousness becomes a frightening, sometimes terrifying experience. And so we attempt to overcome the limits. Sometimes we try to conform the self to the world—we consume, or achieve, or seek self-forgetfulness in sensuousness.

Sometimes we try to conform the world to the self. Probably no "cult" is more pervasive in our culture than the cult of the self. We are quite explicit about it. We value self-expression, self-expressiveness, harmonious self-realization, self-fulfillment. We try to conform everything to the contours of our own needs, to suck everything into the contours of the self. We exalt relevance—by which we often mean immediate relevance, relevance to the grasping needs of the self.

I have had the sublime experience during the past year of teaching with my wife Vicky a third-grade Sunday school class. It is sometimes an experience that makes one return longingly to the Lukan passage that speaks of shaking the dust off one's feet and departing hastily.

During our first quarter we taught the Old Testament. (I use the word "taught" loosely.) We taught largely contents—the stories, the narratives. And that prompted from one parent the impatient response: "How irrelevant."

Now Nashville must have heard similar complaints, for the teachers' text for this quarter is *Transactional Analysis for Tots*. We move from archaic texts to depth, meaning, relevance, self-enhancement. And that is all right, I suppose. *Transactional Analysis for Tots* has nice pictures. The kids will like it. But it does fit into a larger pattern, the pattern of preoccupation with immediate relevance.

We have transformed psychoanalysis into a cult of personal fulfillment (Freud would have laughed sardonically). We have transformed theology into therapy, Jesus into an image of ourselves. We can recognize that transformation when it is vulgarly done: as when Bruce Barton published his life of Jesus entitled *The Man Nobody Knows*, and revealed to us that Jesus was the greatest advertising executive the world has ever seen.

It is terribly difficult to recognize the transformation of Jesus when it is done with refinement and sophistication. And I think that we shall continue to do it again and again. But it is important that we cannot fully appropriate Jesus into our worldview. The Jesus who scandalizes us is as crucial as the Jesus who speaks to us; we would be remiss to smooth over the scandal, to conform Jesus too easily to ourselves.

Now that jeremiad was far too sweeping, but it does prepare the way for the central claim of this sermon, a claim about ministry: *Ministry comes into closest contact with the human dilemma in our time and place when it embodies the discipline of self-denial.*

Back to the Lukan text. "If any man would come after me, let him deny himself...." It is incredibly easy to trivialize this. We are accustomed to the easy language of self-denial. It is a staple of fund-raising drives, special offerings, and the last evening of youth camps (where it is spoken softly as the campfires crackle). It usually is reduced to a program of omissions and abstentions; or it is romanticized as martyrdom; or it is trivialized as a winsome self-effacement (whereupon self-denial comes to be seen as shuffling our feet and speaking in a subdued tone of voice). But in fact these usual pieties about self-denial are generally disguised forms of self-veneration, without the slightest recognition that one insuperable barrier to participation in the kingdom is the relentless intrusion of self-veneration, and that a dying to self is close to the center of the Christian life.

Self-denial is not asceticism (which in many cases is simply another form of self-preoccupation). Self-denial, rather, is the full and attentive exposure of the self to the realities outside the self. Or perhaps one could say—somewhat more cryptically—the full and attentive exposure of the self to the real.

Let me try to suggest something of what this might mean—and then what it implies for ministerial piety and practice.

One dimension of self-denial is simply the repudiation of the self's merciless pretensions. How difficult it is for us to forgive ourselves for having limits; how difficult it is to recognize and accept that there are boundaries (both within and without ourselves) that are not subject to our wishful control.

In another, more important, dimension self-denial is the struggle to attain a selfless regard for the real. Dying unto self is the effort to overcome the relentless insinuation of the self into every vision, every project, every yes, and every no.

Self-denial is a selfless respect for reality: a respect—a looking and a looking again, painfully, carefully. It is the attempt to focus one's gaze on the reality outside the self—even when that reality is a blinding light that burns away the dross of our fantasies.

Self-denial is like unto the vision of God, the vision of Yahweh. It is like unto the vision of God's holiness. But ah, one might say, this regard for the real, this respect for the intractable otherness of things, this is not like unto the vision of God, for the vision of God exalts the self and has nothing to do with commonplace realities. But that is not what the prophets say. Listen to Hosea on the holiness of Yahweh. In Canaanite fertility religion the holy was the separate; for Hosea the "Holy One" was "in your midst" (Hosea 11:9). Or Isaiah: "Holy, holy, holy is Yahweh of hosts; the whole earth is full of His glory."

The prophetic vision of Yahweh is a vision of rivers and whirlwinds, chariots and horses, fires and locusts, and plumb lines and summer fruit. It is a vision of Yahweh in our midst. It is a vision of a world outside ourselves. And far from exalting the self, the vision of Yahweh humbles and casts down. Listen to Isaiah: "the vision" is "stern."

"My loins are filled with anguish; pangs have seized me, like the pangs of a woman in travail; I am bowed down so that I cannot hear; I am dismayed so that I cannot see. My mind reels" (Isaiah 21:2-4).

Self-denial is like unto the vision of Yahweh. But we could also illustrate it with more commonplace realities: The English novelist Iris Murdoch has often written of the struggle for selflessness. It is ingredient, she says, in good art which, unlike happenings, is "something preeminently outside ourselves and resistant to our consciousness. We surrender ourselves to its authority...."

It is ingredient in such a mundane reality as learning a language which is itself an "authoritative structure that commands respect." "Love of a language leads me away from myself towards something alien to me, something which my consciousness cannot take over, swallow up, deny or make unreal," Murdoch writes in *The Sovereignty of Good*.

Now what does all this have to do with ministry? I am calling, I suppose, for a certain kind of ministerial piety. Most of us are products of a specific pietistic tradition that required self-scrutiny, introspection, the examination of motives, and the testing of internal righteousness. Though we may bewail the fact, most of us have become adept cartographers of the inner life.

You see, the pietists were right when they insisted that piety was embedded in honest ministry. But don't we need a different kind of piety? A devotion to the real? To the extent that we approximate this devotion, the activities of ministry become themselves the embodiment and exercise and expression of piety.

To listen, for example, really to listen, and to overcome the temptation to explain, the temptation to fill the void with soothing words and spin a verbal web of self-serving protection, is to commingle piety and ministry.

I can recall visiting in one hospital room with a man involved in an automobile accident in which a young woman was killed. It was an awkward moment. But the minister who came by was crisp, cheerful, smiling, voluble, smooth. He asked the usual questions in rapid-fire fashion; he suggested a word of prayer; he prayed smoothly, quickly; and as he left he gave us a bulletin from his church.

I recall another minister who sat at Emory Hospital with a young couple who had encountered utter tragedy, and the three of them held hands and cried. And thus he said everything that could or should have been said. Because he was with them, he was enrapt in their reality. That was the commingling of piety and ministry.

To study a text—to search the Scripture—is, to the extent that it is honest and careful and painstaking, a suppression of self. Or to look carefully at the people in our congregations and to accept their separateness and differentness, is an expression of devotion to the real. It is so easy to make them extensions of our ambitions; to seize them and use them and appropriate them. The anxious tentacles of the self will reach out for them and fog any clarity of vision. You see, self-denial is ingredient in honest ministry.

But let me add one further word. Such a piety is hard-won. In fact it is never won; it is never possessed. Most of the traditions that have shaped us have spoken of the centrality of a decision—a decision that issues in (according to one's favorite vocabulary) salvation, or authentic existence, or openness to the future, or the acceptance that we are accepted.

But the fat, grasping, demanding ego is not overcome by a decision to be open to the future. If it is ever overcome at all—and I suspect that we are destined to have to be content with fragments and pieces—then it is overcome only with patient persistence; it is overcome from time to time, now and then, but not once and for all. And that is to say that the Christian life—for most of us—is not in fact perpetual openness and freedom and care-less-ness. The sin remains, and the Christian life at its best is a life, rather, of repentance: ongoing exposure of the self to the judgment of the real (with the realization that the judgment is both painful and cleansing).

Ours is a culture in search of the transcendent experience that will erase the creatureliness: Erhard seminar training, primal scream therapies, transactional analysis, Esalen, Gestalt, Emotional Flooding, Encounter, Transcendental Meditation, Assertiveness Training, Bio-Feedback, Hypnotherapy, Rolfing, Bodily Awareness, Revivalist ecstasy, activist crusading, charismatic immediacy, exorcism. And some of these ecstatic movements may bring a kind of life. But all of them offer the temptation of assuming that one can transcend anxiety once and for all by the reconstruction and enhancement of the self.

I suspect that we are far more realistic when we invite people onto the way of repentance, and when we tread that way ourselves. I therefore hope for you a ministry in which, from time to time, you will lose yourself to the reality outside yourself—and help others to do the same. I hope for you a ministry in which there are moments of genuine self-denial.

*Summer 1976*

# III
# Congregational Life

## The Case of the Hidden Body

JAMES F. HOPEWELL

Our ministry support group met down the hall from a gathering of local physicians. In that they arrived in their Mercedeses and we in our Chevys, there seemed reason to hope that God might in justice give us the richer meeting. God did not. We pastors straggled into our meeting, unsure of its purpose. The doctors, however, knew what they came for and got what they wanted.

Our meeting served as a retreat from our jobs: a time for fellowship and support. The doctors instead used their time together to further a skill needed in their profession. They were soon called away to their next appointments, but we lingered on, hugging and joking and wondering whether we had something beyond our personal lives to share.

A curious difference underlying the two meetings was that one featured a body and the other hid a body. The physicians focused their attention upon the human body. Their profession rests upon determining and restoring the health of that body. Learning how to gain its health gives discipline to meetings like theirs down the hall. We pastors hid our body. Although we likewise were responsible for the health of a body whose nature is probably as complex and intriguing as the human body, our gathering nevertheless avoided its mention, except, occasionally, to complain about it.

Each profession depends upon a specific body. Professional associations gain both their rigor and their *raison d'etre* by furthering the maintenance of their particular body. For lawyers this body is the *corpus juris*, the body of law that they must understand and interpret. Doctors serve the human body. The *corpus* whose health is the pastor's responsibility is the local congregation.

The local church is the body whose care legitimates the notion that ministry is a profession. Pastors are not professionals because of their credentials, but because, like doctors and lawyers, they are responsible for the health of a particular body.

There is, however, a sort of conspiracy among Christian institutions to obscure the full reality of this body and what constitutes its health. Judicatory action tends to reduce the local church from a body to a set of numbers—membership, budget, and pastor's salary—and its health to a matter of maintaining these numbers. Seminaries seem occupied with understanding and altering the thoughts of individual students, not the thoughts of congregations. And pastors themselves, needing colleagueship and personal support, readily shift the focus of their gatherings from the health of the congregational body to the health of themselves.

The problem of the hidden body, however, goes even deeper. The church, we discover, knows surprisingly little about the anatomy and physiology of congregational bodies: what really makes them tick, what constitutes their unique personalities and outlooks, how they change, how they move in mission. Through the ages the church has concentrated so much upon what congregations should be that it has neglected to learn what they in fact are.

Candler is giving more and more attention to uncovering this hidden body. Today it teaches more courses on congregational analysis than ever before; it now supports an unprecedented amount of research in this field. Next year it will host the first national conference ever held regarding the study of the local congregation. If your ministry support group is also interested in uncovering the body, please let those of us in Candler's Rollins Center know. We need each other's insight.

*Spring 1981*

# Ministry to Believers

JAMES F. HOPEWELL

A curious blindness about belief afflicts both pastors and professors. Because faith and the belief which attends it are so central to salvation in Christ, we spend our lives discovering and proclaiming what should be believed. So important seems this task that we seldom discern and ponder what is in fact believed, even by those closest to us.

Concerned that their ministry was hampered by such blindness, a group of pastors and laypersons in North Georgia set out this spring to learn all they could about what some people in their congregations actually believed. Before interviewing their friends, however, they practiced on themselves some skills such as those of listening attentively and of refraining from "scorecarding"—that reaction which makes us automatically assign our own value to a belief another person states. Many in the group then started their interviewing process by talking about beliefs with their spouses, and several reported surprise with the unusual depth at which that conversation progressed.

Each completed several interviews and came back with new impressions, including some that raise questions about our own ministry to believers. It was reported, for example, that people of varying degrees of involvement in church activities nevertheless expressed firm confidence in most of the central Christian doctrines. Should not the ministry of preaching to such persons, then, who already share the same major beliefs with the preacher, become a more precise and probing ministry than that now practiced? To qualify as really Good News, preaching to persons whose beliefs equal those of the preacher would seem to require much more than the standard three-point rehearsal of a familiar belief.

It was also reported that these same firm believers went on to express equally strong confidence in beliefs which most ministers do not share with them: convictions about reincarnation, for example, or in astrology, or in the religious efficacy of Masonry. Surviving centuries of both orthodox and academic opposition, these beliefs pose their own question to ministry, and one that has no easy answer. One way of putting that question: when a believer in one of these latter concepts faces a major crisis in his life, should his pastor encourage, ignore, or challenge his reliance at that critical time upon that belief?

Each of us human beings deals with the world around us by constructing for ourselves a wondrously complex system of beliefs, hunches, and suspicions. Little in our theological education has prepared us to deal sensitively with that system in another person; in fact theological education seems to socialize us in a way that makes looking openly at another's beliefs very difficult. Perhaps this blindness is a beam in the very eye of faith.

*Summer 1976*

# While You Wait Expectantly

## JAMES F. HOPEWELL

You believe the world will soon end. You are a friend, not a fanatic; you go to my church, not to some mountaintop. You seem to me less obsessed by your thought than you seem eager to use it, giving sharp meaning to dull puzzles of life in the 1970s. You honor the Bible and, with guides like Hal Lindsey, you find our times and selves to be the final products of promises made in Scripture by God.

I, however, do not share your sense of Christ's imminent return. Were the million-and-a-half-year span of human existence compressed evenly into a single year ending tonight, Jesus Christ would have come the first time only today at noon. So recent an event in the majestic pace of God argues, for me, against Christ's quick return. God's timing seems so wholly different from my own that I do not expect the consummation of this world within the moment of my life.

Our problem is: *How does ministry occur between us?* We could in our conversation avoid the issue of the Second Coming. Believers like you and pastors like me learned long ago the art of polite religious talk which ignores deep issues that stir controversy. To avoid deep issues, however, is to avoid the source of ministry; so to acknowledge to each other our concern over the Second Coming, however different, may open our ministry to each other in surprising ways.

So let you and me vow to talk. I will try the following:

1) I will hear what you say. I will not jump to conclusions before you yourself make them; nor will I use your words to presume to analyze their psychic or social motive; nor will I use your thoughts primarily to improve my picture of you.

2) I will be more intent upon receiving your witness to the presence of God in our midst than upon responding with my own witness. Ministry may occur in the testimony of one to another. It may not occur if, instead of receiving your witness, I counter with my own.

3) I will recognize your witness to be not merely to the presence of God but also to the existence of a world that has an end and reckoning. This essential Christian belief resists increasingly common views about the drift and inconsequence of life.

4) I will not assume that your perception about the End automatically means your indifference to social issues.

5) I will, like Paul, see that "there is indeed no single gift that you lack, while you wait expectantly for our Lord Jesus Christ to reveal himself."

*February 1977*

# Sense Your Church's Total Language

## JAMES F. HOPEWELL

Do you recall how pungently the church of your childhood smelled: its varnishes, musts, and kitchen spices? Churches have not deodorized themselves as we have grown up. We still smell these smells, but as adults we give them smaller place in the total bombardment of sensory stimuli that strike us as we participate in the life of a congregation. A local church is held together by much more than its creed and committee meetings. It emits a total language of smells and sights and tastes and touches which, coupled with words and tones, communicates the fullness of its identity and meaning. If we wish to understand the full story of what's going on in our congregation, we might start by doing some sensitive sniffing and looking and touching around the place.

A language is the code by which a group communicates its models of reality, its attitudes and its actions among its members. That language in a local church is only in part a vocal code involving words. The other part is just as essential to church life and ministry. It involves a rich code of gestures, signs, and symbols perceived by all senses of the human body. Without these latter parts of corporate languages the local church, or any organization, would surely die.

The lowly doughnut shows how things other than words form part of the total language of the church. Take a church troubled by its people leaving abruptly after worship service. A wise committee dealing with this practice works with more than words to get people to linger. It tries to touch more than consciences; it uses more than verbal appeals. The committee addresses the full bodily relationship among members, changing the code by which worshipers may comfortably stand in each other's presence, perhaps by giving each a doughnut.

Neither provided nor consumed for the sake of nutrition, the after-worship doughnut (and the manner of its provision and eating) could become part of the language code of that church. The event could provide new group linkage, influencing the tone, timing, and possibly the meaning of common life. It is one of those signals that, if incorporated in a local church's language, conveys deep messages through organs other than the ear.

The point is not that the code can be changed but that the code works. Introduce a doughnut and almost everyone in the church would know what the gesture means and how to respond to it. The code that links signs with specific meanings in a congregation works, however, only in certain instances. Most substances found in the world would not produce such commonly understood messages. Introducing glasses of water in the church foyer after worship, for example, would probably cause bewilderment, as would the distribution of gum or grits. "What's this *for?*" we would ask, uncertain of the intended meaning. Some substances, however, as well as some shapes and gestures and sequences of these, do serve as signals within a congregation, which by convention understands each to stand *for* something else.

These signals, their combination, and the code regarding their meaning form the full language of the local church. It is a wondrously complex language, built of written and spoken words and phrases, but also including matters as tangible as doughnuts and as mute as handshakes and pouts. Together these form the code by which the congregation communicates itself, enabling it to identify and integrate itself, to express its faith and love, to govern and sometimes change its corporate behavior.

Ministers see themselves as the chief spokespersons in the congregation, their own words being the major signals transmitted in the life of their local church. Within the total language of the congregation, however, these words actually play a significant but minor part. A congregation sustains itself by a much richer language than that provided by its pastor. A good pastor spends considerable time sensing that richer language, learning its smells and sights, tastes and touches, as well as the words that it communicates.

*September 1982*

# Churches through the Looking Glass

## JAMES F. HOPEWELL

At a time when churches view themselves through the mirrors of statistics and solemn data, it is nice to report on a congregation that is pondering its image by means of a fairy tale. The tale in this case functions much like Alice's looking glass, which by giving way to fantasy reflected hard truth as well. Time will tell how much truth this church actually learns, or remembers, about itself through the fairy tale. At present the story seems to provoke an uncommon amount of self-scrutiny.

A particular, powerful story can probably be told about the life of any congregation. That tale would be one that would evoke wide understanding of such deep elements in the life of the group as: what this church fears, what behavior it rewards and what behavior it avoids, how it identifies the sacred, its sources of hope, and what embarrasses it.

As these matters differ greatly from one congregation to another, the story to be told about each is singularly its own. By dealing with the system of values peculiar to that church, the tale describes what pastors and other observers often call the "personality" or character or ethos of the congregation. Although this story on the surface may seem fanciful, its components may nevertheless reveal through nuance the deep culture of that congregation.

The trouble is that this powerful story is hard to tell. It tends even to be obscured by the usual modes of parish description. Little of what a congregation really relishes or is embarrassed about, for example, is exposed in its annual report. Such records may, rather, serve to hide the real joy and chagrin of that group. And the dull recital of names, dates, and safe anecdotes that make up most books of congregational history does little but confirm the suspicion of many folk that history is irrelevant to real life. Even a sociological study of a church done by expert consultants usually describes more keenly the group's structure than it does its culture. The character of a congregation, like that of a person, is hard to portray.

Telling the congregational story is also made difficult by our tendency to regard the more intense social interactions among the group as private, to be referred to in jokes and gossip and not in straightforward, public description. For example, the congregation featured in this article has to face such mortifying matters as the alienation of its pastor from church leaders, its decrease of financial power, doubts about its corporate worship, and questions concerning the wisdom of founding this church twenty years ago.

Issues such as these are likely to be discussed privately and not in a manner in which the thousand or more members of this body may together comprehend the state of their corporate life. How might such painful topics, together with the positive elements of this congregation's culture, be described publicly in a seasoned manner?

One way seems to be that of telling the story through a mythic framework. Whatever else they are, myths are powerful narratives by which a society comes to terms with realities it deems to be even more powerful. Myths survive because of their capacity to mediate facts of life too large and mysterious for ordinary communication. By participating in such myths a human group hears in objective, narrative form what they also experience as puzzling and perhaps deadly forces within their corporate life.

Strong congregations seem the more able to tell strong stories about themselves. One reason for this link appears to be that the story provides a handy, and often compelling, way that members can talk about the nature of their church. Strong stories, even painful ones, about one's family draw its members together, and the same dynamic seems true for the church.

Beyond this obvious reason for finding the story there is also the hunch that powerful stories lessen "scapegoating." When a congregation, wrestling with hurtful forces within itself, does not identify these forces in some comprehensive way, it is liable to personalize its problems by blaming one or another of its leaders as the cause. That leader may be fired in the hope that the problems leave with him or her.

When a strong story is told, moreover, the Christian gospel gains its context. The link between life story and the gospel is assumed in our individual lives and is celebrated in our personal confessions and testimony. In our congregation, however, the link between its corporate struggle and the gospel has been less clear, in part because the strong story that symbolizes its struggle has not been told. The kerygma for the whole congregation may better be disclosed when the myth of the latter is heard as well.

A tale from Western Europe seems to convey the character of the congregation already mentioned. Found in Grimm's collection, "Little Briar Rose" is one of the sleeping beauty stories, featuring the curse laid upon a child long wished for by her royal parents. In their celebration of her birth they do not adequately provide for guests, and an uninvited wise woman interjects a curse of death among the blessings. In spite of the efforts of her parents the girl, in her fifteenth year, discovers a spindle, is pricked as the witch predicted, and with the entire palace falls dead asleep for a hundred years.

A thick briar hedge imprisons the castle and impales a succession of kings' sons who come to rescue the princess. Ultimately a prince comes who makes it through the thorns, which then turn to roses. He kisses Briar Rose, who awakens, etc.

In *The Uses of Enchantment* Bruno Bettelheim describes in convincing detail the underlying message of this fairy tale. While told in families for sheer enjoyment, it transmits as well, Bettelheim argues, a message to children regarding their sexual awakening, their exasperation in adolescence over a period of inactivity that seems to last a hundred years, the peril of premature sexual relations, and the ultimate fruition of the person in conjugal love. The message of the fairy tale, Bettelheim declares, is "Don't worry and don't try to hurry things. When the time is ripe, the impossible problem will be solved, all by itself."

The uncanny resonance of this story with the ethos of the church in question can only be hinted here. Like Briar Rose the congregation enjoyed extraordinary growth during its first fifteen years, but was troubled from the beginning by a poor assimilation of its many new members. Basically healthy and outgoing, it nevertheless experienced an abrupt "bleeding" at fifteen, losing attendance but not membership, suffering a decline in property, paid staff, and vigorous leadership.

A "big sleep" has set in, producing a comfortable and, in many ways, satisfying if fragmented existence for the congregation. Tragedy has struck the present pastor, however, who like a king's son came to awaken the church only to be caught and vocationally killed by its protective thorns. The dream of the congregation is that it will awaken (it held a New Life Mission last month) in maturity through good leadership.

What might a congregation be able to do if it were to hear a strong story like this one? At least the church might be able to use the metaphorical power of the tale in prayer about itself. The story might, moreover, be used to typify the life situation addressed in sermons. In future planning sessions of the church, the tale might also freshen the more usual strategies and pieties employed to move the congregation as Christ's body in an uncertain world.

*April 1980*

# Faith Development in the Parish

JAMES W. FOWLER and ROMNEY M. MOSELEY

We find it useful to speak of faith as a dynamic relationship of trust in and loyalty to three interrelated factors in our lives. First, there is faith and trust in the loyalty to a center or centers of value. Worth and worship are etymologically related. We worship, or give devotion to, that which seems to us to have supreme worth. Worth is determined by the way an entity or a person or a deity confers worth or value upon our lives.

The biblical concern with idolatry has long alerted us to the fact that values other than the God of Abraham and Isaac, of Rachel and Rahab, can take on "God-value" for us. The centers of value in our life may be many things. The biblical call is for us to undergo a process of ongoing conversion in the direction of letting God Almighty be the transcendent center and source of all value, and, in relation to that, we learn through conversation to value other goods appropriately, but to avoid the dangers of idolatry.

A second element in our lives of faith is our operative image of power. We live in a dangerous world, a world fraught with destructive potential. How do we align ourselves in such a world so as to be able to trust that in life or death we will be sustained? Bomb shelters, stock portfolios, tenure in the university, membership in a conference, wealth, power—all of these represent ways in which we can try to position ourselves in face of our vulnerabilities in a dangerous world. A god who has no power is not of much use to us in the kind of world we live in. An important element of any of our faiths is our operational image of power and our alignment with it.

Third, faith involves our allegiance to, our trust in, what we are learning to call "a master narrative." A master narrative is that story we tell ourselves when we are asked the question: "What does life really mean?" A master narrative is our sense of what God is doing in history, and it represents our effort to align ourselves with that moving character of God which discloses itself in the events of history.

Marxists, with their vision of the dialectical movement toward the classless society, offer one kind of version of a master narrative. Those who tell us that the universe is at best neutral (and at worst hostile) to all human efforts to make and maintain meaning have another kind of master narrative. The master narrative of the Christian faith says that God is sovereign in history and that God became flesh in Jesus Christ and lived and died and then negated death in resurrection. This is the powerful master story into which we call people in our ministries.

Faith is always a relational phenomenon, and the shape of the relation into which faith calls us is covenantal or triadic in form. The self forms in its relationships to others horizontal ties of trust and loyalty. But in any lasting relationship we have, we are involved not just in triadic relationships of trust and loyalty, but also in a shared relation to those centers of value and power that transcend us and those to whom we relate in faith. Institutions, causes, leaders, values like love and justice, and political ideologies all can be potentially the "third" with which we and our companions in being share trust and loyalty.

*Fall 1981*

# "Cheating" at Church

FRANK K. ALLAN

When two students collaborate on an examination the word for it is cheating. If at the end of the examination a pledge is signed, it says, "I neither gave nor received help...." Our educational system encourages individualism and competition, not collaboration. And this is only a reflection of our society as a whole. It is no wonder, then, that ministry is so often exercised alone and competitively, "without giving or receiving help." The result is enormous frustration, burn-out, and ineffectiveness for many clergy and laypersons. The New Testament images for ministry are a holy people, a royal priesthood, a body with its members working together. I believe that we need to recover this sense of ministry and thus find freedom from the isolation and burden which so many pastors and laypersons experience in their own ministries.

Let's begin with the word "ministry." The way we use words is not a matter of indifference. When a seminary has "Ministers' Week," who is it for? It is for the ordained, of course. To "go into the ministry" one goes to seminary and gets ordained. And who are the "ministers" in a congregation? Again, the ordained. Therein lies the problem. If ministry depends on ordination then the burden and isolation become unbearable for the few who fantasize that they are carrying the whole load.

Ministry, of course, is *not* contingent upon ordination. Rather, one enters the ministry when one enters the waters of baptism. And in many areas ministry is indeed exercised by the whole body in spite of our terminology, but often this happens haphazardly and nonintentionally. I would plead for us to be clearer and more intentional about this. Not only should we stop using the terms "ministry" and "ordination" synonymously, but we should also begin *acting* in a different way.

The pastor has a very important function in the development of a collaborative ministry. Whether we like it or not the pastor plays a key role in establishing the norms which are operative in the life of a congregation. The pastor is a "symbol person." A symbol ties together (as opposed to a diabol which tears apart). The symbol for ministry stands before the community and represents the ministry which all baptized people have. Paul Ricouer speaks of a symbol as "opaque transparency."

A symbol points beyond itself, but there is a natural tendency for more and more authority to be concentrated in the symbol until the transparency is lost, and the only one who is a symbol for the ministry of all of us becomes *the* minister. Roman Catholicism is often accused of aiding and abetting such a concentration, but Protestantism is equally susceptible to such crypto-papistry. A symbol person must never allow the symbol to get absolutely confused with that to which it points. There is a danger that symbol people will take themselves too seriously. Remember Mr. Nixon: "I am the President." It could as easily be "I am the Bishop" or "the Pastor." Power must be given away. In this sense the pastor of a congregation is a *pontifex*, a bridge builder. Things move across, through, and past him or her, but they don't stop there. The pontifex unites and links together the diversity in the body.

This diversity is represented by three distinct types of individuals in a congregation. The first might be called the *dreamer*—or the fickle individual—the risk taker, the visionary, the prophet. The fickle individual often rubs against the institution and quarrels with it, but it is a lovers' quarrel. Sometimes he or she comes up with the most absurd ideas and is light years ahead of the rest of the congregation. "Instead of building a fellowship hall, take the pews out of the church and give the money for the new building away."

Then there is the *institutionalizer*, the one who resists change and holds on to the past. This is often the bricks-and-mortar person and the one who talks about "the way we've always done things." We need both kinds of people in the church. Out of the wilderness and absurdity of the dreamer, creative and exciting things come. The institutional person, on the other hand, does not let us forget our roots and traditions. It is out of the tension between these two that tempered growth occurs.

The third type in a congregation is the *enabler*, the one who distills the wild dreams and the traditions, mediates between them, and fears neither change nor the status quo. Through the enabler a viable ministry emerges. The enabler sees to it that both institutional needs and prophetic vision come together by holding them in tension with one another. I would suggest that the pastor is primarily called to be an enabler in the congregation (not the fickle individual), and that the church board is also called to an enabling ministry (and not an institutional one).

The leader of a congregation *lets* things happen. He or she doesn't make things happen, but nurtures an environment where growth can take place. I would call this the *maieutic* function of ministry—midwifery. The pastor-midwife assists in the birth and brings to the job certain skills, knowledge, resources, and experience. The pastor-midwife encourages and enables the birth process but does not give birth to the baby.

To determine whether this enabling ministry is happening in our congregations we must ask ourselves some questions: Are there any structures in our congregation which encourage dreams and visions? Do people have authority to make decisions, even if those decisions produce butterflies in the pastor's stomach? Do people have authority to spend money? Are they held accountable by and to one another? If not, we are saying to them that what they do is busy work and ultimately insignificant to the kingdom.

I believe that pastor and people must come together, that visions must be encouraged, needs uncovered, vocations identified, a plan of action developed, and a way to do theological reflection discovered. It is poor leadership, on the one hand, to do everything yourself, or, on the other, to turn the task over to a committee and then disappear without providing ongoing support. The pastor's training makes him or her responsible for equipping the saints for the work of ministry. This is done in administering the sacraments and preaching the word, in teaching, in being available as a biblical and theological resource person and as the person in the congregation who knows what is going on without, at the same time, having to control everything that happens.

Ministry, however, does not take place primarily in the context of parish life, but in the world where people work, play, raise families, and vote, as well as those dark corners of society where few Christians in most of our churches ever go. The Christian community does not exist simply to perpetuate itself or to be a kind of spiritual raiding party which goes out only to bring back captives from an alien and hostile world. Rather, the community comes together as one loaf of bread in prayer, praise, and eucharist, and then the bread is broken as the body is dispersed into the world to exercise the ministry of Jesus Christ.

Need we be reminded that "Jesus was not crucified on an altar between two candlesticks but on the town garbage heap, at the crossroads of civilization, at a place so cosmopolitan that they had to write his accusation in three languages." Ministry, after all, is service, *diakonia* (the other word most frequently translated as ministry in the New Testament is *leitourgia*—public service—liturgy).

Collaborative ministry is exercised as the church interprets the gospel to the world, and clergy can provide profound leadership in equipping the laity for this work; but collaborative ministry is also exercised as the world is interpreted to the church, and the laity provide the dominant leadership in this. Ministry can only bear fruit if both the clergy and laity "cheat" at church, giving and receiving help as we share in the royal priesthood.

*May 1982*

# The Meaning of Church Membership

## JOHN LYNN CARR

In the midst of all this conversation about ordination to the professional ministry, I would like to raise what I feel to be a more important concern: where and how do we in our church life today affirm the ministry of the whole people of God? At first glance, this seems to be an unnecessary question. Over the last twenty years, we have been inundated by addresses, pamphlets, articles, sermons, conferences, and shelf after shelf of popular books on the theology of the laity. And yet, in spite of all this verbiage, the average person in the pew still understands the words "lay ministry" to mean assisting the "real minister" in carrying out the church's institutional purposes. Why?

A full answer would require a careful critique of the whole hidden curriculum of our congregations, the powerful ways in which our patterns of life and work together confirm or contradict our preaching and teaching on the subject. But one fruitful place to begin is with a look at the very visible curriculum of what we do educationally and liturgically with the youth and adults who join our congregations.

*The Book of Discipline of the United Methodist Church* gives an admirable description of the meaning of membership, stating in no uncertain terms that to be a member "is to be a servant of Christ on a mission in the local and worldwide community. This servanthood is performed in family life, daily work, recreation and social activities, responsible citizenship, the stewardship of property and accumulated resources, the issues of corporate life, and all attitudes toward other persons" (paragraph 213).

But look now at "The Order for Confirmation and Reception into the Church" in *The Book of Worship*. How does the above interpretation of membership as ministry get expressed here? In the opening statement we are told that God has created the church "for the conduct of worship and the due administration of his Word and sacraments, the maintenance of Christian fellowship and discipline, the edification of believers, and the conversion of the world. All, of every age and station, stand in need of the means of grace which *it* [italics mine] alone supplies." The mission of the church is expressed here, although in language which reinforces a fairly narrow definition of what that mission is; however that little word "it" implies that this mission belongs not to a people but to an impersonal institution.

In the questions which follow the above passages, one looks in vain for any explicit recognition that these persons are by their confirmation called to ministry. Then we come to the "bottom line," the vow which those transferring their membership from other denominations are asked to make, a vow which the whole congregation is asked to renew: "Will you be loyal to The United Methodist Church, and uphold it by your prayers, your presence, your gifts, and your service?" Ministry is mentioned here, to be sure, but it is a ministry of supporting the church, and not one of being the church. The emphasis is on maintenance, not mission.

What then of our efforts to prepare persons to participate in this liturgy? My informal survey of membership preparation programs reveals that, with some notable exceptions, orientation to the denomination's beliefs, history, and policy and to the congregation's program is their major emphasis. Assimilation is their goal. Participants hear what they ought to believe, how the church can meet their needs, and how they can help the church with its ministry. The biblical message that they are called into the church that they may fulfill *their* ministry gets short shrift. In short, when we look at the two most obvious liturgies in which we communicate the meaning of membership, it is not hard to understand why the general ministry of all Christians is so generally misunderstood.

In two courses offered through the Institute for Church Ministries, my wife, Adrienne, and I have worked this past year with the pastors and people of two congregations and seminary students in experimenting with some new approaches to preparation for membership. Their responses to what we have tried have excited us about exploring two particular directions further. The first is stressing not what people ought to believe and do but what they *are* in Christ by virtue of their baptism. The New Testament strategy of making astounding affirmations about us and then calling us to recognize and respond to them really works!

The second, related direction is genuinely valuing people's experience in ministry. The baptized persons in our membership courses have already received their commissions as soldiers of Christ. They are already engaged in the battle for shalom on the frontlines of work and home and larger community, many of them quite faithfully. The fact that some need to broaden their fronts, others are fighting poorly, and some are deserters doesn't negate their calling. We have found that when we try to help them share and evaluate their experience of ministry in the light of the gospel—prompting them to identify the kind of support and equipment they need from the Christian community in order to grow in faithfulness and effectiveness—they begin to take their calling with a kind of seriousness that all our lectures on lay ministry have been unable to engender.

We closed our second course with a liturgy in which students and laity came to the communion rail in groups of three. The pastor, Adrienne, or I addressed each of them by name, affirmed his or her ministry in a two-sentence statement, and gave each an equally brief charge based on what we sensed to be that person's particular growing edge. Then as he or she knelt, we and the two others in his or her group laid on hands and prayed: "We recognize and rejoice in your unique ministry and pray that God's powerful Spirit will equip and strengthen you for it. Amen."

The powerful impact of that little service has deepened my conviction that we need liturgies for membership reception and renewal which get far more specific, personal, and dramatic about each person's ministry. Considering the fuss we make over the ordination of Army cooks, it's about time we gave far more serious attention to the affirmation of frontline soldiers!

*March 1978*

# Biblical Call to Stewardship
## Interview with Rebecca Youngblood, Ed Loring, and George Ogle

*This conversation, published in the July 1976 issue of* Ministry & Mission, *took place among the following people: Rebecca Youngblood, a recent Candler graduate at the time and newly appointed associate minister at St. John's United Methodist Church in Greenwood, Mississippi; Ed Loring, who was pastor at Clifton Presbyterian Church in Atlanta and a teacher at Columbia Seminary; George Ogle, then professor of world Christianity at Candler and a former United Methodist missionary in Korea; and Barbara Brown, editor.*

**Brown:** Becky, what responsibilities do you expect to carry at St. John's?

**Youngblood:** It's not clear to me right now what my role will be in directing stewardship. Saint John's is a gigantic building, so energy itself is bound to be a real issue. In the latest issue of the church newsletter, I was interested to read an announcement that said, "Summertime is here. Please feel free to come without coat and tie to worship services on Sunday morning and be comfortable."

So my suspicion is that for St. John's and for a lot of churches, simple maintenance is an issue of stewardship: how do we keep this building functioning and manage to pay our bills too?

**Brown:** When I think about stewardship I think about all kinds of gifts, and about listening for what people can do and plugging in their abilities. Is that consistent with your ideas of stewardship?

**Youngblood:** Yes, my own understanding of stewardship includes gifts in terms of what one can do. It's my impression that our understandings of stewardship are often too narrow in the sense that we focus on money most of all. We sometimes use money in order *not* to do something. We give our money and then consider ourselves to be off the hook.

I hope that a part of my ministry will be to draw out and to enable people to offer other kinds of gifts. I guess for me stewardship is not that much different from discipleship. If you live a life of discipleship, the word stewardship becomes superfluous. Because a life of discipleship entails a total use of energies and a total use of material possessions in light of what Jesus taught. So that life is not divided up into so many working parts, but what one gives or does for the church is a part of one's total way of life.

*Loring:* I would like to add an "and, yet" to what Becky is saying, because generally speaking I agree with the broadened term of stewardship and making it synonymous with discipleship. On the other hand, biblically speaking, the main issue that is addressed in the life of the people of God is idolatry, and the second one is economics. So stewardship does have a particular focus on our economic lives. "Steward" is very close to the word "service." The origin of the word is really "one who waits tables," and it's used very often in Scripture to describe what the Christian is like. But it does seem to me that there is a particularity about our economic lives.

Stewardship is not simply focused on giving money but is a response to the economic reality in our lives through which we express the lordship of Christ in our lives and over the economy of our nation, of our world, wherever there's the exchange of goods. The New Testament, it seems to me, does not suggest a 10 percent tithe, although that is what we work for in our congregations. Instead of handing down a law for stewardship, the New Testament seems to say fairly clearly that the loving response to the call of Christ in our lives is sacrificial giving. For some people that's 10 percent; for the widow with one penny, it was 100 percent, and Jesus blessed her.

To give less than sacrificially is less than what the Bible calls us to do. I think that one of the struggles to take the biblical command or the biblical call to stewardship seriously in our own time is that it sets us up against mainline institutions. It sets us up against our culture in terms of our whole sense of economic self-worth, or it sets us up against institutions that capitalize on the idea that "bigger is better" and what that teaches us about fulfillment or success.

To give sacrificially is not simply a matter of an individual putting money in the offering plate as it goes around on Sunday, but it is also, and even more importantly, the way that the congregation disperses its own funds. The size of the church building, what one does in that building, how one furnishes that building, are directly biblical issues. And at each point, it seems to me, we are called to give sacrificially—when we put our money in the plate and when we disperse it through the life of the church.

I think stewardship also calls us to look seriously at how willingly we pay our taxes, how we render unto Caesar that which is Caesar's and unto God that which is God's. Many of us give more money to Caesar than we do to God, and we have to look at that. Our whole participation in consumer society is another form of rendering unto Caesar.

*Brown:* What do you say to someone who believes that part of what he or she pays in taxes every year already goes to the widows and children, to welfare, social security, to many of the groups the Bible charges us to take care of?

*Loring:* Well, we seem to elicit a lot of criticism about our stand, but at Clifton we conceptualize ourselves as a community that does its sacrificial giving through the people of God, and not through the government. We pay social security—everybody in our congregation does—and we have plenty of people who have United Way money taken out of their paychecks. But if you ever let your left hand know what your right hand is doing, according to Jesus, you're going to get to the place where you're going to have to chop off one of your hands.

So we try to conceptualize or "theologize" about our giving in a corporate way. It is not necessarily what we're doing with social security or how we're helping the widows and so forth by paying our taxes, but what we, as the people of God, are doing with our resources to witness to God as God works through this community.

We have had that struggle in stewardship education. One of the largest givers in our church is a woman whose father is prominent in the Presbyterian church and who raised his children to tithe. But in his understanding a tithe meant about 5 percent to the church and a couple of percent to the United Way and so forth. It's been a real struggle for us at Clifton to say that on the other hand, we intend to give 10 percent to the church and to do these other things as well. But that's just a place where we've made some internal decisions about our own lives, and to put that in a newspaper or preach that somewhere—I don't know how helpful that would be.

*Brown:* George, what is your response to all of this?

*Ogle:* I guess I want to start off by saying that I would locate the area of stewardship outside the church as well as inside.

*Brown:* In other words, money should come from inside the church to go outside the church?

*Ogle:* No, I'm thinking in terms of stewardship as the responsible use of natural, environmental, and social resources. And I take all of these categories to be resources given to us, not things that we have created or somehow made on our own. We are somewhat involved in the creation of them, but they are still primarily given to us. Several of the crucial areas that come to mind in terms of stewardship are natural resources: matters of oil and energy, land, air, our environmental resources. But social resources also come under the rubric of God's creation, given to us to use for the common welfare.

By social resources, I guess I have primarily two things in mind. One is the social resource of technology. We live in an era when it is quite possible for us to eradicate a lot of the suffering in our world, but we don't do that. It seems to me that technology is in our hands and should be used, as Scripture directs us, for the common welfare.

The other social resource is the resource of organizations. We know how to organize people, to organize jobs, to put things together so that it would be possible, again, to help ameliorate an awful lot of the suffering in the world. Instead of using our organizational power for that, we tend to use it for in-group interests. So it seems to me that at least one dimension of stewardship is for one to address these resources that are not traditionally thought of as church resources.

*Loring:* I'd like to make a comment, if I may, on the practical side of stewardship, of how we actually get to work. The kind of thing that I'm excited about is the message that comes out of the second and fourth chapters of Acts; that of a sharing community. What develops under the lordship of Christ is a common life, so that one shares common concerns and common prayer for the community and the world.

It seems to me, then, that any understanding of stewardship or of such a common life begins with serious Bible study. Study whatever you want to in the Bible, but study seriously; and pursue a common prayer life and you will discover the basis of commonality, of common life, the body of Christ, the Holy Spirit, the Bible, prayer. That's what the corporate pilgrimage in faith is about.

Secondly, I think, common life grows when we begin to share meals together. I use meals—food—in a symbolic sense as well as in the literal sense that we inherit from our faith: namely, that to share food is the basis from which we share life. Out of eating together, and understanding that meal through Bible study and prayer together, comes a wider sharing. And then, given that prayers have some direction and table talk some focus, there begins to emerge a natural sense of mission, of the servanthood of God in the world. And that mission has a particular focus as it grows out of a common life.

When one begins to move into such mission—actual servanthood with that kind of be-not-anxious quality about it that Jesus advocates—issues of stewardship really become lively, because you get so involved with the Bible, with prayer, with eating together, and with mission that you begin to raise the kind of questions Becky was talking about, about the giving of money, and the giving of time, and presenting your body.

**Youngblood:** And that doesn't happen if you start at the other end, if you start with an understanding of giving as an individual activity by individual families. None of that common life is there, and stewardship becomes more like a duty or an obligation than a faithful response.

**Ogle:** One variable pops into my mind as I listen to Ed and think of the situation that Becky will be going into, and that variable is size. Not only the different sizes of their church congregations, because the bigness or smallness of the church itself doesn't seem to make a very big difference in the whole rhythm of life, but I would guess that a fair proportion of Becky's people will spend most of their weekday lives in rather large organizations. And again, it's strictly a guess, but I would guess that most of Ed's folks relate to smaller and more immediate organizations. I guess what I'm getting at is that the message of common life, common life under a common commitment, is an urgently needed message in our day, but that it's a message out of the wilderness. Maybe it is not completely outside of people's experience, but still to a fair degree foreign to those of us who spend our days in large organizations.

**Brown:** How about a pep-talk for people who have worked within institutions and have been continually disillusioned by them?

**Ogle:** Of course institutions are evil. How could you expect to have anything but evil institutions in a world of evil people? But we don't write each other off because we're sinners and have committed a variety of evil acts in our days, so I don't think we can write institutions off either. In the first place, those organizations are, in some mysterious way, under the creating lordship of God. And secondly, people very seldom go to hell easily. They try to drag you down with them.

As organizations get bigger, as Reinhold Niebuhr says in *Moral Man, Immoral Society*, they have embodied within them more potential for evil than individual persons. The main reason for that seems to be that individuals tend to have some sort of conscience, but that a similar sort of internal conscience is almost impossible to locate in a powerful institution. It doesn't do any good to say, "Look, we've tried this and we've tried that and none of it has worked. All institutions are evil and I'm not going to get messed up with them." Whether we want it or not, we *are* messed up with them. And along with all their evil possibilities, we need to affirm the reality of redemption. The drama of redemption is played out in the battle between the Lord and the principalities and powers, and we are the Lord's proxies in the world, as individuals and as individuals involved in organizations.

**Brown:** So instead of giving up on those powers, we need to offer them up with some hope for their redemption?

**Ogle:** Yes. The gospel comes to each of us in the first place as a judgment, as a demand for repentance, and, in relation to stewardship, as a command to use the resources available to us for love and justice, for the common life. It seems to me that the same word comes to a big corporation, or to a political movement, just as surely as it comes to an individual.

**Loring:** May I respond to that? I was a very faithful student of Reinhold Niebuhr's works for a while and went through the civil rights movement and have struggled with the kinds of questions we have been asking about empowerment and care for the world, changing the world, staying engaged in the world. And I guess the most liberating thing that has happened to me in response to those questions—which has happened to me in this community experience I've been talking about—is the realization that we're not called to change the world.

We're not called to create a conscience for Exxon, but we're called to do something I consider much more radical than that, and that is to be everywhere in the world where Exxon is and to witness to the lordship of Jesus Christ who calls us all to be reconciled. One thing this has meant to me that is different from when I was taking the academic route in my life is the whole issue of courage.

I don't know what courage means exactly, but the whole idea of presenting our bodies to Jesus Christ and living out our faith goes back certainly to what Becky was saying about discipleship. To say it another way: the beginning and end of social ethics is our announcement that the kingdom of God is at hand. And that we live out that reality. And never mind whether gas is going to be one-fifty tomorrow or two-fifty next week.

Reading the newspaper today, we see the powers and principalities really trying to keep us frightened. Coffee's going up, beef is going up, something else is going down—the message you get from the world is: be afraid.

But the main thing I hear in the gospel about how to live in the world is: be not afraid. "Do not be afraid, little flock, for your holy parent in heaven is pleased to give you the kingdom of God. Go and sell all that you have and give it to the poor. And be joyful."

*Brown:* One of the final questions I'd like each of you to address is how we can educate for stewardship. Ed, you've talked about the importance of Bible study and the common life. How else might ministers begin to educate their congregations to the importance of stewardship?

*Loring:* Clifton church would be a very different place if it were not true that the experience and education of stewardship has not fallen on my shoulders. It has, in fact, been something that has come out of the Bible study and prayer group. So education for stewardship has not been one of my particular duties. I continue to be impressed, however, that those of us set aside to do other kinds of duties must continually critique our own self-interests.

What are our salaries? What do we do with our annuities? I am aware of a real ethical question that I have not faced, that haunts me, about the disposition of my denomination's annuities. As one of my good friends in the congregation said, "Do we pray for peace and pay for war?" Do we pray for stewardship to increase in our church and then pay for luxuries?

Because the problem with that is that God's going to damn us. Damn us. Any money we spend on ourselves unnecessarily is taking food out of the mouths of the hungry. So before we start stewardship education we, as leaders, have really got to be clear on what we're about and our own witness to sacrificial giving—much of which I have yet to discover.

*Youngblood:* There was an interesting figure that Nelia Kimbrough, a friend of mine, shared with me recently. Someone she knew had done considerable research and found that if every church in this country took care of eleven needy families, there would be no need for welfare. That sets you back a little bit. Eleven families. And it makes you realize that our stewardship really could make a difference. As Ed said, the way we spend our money really does have something to do with whether or not hungry people get fed.

*Ogle:* But let's just say that through some miracle we were able to divide up all the welfare families. We would be involved in a good ministry, but I'm not sure it would substantially alter our wider responsibility of changing the system. Because we would still be cranking out welfare people, poor people whom the system assists but whom it does not really want to change. It seems part of our wider stewardship to be concerned with that which creates the problem in the first place.

Going back to our original question, Barbara, I want to say that I agree with Ed that education about stewardship may be a contradiction in terms. You may not be able to get people together and somehow instill in them a sense of stewardship. I think the context from which they come the other six and a half days of their weeks pretty well determines stewardship for them. Unless there is indeed the sort of common life that Ed is talking about—whether it takes the form of a small church or a small group within a larger church—unless there's some common life in devotion to the Lord who created heaven and earth and saved us from the cross, I'm not sure we can really teach stewardship.

*Loring:* I remember when I finished graduate school and started teaching and was giving very little money to the church. One of the ways I dealt with that was by telling myself that I had been a student for a number of years and had spent so much time and preparation already that I would postpone significant giving to the church until I paid off my educational loans. And I still haven't paid off my loans. That was really just an attitude. You've got to be humbled some way; the Lord has to break that spirit because it's really true that the old nature in us, the nature that Paul talks about, is simply going to find one thousand and one ways why we can't give any more, and every one of them is legitimate. There won't be a one that isn't legitimate, because that's the power of the mind: it can legitimize anything.

# Preaching What the People Want to Say

## FRED B. CRADDOCK

When viewed as an act of worship within a context of worship, the sermon is most often and most closely allied with the reading of Scripture. This is as it should be, and any moves to sever that relationship must reckon with negative consequences for preacher, for listeners, and for the sermon itself. Just as the Scripture informs and authorizes the sermon, so the sermon fulfills the Scripture, providing for the text a future. Apart from the text the sermon is orphaned, without mother or father, easily becoming a battery of parentless opinions, however eloquently arrayed.

However, when viewed as an act of worship within a context of worship, the sermon needs to be more closely allied with the pastoral prayer or the prayers for the people of God. In its association with the reading of Scripture the sermon is *to* the people, but in its association with the prayer, the sermon is *for* the people. As the prayer lifts to God the joys, sorrows, pain, frustration, faith, doubt, commitment, and cowardice of the people, so does the sermon. Thus understood, the sermon expresses what people wish to say and what they would say were they able to do so.

Mind you, this is not to suggest preaching what the church wishes to *hear* but what the church wishes to *say*. After all, the church has something to say, a witness to make, and through the preacher that witness is made. The preacher is the voice of the church, proclaiming the life and love, faith and values, nature and mission of the people of God. The faith community existed before the preacher arrived to lead it; the appearance of the preacher did not create the community and give it identity. The sermon therefore arises out of the church's confession and self-understanding, and when the preacher publicly states that, the people say "Amen." Healthy preaching, therefore, contains much which the congregation already claims as its own. In other words, the preacher affirms and implements the principle of familiarity.

The principle of familiarity is simply the recognition that people enjoy, celebrate, own, affirm, re-appropriate, and sometimes painfully learn what they already know. People attend concerts featuring artists already familiar to them, and they expect from the performers the well known. It would be a bitter disappointment to go hear Tony Bennett and get from him totally new songs instead of "I Left My Heart in San Francisco." The familiar is moving and powerful because everyone knows it and owns it. It is *our* song. Regretfully, there are too few occasions in the church in which the congregation can say, "That is *our* sermon." Why?

Sometime, somewhere, someone convinced homileticians that the power in preaching lay in its novelty, in its being new to the listeners. The premium was placed on "I'll bet they never heard this before." Unconsciously competing with all predecessors, the preacher was on the search for new and different subjects, texts, ideas. Combing through Leviticus and Jude, exploring the dark side of Nahum, many preachers went in quest of the Holy Grail: an unused text, a novel idea. And quite characteristically, these same preachers often chastised their listeners for never saying "Amen." How could they? They never heard any of it before. The entire transaction was not unlike a weekly leap off the pinnacle of the temple.

Traditionally black preaching has remained innocent of this error. In many black churches, the principle of familiarity is operating in full force. The listeners recognize the sermon as their own; some of it they could repeat and some of it they do repeat. They know when the preacher proclaims their sermon well and they know when the preacher does not do well. And they are concerned because this is their message, their faith, their mission, their identity.

In such churches, when a biblical story is related it is done so in full, with sufficient time to savor its details. Why? The listeners already know the story. That is exactly the reason. While a white preacher might glancingly refer to a biblical account, offering no detail "because they know it," the black preacher gives full narration for the very same reason. And who benefits? Any persons present who do not know the story are able to learn it; all those who already know it relish it anew. Even the children nudge each other and show their pride in hearing something they know coming from the pulpit. If a preacher merely refers in passing to Jesus and the woman at the well or Paul on the Areopagus, who benefits? No one learns; no one remembers with joy.

Someone may object that preaching so characterized would be lacking in prophetic edge, a caressing word that sent listeners down memory lane. Of course, such could be the case, but not necessarily. Consider, for example, the story of Jesus in Nazareth according to Luke 4.

The time and place and occasion and audience are all familiar: Jesus, as is his custom, is in the synagogue on the Sabbath. His relatives and friends are there. He reads from a familiar and favorite book: Isaiah. He tells two Bible stories, one about Elijah and one about Elisha. Every child in the room could have told the stories, they were so familiar. But the audience rose up in anger and took Jesus to the brow of a hill, intending to throw him to his death. Had he been a stranger in town, reading from an unfamiliar book, telling stories never heard before, the people of Nazareth could have disregarded it as easily as you and I do when the unfamiliar share the unfamiliar. But when we are confronted with what we already know, the truth is inescapable. What we already know not only nourishes but judges us.

There is in what we already know sufficient raw material to alter a life, a home, a church, a nation, a world. Then why not play it again, Sam?

*May 1983*

# Love: The Motive for Evangelism

GEORGE E. MORRIS

Harold DeWolf, former professor of systematic theology at both the Boston and Wesley schools of theology, once said, "The New Testament church engaged in evangelism as naturally and normally as a robin sings or a happy child plays" *(The Aim of Evangelism)*. In making this comment, Dr. DeWolf was trying to offset the popular notion that evangelism is a special ministry that must be done by special people at special times and in special ways, rather than the normal ministry of the church.

It is the recovery of this normative aspect of evangelism that is consuming much of the energy and creativity of evangelism leaders in the church today. These leaders dream of a church that will view its evangelism mandate not as a special chore, but as the natural, faithful, day-by-day manifestation of the church's authentic life.

Evangelism is not a program of the church. To the contrary, the church, if it is faithful, is a program of evangelism. If the gospel is utterly normative, then evangelism does not take its shape, style, and content from the church. The church, to the contrary, must structure itself as a means of evangelism. I am convinced, however, that evangelism will not become a normal part of the life of the church until the motives for it are clarified. The motives are not clear to multitudes of laity and clergy, and this is producing a halting response to the appeal for evangelistic effort.

***Death and Doom.*** The driving motive for much of 18th- and 19th-century evangelism was that of preserving souls. With a vivid belief in the substantive reality of heaven and hell, Christian evangelists sought to rescue people from eternal punishment and to open for them the door of heaven before it was everlastingly too late. But are these motives credible? I question this death-and-doom motivation on two accounts.

First, given the fact that lengthening life span is pushing death farther into the future, is death the threat it once was? It is one thing to use death and damnation as motivational prods when one's auditors are very death-conscious. It is something else to find oneself confronted with a life-conscious "Pepsi generation," whose fundamental question is not "Is there life after death?" but "Is there life after birth?" Second, I question death and doom as motivation because I find it difficult to square the concept of hell as everlasting torment with a God of immeasurable love. While I realize that the judgments of God are abroad in the universe, I also know that the Bible never tires of saying, "The mercy of God is from everlasting to everlasting" (see Alan Walker, *The New Evangelism*).

Moreover, I am skeptical regarding hope-of-reward motivation. This tends to play into the hands of our consumer mentality, that mentality that causes us to ask, "What's in it for me?" Instead of addressing itself to our basic needs such motivation tends to pander to our selfish wants. Though there are sporadic outcroppings of fear and reward motivations, I am convinced they are inadequate of their very nature.

***Institutional Preservation.*** A popular motivation in our own generation has been that of preserving the institution. Shortly after I received an appointment to a church in a southern state, one of its leaders came to me and said I ought to visit a certain lieutenant colonel who had moved into our community. "You had better get over there and get him before the Baptists interfere," he said. "If we could enlist him in our church, he surely would help us with the budget." Obviously, there was little concern for the person; the real concern was for the institution and its preservation.

When preserving the institution becomes the basic focus of evangelism, then the institutional church becomes the basic reason for doing evangelism. Therefore we recruit people for the sake of the institution, in order to preserve it and its ideology. The more threatened the institution becomes, the more defensive it becomes, and the more we must recruit in order to preserve it. The church becomes a seducer rather than a converter, and the whole process ends in a style of cultural accommodation that tends to abandon the radical claims of the gospel.

***Americanization.*** Another popular motive in this country has been that of the expansion and preservation of our American way of life. The expansion motive was best illustrated in the doctrine of "manifest destiny." As Martin E. Marty has said, "While America was expanding its domestic empire, an advance guard of missionaries had begun to carry the Christian gospel and Yankee go-ahead determination to many parts of the earth" *(Religious Empire)*. Some spoke of America as the "new Israel" which had received the heathen as her inheritance. For others, the idea of expanding the empire became the equivalent of the growth of the kingdom of God. Thus, some missionary work was a blending of evangelization and Americanization. To evangelize was a means of spreading Anglo-Saxon civilization.

Today, however, we are beginning to realize that there is no such thing as a "Christian nation." There never was one. A new mood of humility now pervades our missionary boards and agencies. We now go around the world not to exhibit the virtues of the American system, but to share the witness, the service, and the struggles of other Christian sisters and brothers.

If these motives are all questionable, what would constitute legitimate motivation for evangelizing? I wish to state a three-part thesis and defend it: Evangelism is founded in God's love; it fulfills the Great Commission; and it focuses on total redemption.

**God's Love.** Both of the words, *God's love*, are crucial to our understanding. The first says that the responsibility for evangelism ministries is rooted in the very nature of God. Therefore, evangelism ministries are necessary because of who God is. What was the first verse of Scripture you learned as a child? For most of us it was "God is love." But what do we mean? The question must be raised because we who speak the English language use the word "love" in a very sloppy fashion. I have found it very helpful to look at the meaning of love by employing the ancient Greek language, which has several words for love.

*Eros.* When most of us hear that word we think of sensual or sexual love because we get our English word erotic from *eros*. In fairness, I think it necessary to say that the word meant more than sexual love in Greek antiquity, but two characteristics of *eros* remain fairly steady throughout its history: it is a love that desires to possess the object of its devotion for its own sake, and it is therefore quite egocentric.

*Phileo* or *phila*. This means social love, or the mutuality of friendly affection. It is usually understood on the horizontal level. This form of love also has two general characteristics: it is reciprocal, and, of its very nature, is seated in the emotions.

*Storge.* In the New Testament this word usually appears in the negative sense as *astorgos* (without natural affection). In the positive sense it means natural affection, the kind of affection parents naturally feel for their offspring.

However, with the advent of Jesus Christ some two thousand years ago, the Greeks were faced with a dilemma. Jesus was both the exemplar and exponent of a love so unique that they did not have a word for it. Their solution was to resurrect an old word and pour new meaning into it.

*Agape.* This word indicates a love shown by the desire to help the object of its devotion rather than to possess or enjoy it. Here I would like to share with you a four-point understanding of *agape* that has been inform-ing and shaping my life for years. I believe that its implications for evangelism are both natural and crucial.

In order to grasp the meaning of *agape,* one must first realize that it is not a natural endowment. If it were a natural part of us, then all that would be necessary would be to get out the bellows and stoke it up a bit. But we cannot conjure it up on our insides. There is only one way to ex-perience *agape* and that is to receive it as a gift.

The second part of my understanding is the realization that *agape* is a gift from God. This is best understood in the familiar words of John 3:16: "God so loved the world that God gave...." There is no way to earn or merit this love. Because it has been poured out as a gift, our only legitimate response is one of grateful stewardship. We become stewards of God's love in us, and this brings us to point three.

*Agape* love of its very nature makes both the giver and the recipient vulnerable. In pouring out this love upon us God takes an awesome risk. God risks the possibility that people will not respond to this love, and many do not. However, this does not deter God. God gives the gift whether we receive it or not. This is what we mean when we talk about the vulnerability of God.

If I open my life and receive God's love there is only one way I can ex-press my overwhelming gratitude for such an unmerited gift, and that is to turn that love loose upon others. In so doing I find myself sharing in the vulnerability of God. I find myself sharing the pain of rejection and the joy of acceptance, and loving the unlovable—even loving those whom I do not particularly like. It ought to be obvious that love so deep is more than just an emotional jag, which brings us to point four.

*Agape* is seated more in the active will than in the emotions. That is the reason *agape* is a verb. It means that we take action for the sake of the other even when we do not feel like it. It also means that we are willing to take responsibility for our actions.

Thus, my primary motive for evangelism and all discipleship is founded in God's love. But subordinate to that primary motive of gratitude is that evangelism fulfills the Great Commission. It seems to me that this is the proper order lest we allow the Great Commission to become a new form of legalism, a duty rather than a response to grace. Law grows out of grace. The Christ who called people to follow him in grace is the same Christ who turned around and taught people how to live with him responsibly. So law and gospel belong together. Both are needed, but the order of the two is crucial, and I am suggesting to you that gospel comes first. The in-dicative precedes the imperative. Without the announcement of God's love, one has neither the motivation nor the ability to obey commands and commissions.

The redemption of society is a powerful motivation for me because I ad-vocate a whole gospel for the whole person in the whole world. When I see the dire needs all around me, I am deeply moved. My heart aches because millions are forced to live crippled, unfulfilled lives in poverty, hunger, oppression, and racism. I am deeply concerned when I see the threat of pollution and nuclear destruction hanging over the whole earth. In Christ I see the answer to these and other deep personal and corporate needs. Thus I am moved to spread the gospel by both word and deed.

*Winter 1981*

# Educating Christians to Share the Gospel

## JOHN LYNN CARR

If George Morris is right about the motive for evangelism and about its being the body language of the whole Christian community [see preceding article], we have quite an educational task on our hands. For it is clear that the average person in the pew sees evangelism as the job of the traveling celebrity preacher, the pastor, the special committee, and the laity making house calls—anything but his or her personal responsibility. And it is equally clear that institutional preservation and success are perceived as the dominant reasons for evangelizing.

How can we turn this situation around? How can we educate our people to be evangelists in the true sense of the word? First, by understanding something about where our people are and why. Faith development theorists tell us that we grow in faith by expanding through certain predictable stages much as an oak tree adds rings. No stage can be skipped, and when we move into a new stage, the needs of previous stages must continue to be met.

In John Westerhoff's popularization of James Fowler's research we move from the experienced faith of early childhood to affiliative faith in childhood and early adolescence. The primary characteristic of this stage is the definition of one's identity through belonging to a self-conscious community. The big need is to feel wanted, needed, accepted, important to a group. Fowler writes: "This is a conformist stage in the sense that it is acutely tuned to the expectations and judgments of others, and as yet does not have a sure enough grasp on its own identity and autonomous judgment to construct and maintain an independent perspective." Then, if the conditions are right and the needs of previous stages have been met, our faith next expands in late adolescence into a searching phase, a time of questioning, doubt, and experimentation. Real adult faith only occurs when we have passed through this searching stage, claim for ourselves the faith we have been given, and commit ourselves to living it out in word and deed.

In light of this understanding, our problem, as I see it, is not that our congregations lack faith. Our problem, rather, is that they do not have an adult faith, that they are stuck in an affiliative stage and have been led to believe that this conformist faith is as far as they need to go in their growth as Christians. Among the many factors that have contributed to this situation, our educational approach has been a major influence. Take, for example, the way we go about education for confirmation, supposedly the rite of adult faith. We direct our programs at young people precisely when they are in the midst of the affiliative faith stage. And what do we do with them? We try to teach them everything they need to know, believe, and do in order to be proper members of our group, reinforcing their conformity precisely at a time when they need to be encouraged to question the faith they have been given and begin the search for their own faith perspective. And after this, they're in!

Or take the way in which we deal with adults at the point of membership. Often we do seek to provide some kind of educational preparation. But generally these membership classes deal with orientation to the institutional church, with getting acquainted, and with "what United Methodists (or other specific denominations) believe," again an affiliative emphasis. Or, finally, look at our adult Sunday morning classes. The primary need that they meet, as church-school studies conclusively demonstrate, is affiliative. These homogeneous groups with their largely teacher-and-content-centered approach to learning help people feel that they belong.

In short, our people are where they are in their faith development, not because our educational efforts have failed, but because our congregational curriculum does all too good a job of getting them there and keeping them there. And if we would educate them to be evangelists, we are going to have to find ways of helping them move through searching to owned faith.

How can we do this? We can give top priority to the creation of educational contexts in which: 1) People are helped to get in touch with and share their own faith pilgrimages with one another. Until they feel that their own experience is valued and heard, they will not be able to move beyond it. 2) People are helped not only to understand but to experience the gospel in new ways. Knowing about the Christian story is not enough. People need to be enabled to get inside of it, to feel its transforming power. 3) People are prompted to try common experiments in Christian living and honestly to talk together about the results. In a very real sense faith is a hypothesis whose truth and power appear only when we try living as if the hypothesis were true.

We can work to make these elements present throughout the church's educational program. But realistically, we can begin by developing a core course in which we seek to involve not only persons considering membership but also, over a period of time, every present church member in reexamination and renewal of his or her faith. Such a course can be advertised to the community at large in a way in which honest searchers, and skeptics even, can take a serious no-strings-attached look at the gospel.

In my experience this sort of educational effort produces evangelists, persons who spontaneously witness to the difference this new encounter with Christ in his body has made in their lives, persons who invite others to "Come and see."

*Winter 1981*

# Are Parishes Political?

## THEODORE R. WEBER

In order to write about "parish and politics," one must clarify two points at the outset. First, the references are to white Protestant experience. Black experience and Roman Catholic experience often are quite different. Second, the subject matter is not "parish politics," but the responsibility of the congregation for the politics of civil society.

With these clarifications in mind we can assert that, with respect to fundamental orientation, the prospective view of "parish and politics" is not basically different from the retrospective view. White Protestant congregations do not, in most instances, think of themselves as "political." They do not involve themselves directly and intentionally in the political process. They do not support—in an explicitly partisan manner—candidates, parties, factions, or programs. On those rare occasions when they break out of this pattern to support or oppose (usually the latter) some issue of public policy, they characteristically insist that they are "taking a stand on a moral issue," not "engaging in politics."

Of course they are more political than they think they are, because they serve an important social function as conservators of community institutions, mores, social divisions, and values. Their failure to recognize this is a serious theological weakness and not simply a matter of sociological ineptitude. Nevertheless, their predominant self-image is nonpolitical. That is the way it has been and is, and the way it is likely to be.

Principal carriers of political consciousness in white American Protestantism are the denominational social action agencies and the seminaries. Although both types of institutions seem well positioned to transfer this consciousness to the local church, neither has been particularly successful in doing so. The power of tradition, community influence, class values, and self-survival (for both pastor and local church) usually have been adequate to resist efforts to modify the nonpolitical self-image.

The one point in the local church structure, with the possible exception of the pastor, which frequently provides the means and setting for the enlarging of social and political consciousness is the women's organizations. In what sometimes appear to be religious tea parties conducted by conservative women with adamantly conservative husbands in defiantly conservative communities, the use of study books and the acceptance of service projects often produce a sensitivity to human need and an awareness of Christian mission which surprise and embarrass the liberal critics of the church.

However, even if we accept the hypothesis that fundamental change in the relationship of the parish to politics is unlikely, we should be aware of developments since 1960 that open up the relationship to new dimensions of responsibility. I shall list and comment briefly on a few of these developments.

*1) There has been a "shaking out" of some issues which have been political preoccupations of American Protestantism.* One of these is the fear of political Catholicism. In November of 1960, John Fitzgerald Kennedy became the first Roman Catholic to be elected President of the United States. His election and subsequent presidency helped to dispel most of the Protestant anxiety over the prospect of a Catholic-dominated America.

Other political preoccupations have included legalization of the sale of alcoholic beverages and of commercial gambling. These continue to be "hobby" political issues for some Protestant groups—or more precisely, their pastors. But the ability to mobilize support has declined. However one might feel about the merits of these issues, the fact remains that they are slipping away as Protestant political preoccupations. And their passing opens the possibility for broadening the scope of moral responsibility in politics.

*2) The traumas of the sixties—civil rights and black power, campus riots and killings, Vietnam—affected the political consciousness of local parishes in ways that cannot be fully determined.* We can speculate on some consequences: The members of congregations have been forced to look at and acknowledge some problems, issues, and points of view which previously were invisible or repressed. Many of them find themselves much farther along in changes of attitude than they or anyone else would have guessed was possible.

But they have not been radicalized, and they are not interested in promoting or supporting radical solutions. They may accommodate themselves to a moving center, but they want the security of the center—and of orderly rather than precipitous movement. They are much more reluctant now to support foreign policies which might commit the United States to armed struggle, but their reluctance has more to do with unwillingness to send their sons off to foreign wars than with a more astute perception of the proper role of the United States in world politics.

*3) Conservative Christianity has discovered political responsibility.* In the past the call for Christian political involvement has come rather overwhelmingly from liberal Christianity, whether in its idealistic or realistic (Niebuhrian) forms. Examples of the latter were William Muehl's *Politics for Christians*, William Lee Miller's *The Protestant and Politics*, and John Bennett's *Christians and the State*. "Conservative" Christianity had its political expressions, to be sure, but they tended to be of the militant anti-communist, nativist, anti-welfare, anti-black type that split the world into manichaean forces of light and darkness and showed little if any sympathy for the poor and oppressed.

Now, however, we are reading highly sensitive and theologically competent "evangelical" works such as Paul Henry's *Politics for Evangelicals* and Richard Mouw's *Politics and the Biblical Drama*. In a socially more radical vein, but still "evangelical" in its theological commitment, one finds the excellent new journal *Sojourners*.

But the propensity for identifying conservative Christianity with conservative politics and economics, and making orthodoxy in one a test of orthodoxy in the other, certainly is not dead. To the contrary, it now is more explicitly and aggressively political, more highly organized, more determined to bring the various levels of government under control. For a report on this type of conservative Christian politics, represented in Bill Bright and the Campus Crusade for Christ, Third Century Publishers, and Christian Freedom Foundation, see "Politics from the Pulpit" in *Newsweek*, September 6, 1976.

One of the prospects for the "parish and politics" is that local congregations may be split, not between liberals and conservatives, but between or among the varieties of conservative Christianity. I note in passing *Newsweek*'s report that Billy Graham has dissassociated himself from Bill Bright and his political movement.

Having pointed to these developments, and especially the last one, I may thereby have undermined my earlier assertion that the fundamental relationship of parish to politics is not likely to change. But I don't think so. I expect—and hope for—a heightening of the consciousness of Christian political responsibility at the parish level, but I doubt that most parishes will surrender their self-image—and corresponding disposition—as essentially nonpolitical.

Ironically, if local parishes are transformed into power-wielding political organizations, that transformation more likely will be carried off by religious-political fundamentalists of the Bill Bright variety than by the traditionally more politically conscious liberal Christians. But if the political biblicists have some measure of success, it surely will be at the price of dividing and destroying a number of congregations, and probably also of fouling both the political process and the concept of Christian political responsibility.

The optimum to hope for is increasingly visible, sophisticated, and constant conversation at the parish level (and elsewhere) among the varieties of liberal and conservative Christians who are willing and able to talk with each other. We may then move toward a deepening of our theological understanding of human nature, historical expectation, and Christian mission, and a sharpening of our awareness of and sensitivity to the interrelationships between political process and human need.

*June 1977*

# Ten Ways to Help
# Your Congregation Go to Hell

JOHN LYNN CARR

Is there ever a time when someone should be told to go to hell? In their book *Christ's Suburban Body*, Wilfred Bailey and William McElvaney suggest that

> In addition to the time-honored greeting of "grace and peace," we should be saying to each other, "in the name of Jesus Christ, go to hell"—to where principalities and powers are robbing men of their humanity, into the suffering, the humiliation, the injustices of the world where God is at work freeing the captives. "He descended into hell" in the Apostles' Creed is a much-needed reminder of a missional style of life held before us in Christ.

Here, then, are ten ways in which a congregation can be helped to hear and respond to such a word.

1) Read John 21:15-17 and point out that Christ's love for Peter was given not to be paid back but passed on. Divide into groups of three or four with the task of identifying persons in the neighborhood, church, community, nation, or world who need to be fed. Make a newsprint sign with felt marker for each one in the form of an "I am" statement: "I am a four-year-old in Bangladesh who is starving." "I am a Brazilian imprisoned for my views on humane treatment for Indians." After taping signs to the walls of the room, hold a silent intercessory prayer walk, followed by spoken prayer and debriefing.

2) Design field trips to provide the kind of personal exposure to situations of human need in your community which your people would not ordinarily get: nursing homes, correctional facilities, health institutions, crisis centers, welfare offices, etc. Place the emphasis on person-to-person contact and avoid as much as possible the "tour of the building and pitch for volunteers." Equip participants with questions such as "How does it feel to be where these people are?" "Why do they find it difficult to believe that they are valuable human beings?" "What might it mean for you realistically to embody the love of God in this situation (either individually or as a part of some corporate effort)?" Debrief together.

3) Use simulation games such as "Starpower" (do-it-yourself instructions available from SIMILE II, P. O. Box 1023, La Jolla, California 92037) or "Bread" (from *Gaming: The Fine Art of Creating Simulation/Learning Games for Religious Education*, by Dennis Benson, Abingdon, 1971) to raise consciousness of the realities of our unjust world fast.

4) In a sermon or, better yet, a study group, take a cue from Jesus and use a modern parable such as "Mislaid Mission" or "Lying Offshore" from G. William Jones's *The Innovator* (Abingdon).

5) Explore the possibilities of alternative celebrations at Christmas and at Thanksgiving. The *Alternative Christmas Catalogue* (1500 Farragut Street, N.W., Washington, DC 20011) is full of ideas for transforming our annual festival of conspicuous consumption into an expression of concern for the world Christ came to liberate. And what about including prisoners, nationals, senior citizens, or folks from an inner city center in an intergenerational worship service followed by a congregational potluck?

6) Locate a small group of persons willing to invest some real time and energy in being trained and empowered to become loving critics, agents of change in the organizations and structures of which they are a part. Work together to find printed and human resources to help (denominational staff and local educational institutions are good initial contacts). See if you can't develop a modest model for change-agent training and support groups.

7) Ask people (perhaps as a part of your stewardship drive!) to list all the groups, organizations, and activities in which they are involved this year and the average number of hours they invest in each per month. Then, ask them to put a plus beside those things which truly nurture or recreate them, a star beside what meets a crying human need, and, finally, beside each item which they have not marked, an explanation of why they are doing it! Discuss!

8) In the way you speak about and deal with people's time, make clear to yourself and to them the all-important distinction between "church work" and "the work of the church" and the importance of evaluating the former by how it serves the latter; e.g., replace the usual announcements in worship with a period just before the prayers in which concerns for persons, issues, situations are shared and ministries of your people celebrated.

9) Use the power of personal particularity by promoting those giving projects which link your congregation (or groups, families, and individuals within it) to specific people and situations, making possible personal correspondence, visits, focused study, etc. Encourage the task-force approach to mission: a small group of people studying, caring for one another, and focusing intensively on responding to one specific need or issue.

10) Remember that none of the above or any of the other many possibilities is likely to make a dent unless people are not only hearing but experiencing the Gospel of Liberation themselves. The only adequate soil for the above catalogue of seeds is the kind of Christian community in which persons can receive the power to face and fight the principalities and powers which dominate and dehumanize them.

*June 1977*

# IV
## Matters of Belief

## Healing as Transformation

CHARLES V. GERKIN

There is probably no word in the English language with more ambiguous meaning than the word *healing*. The human wish is, of course, that it might mean to be cured. And now and again that can happen. Something goes awry with the body or the psyche of a person and the cause of the problem is found; the cause is removed or overpowered by insight, a surgical knife, or chemicals and the problem is resolved, the person healed.

But many, if not most, human ailments seem stubbornly to resist cure. Modern medicine spends much of its time and energy dealing not with illnesses of the body that have a single, eradicable cause, the removal of which can issue in a cure, but with diseases related to the aging process and the wear and tear of life's stress. Cardiovascular disease, pulmonary ailments, the deterioration of glandular, kidney, or liver function do not submit themselves to cure in the sense of healing that removes the problem. For a time measured in months or many years they can be controlled, managed, but they can seldom be cured. Likewise, the psychic and interpersonal ills that affect the self's ability to function and that interfere with the full flowering of relationships seem often to ebb and flow; their constant suffering heightens in some periods of the life cycle and recedes in other, less stressful times. To be healed of these ills is not a one time, once and for all, thing.

All of which is to suggest that healing, if it is to have meaning for much of what ails us, must be grasped in a sense other than the wish to be cured. Life is a process that ebbs and flows, and it carries us ever toward death for which there is no cure save the hope of resurrection.

There is another quite different direction our wish to be healed can take that is more congruent with the Christian vision of reality. It is the wish to be healed in the sense of the desire to be made whole. To wish to be made whole is to recognize the broken, fragmented, imperfect state of finite human life—a state for which there seems to be no cure short of the coming of the kingdom—and to look for the transformation of that state into a life of wholeness. To wish to be made whole has an "in spite of" quality about it that looks for the healing of what cannot be healed in the sense of being "cured."

A woman with terminal cancer comes painfully to terms with the reality of approaching death. No longer denying her state she stops praying for rescue from her plight and begins to pray for strength to live fully until death comes. She shares her feeling of having been cheated out of her future with her family, and in the sharing she finds herself having to rethink a lot of old resentments and scale down some old understanding of herself as indispensable to her children. The closing in of life's boundaries forces a process of reassessment of herself and the significant relationships in her life. That process also begins to include a rethinking of her relationship with God that up to now had at its core a childlike desire for protection from life's pain and the threat of death. She becomes in the profoundest sense a more whole person. All is in one sense the same with her: She is sick unto death. But all is transformed. What happened? Has she been healed?

The best answer seems to be that the woman has been healed, although dying, because her life has undergone transformation. The meanings that have clustered in the past around her understanding of self and others, God and God's activity, have undergone transformative change. She experiences everything in her life from a new standpoint. She may be sick unto death, but she is more whole than she has ever been.

Some years ago I awoke in the night with acute and severe pain in my lower right abdomen. A doctor was called and by three in the morning I was on an operating table to have my appendix removed. It had ruptured suddenly, but surgical skill quickly removed the culprit and I have never had that same pain again. Healing, however, seldom comes that way. More often it comes in the process of coming to terms with the way things are with us, whether that be our sick or aging bodies or our inability to live in love with our neighbors. Our lives are transformed and what has been fragmented and contradictory becomes more whole.

*September 1978*

# "Arise and Walk"

## RICHARD B. HAYS

Anyone who has sat through an introductory Bible course with moderate attention knows that the Scriptures undercut our deeply in-grained cultural tendency to think in terms of anthropological dualisms: "body" versus "soul," and so on. In general, the biblical writers think of the human person as a psychosomatic unity, a living *nephesh* whose right relationship to God, whether we call it *shalom* or *soferia*, encompasses all dimensions of existence, the physical and the spiritual together. Indeed, we are fond of wielding this truth in order to explode the tiresome false dichotomy between "social action" and "evangelism," which everyone in-volved in ministry encounters. "No!" we exclaim, "concern for the salva-tion of individuals cannot be separated from concern for their practical well-being." And so we press on to insist on the appropriateness of Chris-tian involvement in political projects. So far so good.

But I wonder whether we have reflected deeply enough about the im-plications of this same point for the church's practice and theology in rela-tion to physical healing. Oddly enough, at this point we start to get nervous and retreat into a spiritualizing dualism. We pray for God to "comfort" the dying cancer patient, to give her the grace to be at peace in her affliction, to help her family to cope with the tragedy. But do we pray corporately, as the gathered community of faith, for God to heal her? We might dare such a prayer in our private desperation, but to pray it in the congregation would usually be viewed as a shocking transgression of clerical etiquette.

In order to place this contemporary situation in its proper perspective, let us reflect a bit on the New Testament witness in relation to healing. The four Gospels, of course, are unanimous in portraying Jesus as a healer; we have long accustomed ourselves to this fact. But the fact with which we reckon all too little is that these same Gospels also insist that Jesus commissioned his disciples to carry on his ministry of healing. (Cf. Matthew 10:7-8, John 14:12, etc.) The narratives of Acts give us a vivid description of the way in which this commission was carried out. Let us concentrate for now on the story of the healing of the lame man by Peter and John in Acts 3 and 4, asking what the meaning of this story might be for us.

The healing in this story serves as a *sign* by which the power of God is made manifest and the role of *Jesus* as the effective mediator of that power is authenticated. "Be it known to you all . . . that by the name of Jesus Christ of Nazareth, whom you crucified, whom God has raised from the dead, by him this man is standing before you well" (Acts 4:10). This car-ries several implications:

1) The healing is *not* an illustration of the power of mind over matter or of the wholeness that results from some harmonious resonation with the

cosmic energies; it is a miracle which attests that through Jesus Christ the kingdom of God is already impinging upon human reality. The healings in the early church's experience were always interpreted in this eschatological context. This was true of Jesus' own ministry: "If it is by the Spirit of God that I cast out demons, then the Kingdom of God has come upon you" (Matthew 12:28).

When the disciples of John the Baptist asked, "Are you he who is to come, or shall we look for another?" Jesus answered simply by pointing to the miraculous healings that attended his ministry (Luke 7:18-23). Just as these signs were the credentials of the Messiah, so also the miraculous healings in the early church were understood as evidence that Jesus the crucified one, in whose name the healings were performed, was now exalted at the right hand of the Father, hearing and answering prayer. Thus the church's faith in God's healing power was intimately bound up with its consciousness of itself as an eschatological community in which the signs of God's coming kingdom were already appearing.

2) The ministry of Peter and John was "legitimated" by the healing done through them.

> Now when they saw the boldness of Peter and John, and perceived that they were common, uneducated men, they wondered; and they recognized that they had been with Jesus. But seeing the man that had been healed standing beside them, they had nothing to say in opposition (Acts 4:13-14).

3) A corrective supplement to the previous point: The healing miracle is not the occasion for a cult-following around the faith-healer. "Why do you wonder at this," protests Peter, "or why do you stare at us, as though by our own power or piety we had made him walk?" The focus is on Jesus as the healer, and the healing is in no way dependent on the holiness either of Peter and John or of the lame man.

To sum up, we see in this Acts narrative that the healing of the crippled man serves as a dramatic, visible expression of the lordship of Jesus Christ over creation. The appropriateness of the sign is undeniable; in the healing of one man "lame from birth," we see figured God's will to heal creation. But this brings us to one more point that figures prominently in the New Testament perspective on healing. Healing is understood as something which takes place in the context of the Christian *community*. Paul in 1 Corinthians 12 speaks of "gifts of healing" among the interdependent manifestations of the Spirit which serve to build up the body of Christ. And in the letter of James, we find this exhortation:

> Is any among you sick? Let him call for the elders of the church, and let them pray over him, anointing him with oil in the name of the Lord; and the prayer of faith will save the sick man, and the Lord will raise him up; and if he has committed sins, he will be forgiven. Therefore confess your sins to one another, and pray for one another, that you may be healed (James 5:14-16).

There is a challenge for us! We like to psychologize passages like this and explain that there is great therapeutic value in this kind of close community of mutual concern. This is true, of course, but we must not overlook the eschatological horizon of this exhortation. The very existence of this community of mutual concern is itself a sign of the coming consummation of all things, and God's healing activity in this community is understood in light of this hope.

What are the implications of all this for us? It seems clear that, if we are to be faithful to the New Testament witness, we ought to pray for God to heal people in our churches, especially within the gathered community. The wholeness offered in Christ may very well include physical healing.

The scary part, of course, is that the healing will often *not* be granted. The teaching that we sometimes hear about "claiming your healing" as if it were a right or an assured result is not on firm biblical ground because it dissolves the eschatological tension. The consummation, after all, is not yet here, and God has not yet wiped away every tear from our eyes.

We find Paul recounting his unsuccessful prayers for healing (2 Corinthians 12:7-10), and we do well to remember that God's power is sometimes "made perfect in weakness." But we should not forget that Paul's grasp of this theological point did not prevent him from praying three times for the "weakness" to be removed! We should ask in simple trust and leave it to God to choose in specific cases whether to heal or not.

*September 1978*

# Theology's Task

## WALTER LOWE

A favorite theologian of mine, Soren Kierkegaard, once made a remark which sticks with me. Most people, he wrote, "are subjective toward themselves and objective toward all others, terribly objective sometimes." Compassionate toward ourselves, we can be coldly analytical toward others. "But the real task," he added, "is in fact to be objective toward oneself—and subjective toward all others."

The task is to become subjective toward others. Clearly this is what one segment of the seminary curriculum is about. In learning to counsel with others, we learn to be with the other person. To counsel is first to listen, to feel what the world is like from another's point of view. But I would urge that this business of getting inside another person's world is just as important in the "academic" area as well. Nothing is more vital to scholarship than an empathy of the mind. We may think of books as so many dead objects, like blocks of ice upon the shelf. But any writing worth reading needs only the warmth of passionate attention in order to "melt," to become fluid and nourishing.

Just as counseling is a matter of listening, scholarship is a matter of reading in a style which is at one and the same time active and receptive. And in the one case as in the other, the key lies in our being willing to bet that the other person, the speaker or the writer, is as real and as alive as we. The task, too, is to become objective toward oneself. To listen we must let go of our prejudices and preconceptions, the pat answers we may bring. And to let them go, we must know what they are. We must see ourselves objectively.

Christian social responsibility, it seems to me, involves cutting free of the natural tendency to think oneself the center of the world. In a time of global interdependence, it is more than a theoretical necessity. This year we at Candler will be giving special attention to world hunger. When I spoke of this recently at a youth retreat, one person replied, "I am not going to feel guilty about eating a good meal. I work hard for what I eat." That sounds fair enough. But the fact is that many of our sisters and brothers work hard as well, and they remain hungry. To be mindful of this fact, and to feel something of what it means, is an initial way of pulling together the two strands of which Kierkegaard speaks.

But we as Christians do not pull our lives together by ourselves. Kierkegaard would say the "that" of Christianity, the substance of the faith, lies in the "how" of our relationship to the Lord Jesus Christ. Theology did not invent that good news. Theology trots along afterward, understanding as best it can. But the news may give you a sense of why I find the study of theology, too, to be worthy of passionate commitment. For the notion that the way to true objectivity, the way to seeing things as they are before God, *coram Deo*, is by following with all our subjectivity the person of Jesus of Nazareth—that is a notion which never ceases to stagger and to nourish my mind.

*November 1976*

# Scholarship and the Spiritual Life

RODNEY J. HUNTER

The discipline of scholarly work is usually viewed as either unrelated to spirituality or its direct antithesis. Academic pursuits, as the very word "academic" has come to suggest, are assumed to be narrowly and technically intellectual, as far removed from spirituality as they are from the "real world" of lived experience, concrete relationships, and historical events. While learning in the church may be valued for its own sake or, more often, for its real or imagined social and professional benefits, there is today little sense of scholarly work as in principle a spiritual discipline, an activity to be undertaken with commitment and accountability, for transcendental or spiritual ends.

In my view this is unfortunate, and is perhaps one of the reasons why spirituality is so little understood or valued among us except in narrowly pietistic forms. What is missing is a sense of scholarship as a tangible and necessary cultural expression of the love of truth, without which spirituality in any developed sense is impossible. But the idea of loving truth has fallen upon evil days. For many, the love of truth sounds vaguely like a nostalgic appeal to narrow-mindedness and fanaticism, or the threat of abstract intellectualism replacing the playful liveliness of imagination, restraining the richness of lived experience. For others more philosophically inclined, the idea of loving truth may seem either mystical or naive in an age when the notion of truth itself and the human capacity for truth are frequently suspect, complicated, and qualified by innumerable considerations.

One can surely grant more than a small measure of validity to these concerns. Yet important and necessary as it is to clarify distortions in the meaning of truth and what it means to love truth, and to avoid presumptive claims to possessing the truth, it is equally necessary to honor the fundamental moral and spiritual nerve of the idea. This, as I see it, has to do with a devoted willingness to be related to the world at its historic and cosmic actuality, which invariably calls into question our own conceptions of it. To love the truth does not mean to love our own truths but to love that which our truths seek. It means seeking a right relationship with reality—the whole of life and the world as given to us and transformed by us—even at the cost of being challenged, changed, and transformed ourselves in the process.

Rightly understood, this is the proper aim of scholarship, which may be defined as the cultural discipline of the love of truth. As such, scholarship gives specific embodiment to this spiritual principle in the form of particular disciplines and traditions of inquiry and reflection, without which the love of truth would be a mere formless ideal. Yet the love of truth cannot be contained by these disciplines or simply equated with them, and scholarship at its concrete enactment cannot be reduced to the historically contingent and fragmentary conventions of academia.

The practice of true scholarship as the cultural discipline of the love of truth is in some respects as rare among professional academicians (even theologians) as it is among nonacademics. Going through the motions of scholarly work, however skillfully and impressively executed, gives no guarantee of authentic inquiry, as the current deluge of competitive, repetitive, and often trivial publications in academic journals attests. Nonetheless, there is no way to love truth seriously apart from specific means and occasions for doing so, whether these are institutionally organized and formalized or individually undertaken in unique and personally variable ways. In any case scholarship in some form and degree is integral to the love of truth and hence, in its deepest and truest sense, is a spiritual discipline.

This means, however, that insofar as ministry involves spiritual discipline it involves scholarship, not simply as a practical means of furthering professional or institutional effectiveness, but as a necessary expression of the life of faith itself. The scholarly love of truth, shorn of dogmatic and self-righteous pretensions, in principle if not always in fact, protects faith and ministry from illusion, sentimentality, and idolatry by orienting us outward from ourselves toward the sovereign God of a universe and a human history we cannot ultimately master and control, nor yet fully comprehend. Conversely, when ministry proceeds without a love of truth disciplined in scholarship, its worship becomes clannish and idolatrous, its proclamation an authoritarian demand, its education degenerates into indoctrination or the celebration of pious ignorance, and its personal guidance and care slide into sentimentality, technical gimmickry, and superficiality.

It may well be that the apparently troubled state of the church's and the ministry's spirituality, its agonized uncertainties about spiritual life matched by chauvinistic enthusiasms, results in part from a misperception of what true spirituality is, that is, from a certain unwillingness to be disciplined in the quest and discovery of truth, and to subject the whole of our religious and moral life to the question of truth. The spiritual enthusiast is perhaps too quick and presumptive in claiming to possess or be possessed by the truth; and the doubter not venturous enough in the love of it. In either case the love of truth and its concrete expression in the disciplines of scholarship serve in their own unique ways to bear witness to the sovereignty of God who is beyond all our truths yet graciously invites us into the truth of the divine being and history. Far from representing an artificial or abstract evasion of life and ministry, scholarship rightly conceived as a disciplining of life by divine reality as it meets us in history and cosmos, is an integral, indispensible feature of a developed life of faith in the spirit of God.

*February 1982*

# Theology and the Life of the Community

## THEODORE W. JENNINGS

There is a wide separation today between the work of theology and the life of the Christian community. There are many reasons for and symptoms of this separation. In order to meet the standards (real or imagined) of academic study, theology has preoccupied itself with questions of method and of presuppositions to such a degree that the actual work of interpreting the Christian faith seems endlessly deferred or postponed. At the same time a bewildering succession of theological proposals marches past, each idea claiming to represent the new wave of future theology, each pronouncing the others to be hopelessly out of date, out of touch, or just "out of it."

The life of the Christian community, on the other hand, exhibits a preoccupation with questions of institutional extension or preservation which obscure the questions of Christian identity and faithfulness. How to make our church grow, how to get more people more involved, how to raise the budget, how to effect necessary retrenchments—these are often the kinds of issues which consume the energy of the community. One gains the impression of a compulsive busyness without a clear commitment to anything but the life of the institution.

The result of this double malaise is that theology as a reflection upon the basic character of Christian faith seems nearly to have disappeared, while the community of faith takes on the character of a voluntary association whose specific Christian identity is simply assumed but seldom made evident. We must not suppose that this connection between the poverty of theology and the barrenness of church life is only a historical accident. The vigor of theology has always been closely tied to the vigor of the church's life and witness. The one cannot long survive without the other. How then are we to overcome this gulf between theology and the church, so fatal to both? It will not do simply to "translate" theological statements into the popular jargon of the institution. A dialogue between sterile theory and blind practice can produce nothing of value.

I believe the astonishing vigor of theology in Europe in the first half of this century is related to two principle factors. The question of Christian identity was raised in an especially radical way by the debacle of the First World War and then by the emergence of quasi-religious fascism. The response was to produce a theology directed toward the practice of the church in proclamation and witness. Thus the ideologies of Barth, Brunner, Bonhoeffer, and Bultmann were preeminently theologies for preaching, theologies which sought to serve the proclamation of the church through a critical reflection upon the foundation, the fidelity, and the goal of proclamation.

Similarly, the most important theology of the Christian community in the last decade has emerged from a situation of crisis in the Third World. The "liberation theology" of Latin America, Africa, and Asia and the "indigenizing" of theology in the same churches correspond to the cultural crisis of post-colonial cultures seeking to discover their own identity and the attempt to disengage the church from its legitimation of colonial, neo-colonial, and neo-nationalistic structures of oppression.

Common to these theological movements is the determination to oppose political, cultural, and economic forms of exploitation and oppression in the name of the Jesus who announced deliverance to the captives. What is important here is to notice that theological vitality is the handmaiden of a vigorous church struggle to determine the concrete forms of faithful discipleship. A vigorous theology corresponds to and contributes to the vitality of a church seriously concerned about Christian identity and faithfulness.

What do these examples of the marriage of theology and the life of the church, taken from situations quite different from our own, have to teach us in mainline American middle-class Protestantism? Only by way of serious attention to the identity, the life, the actual practice of the Christian community can theology once again become a meaningful and vigorous discipline. Only by way of a critical reflection upon the basis and aim of its practice can the church acquire a compelling sense of its own identity and mission. For us, as for the Europeans of the earlier decades of this century, this will have to take the form of a theology for preaching. For us, as for the Third World Christians of the last decades of the century, this will have to take the form of a theology for an authentic Christian practice of liberation. Yet in all of this, we will have to find our own way as well.

One place to begin is to engage in serious theological inquiry concerning our practice of worship. What does it mean to pray for the coming of God's kingdom? What does it mean to announce and to enact the forgiveness of sins? What does it mean to join together in eating bread and drinking wine "until His coming again"? Worship is something we do almost without thinking about it. Perhaps by beginning to think about it, about why we do what we do, about who we declare ourselves to be by doing these things, we may find clues to our identity as Christians and about the basis of that identity in what God has done for us in Christ.

A recovery of the relationship between serious theology and the life and praxis of the community, whether our focus is upon preaching, worship, formation, or liberating mission, will require of us in the seminary that we reconsider the relationship of historical and theological disciplines to the "practical disciplines." I think it will mean that we will have to break down the airtight compartmentalization which separates historical-exegetical inquiry from theological reflection. We will have to challenge the separation of pastoral care from social ethics and of both from worship. Above all it will mean that theology itself recover from its narcissistic self-preoccupation to turn toward a genuine theory for practice, a critical reflection in the service of life, a theology for the church. I believe that these things are beginning to happen.

But they cannot get very far if the churches remain intellectually dormant, if they refuse to ask serious and probing questions, if they seek only to be consumers of theology rather than its producers. Serious wrestling with the question of Christian identity will not make our churches grow, but it may help them to grow up. It will not get folk involved in our program, but it may involve them in God's mission. It will not make us successful institutions, but it may help us to become vital communities of faith. It will not help us provide havens of nostalgia, but it may drive or lure us into God's future. Theology is a risky business. It does not give us answers, but it places us before questions we cannot evade. It sets us before the One who asks "Adam, where art thou?" and "Who do you say that I am?" In the church and in the seminary we may engage in this kind of theology because we are persuaded that it is only the Truth which can make us free and give us life.

*April 1980*

# Church Education for Creative Discipleship

JAMES W. FOWLER

The theologian's job is to help us think straight and act true in our efforts to be the church. The theologian lives between the Scripture, the tradition, and the unfolding present.

He or she must have the courage and faith to bank everything on the word of God and on the history of its interpretation. He or she must exercise the imagination, sustained by prayer and spirituality, to release the power of the original events of God's self-disclosure. Then there must be the artistic power, fueled by a Spirit that is Holy, so to communicate the master-images of the Christian faith that our minds' eyes and souls' eyes are illumined to see God's work in the present, and our hearts are moved to *do* the truth.

Education in the church consciously or unconsciously reflects the church's operative sense of mission. Teachers, curriculum, and program of course represent the major intentional foci of our educational efforts. But the larger medium is the message: Our *real* sense of mission in churches comes to expression, for young people and adults alike, in the priorities guiding our allocation of lay and professional energies, in the procedures by which corporate decisions are made, in our attention (or inattention) to issues of justice and fairness in the larger community, and in our seriousness (or lack of it) about being aggressive pioneers of expanding colonies of the kingdom of God.

Church educators need the critical and constructive help of church theologians. We need them in our efforts to find creative methods of engaging persons in the processes of becoming Christian. We need them in the efforts to stimulate development in faith. We require trusted brothers and sisters who know the Script and who know the present era, and who therefore can risk formulating the Christian story's present meanings.

The church without lively theological reflection and guidance in the shaping of its mission is vulnerable to two kinds of failures. It will either pursue the route of institutional idolatry, in which we produce good church women and men for whom the church is an end in itself; or it will become a conforming cheerleader for the class and social interests of its members.

In this era, we have good reason to be grateful for the efforts of church theologian Jurgen Moltmann. Here I want to consider with you the import for the work of church education of some of Moltmann's bold efforts to guide us aright toward present and future faithfulness in our mission to the world as followers of Jesus Christ. My working title is "Future Christians and Church Education." With reference to "Future Christians" I mean a double play on words. I want to speak about Christians of the future, that is, the shape of Christian discipleship in the coming era. But then I also want to speak of Christians *of* the future, that is, Christians who lean into life, nerved and kept alert by the ever-fresh horizon of the coming kingdom of God.

The recovery of eschatology as the primary context for understanding Jesus' teachings about the kingdom of God is a great contribution of the theologians of hope. When we begin to get their message we find that they have interrupted our sense of time in some very fundamental ways. In common-sense ways of thinking, we take for granted that the present is the result of things that happened or didn't happen in the past; and the future, we assume, will result from and be shaped by things that happen or don't happen today. Cause intersects cause and they produce effects. The present came to us out of the past; the past and the present will give us the future. Church education is, or ought to be, education for creative discipleship in the context of the coming kingdom of God.

From the first this way of imaging church education pushes aside some other organizing themes or goals that have consciously or unconsciously guided the church's educational efforts. Education for creative discipleship in the context of the coming kingdom of God cannot be translated, without serious loss, into "education for character development" or "education for values and citizenship" or "education for self-actualization." Nor can it be translated, without deformity, into "education for church-personship" (to coin a phrase). Neither "intentional religious socialization" nor "education for faith development" can contain the normativity and radicality which we intend. Though each of the educational approaches we have touched on here may have important contributions to make to our task, the breadth and depth and thrust of what Moltmann intends necessarily spill over and make relative the categories of these other strategies.

Education for creative discipleship in the context of the coming kingdom of God is both a *function* of a church whose mission is centered in the coming kingdom and a *means* to the clarification and intensification of that mission. Unless the church's corporate vision already looks to the horizon of the coming kingdom, church education's work will inevitably tend to fall into the service of more limited and more self-serving commitments. On the other hand, unless church education, understood in the broadest sense, is stimulating, goading and guiding the extension of vision to the horizon of the future kingdom, there will be little chance of the church's finding its authentic mission.

Does education for creative discipleship in the context of the coming kingdom of God necessarily stand critically over against culture and society? Or are there times and ways in which it must guide Christians into the tasks of maintaining and re-forming the *saeculum?* Christian education cannot, I believe, determine in advance to be either consistently opposed to secular society (H. Richard Neibuhr's "Christ Against Culture") or consistently aligned with it (Neibuhr's "Christ of Culture"). Rather, what Christian education, as we are proposing it, calls for is an alert leaning into life, receiving it from God, and attempting to respond faithfully to the movements of the coming kingdom in the present. Such a stance requires a committed flexibility, born of and tested in an honest corporateness and centered in an imaginative, shared discernment of the church's present calling.

Responses to the inbreaking kingdom will never allow the sacralizing of the economic, political, or ecclesiastical *status quo.* Christians are called to constant and ongoing self-critical submission to the kingdom's imperatives of love and justice. These are corporate, social-structured imperatives. Moltmann and Segundo are right when they urge that Christians must identify with the oppressed and the exploited if we would really hear faithfully the liberating imperatives of the kingdom of God. But response to the kingdom has its constructive moments as well as its critical ones.

Faithfulness to the kingdom may require profound investments in the building or rebuilding of the structures that maintain and protect the common life. Just as it may, in other contexts, require determined resistance, resolute opposition, or even dead-serious efforts to overthrow these structures. What is certain is that taking the emergent kingdom as the organizing principle for the church's mission and its education will mean for us to live in ongoing tension and transformational engagement with the surrounding world.

*March 1979*

# Is the Bible True?

## WILLIAM MALLARD

That question may very well come from a member of the congregation that one is serving. Most denominations or communions have a statement of commitment or belief on this matter that the pastor and the member already share and that can be a useful meeting ground for discussion. For example, in the United Methodist tradition the question is raised of the candidate for membership or confirmation, "Do you receive and profess the Christian faith as contained in the Scriptures of the Old and New Testaments?" If a member asks, "Is the Bible true?"—or an equivalent question—it is useful to recall that both the pastor and the member have at some time said, "I do," to the question in the confirmation service as given above.

Then the question becomes a matter of discussing what is meant by "receiving and professing the Christian faith" as contained in the Bible—both Testaments. Is the Bible true? In light of the membership vow, this question asks the truth of the Christian faith "as contained in" the Bible. For one baptized and confirmed, all other questions of truth in the Bible must relate to this one, and this one is the most important. "Is the Bible true?" becomes the question of whether or not the Christian faith is true, as given in the Scriptures.

*The* faith? But surely the biblical books express a variety of faiths, not just one. Does Judges fit with the Gospel of John? Ecclesiastes with Luke-Acts? Imagine a long shelf—full of books in someone's home. One sees there history, poetry, drama, hymnody, religious handbooks, law, epic accounts, oracular literature, and collections of letters, standing side by side, but no Bible. Then one realizes that the whole shelf is the Bible, with its books bound separately.

The Bible is a library. What library that you know expresses one faith? How can you declare to be true *the* faith contained in this Bible-library? Professor Northrop Frye says, "Why does this huge, sprawling, tactless book sit there inscrutably in the middle of our cultural heritage . . . frustrating all our efforts to walk around it?" (*The Great Code*)—or to walk a straight line through it? Professor Frye himself helps to provide an answer. No straight line may go through the entire Bible; yet Frye finds something across its sprawling mass that he calls a series of cycles. For example, one is the socio-political cycle, from the promise to Abraham, through Moses and the Law, to the Holy City in Revelation; one is the sexual cycle, from Adam and Eve, through Israel the faithless wife (Hosea), to the new Jerusalem as a bride (Revelation). Another of these Frye calls the cycle of "the heroic quest of the Messiah" (*Anatomy of Criticism*), from the promise in Abraham's Isaac all the way to the second coming of Christ Jesus at the end.

He calls for a "literary criticism which would see the Bible, not as the scrapbook of corruptions, glosses, insertions, conflations, revealed by the analytic critic, but as the typological unity which all these things were originally intended to help construct . . , a single archetypal structure extending from creation to apocalypse." In that case, revelation is not limited to original, discrete events (crossing the Red Sea, or the "Christ-Event," as we have been taught to call it), but includes the assembling of the Bible as a whole. So Frye: ". . . if the Bible is to be regarded as inspired in any sense, sacred or secular, its editorial and redacting process must be regarded as inspired too."

Suppose we say that in these cycles in Scripture lies a basis for *the* faith. What is that faith? Is that faith true? The faith is that God's Messiah has come and will come again. Among other things, consider the surprising singularity of this Messiah. Child of the universal, creator-God, and therefore universal himself, the Messiah is not only humble and rejected (scandal enough), he belongs to a particular time, place, and people, never to be fully unloosed and abstracted from them. Such parochialism seems even a greater scandal.

He is the concrete result of a frightening covenant made with a particular, ancient nomadic group ("It is terrible what I am about to do with you."—Exodus 34:10). Yet for all this particularity, the Bible stories mean to be interpreting universal history. Erich Auerbach says, "Into [the Old Testament] everything that is known about the world . . . must be fitted as an ingredient of the divine plan; . . . the reader is at every moment aware of the universal religio-historical perspective which gives the individual stories their general meaning and purpose" (Mimesis). Is it not arrogant to propose that the Bible, one narrow strand of narration, inexhaustibly holds the key to the world's complete history, and must be returned to again and again? Christians convinced that their Bible held the key to all of truth have done terrible deeds to others (the Crusades, European conquest of America, the African slave trade). But they abused the Bible to their own ends.

The point of the Bible is the opposite, is the humility of knowing one's own appropriate limit and calling. Appeals to universal, rational truth, on the other hand, have often become isolating (elite) or dominating (tyrannical). Focused, stubborn, biblical narrative exists to humble both the elite and the tyrannical, the church and the world, whenever any of these—reaching past the simple stories and parables to the naked "truth"—have attempted to unseat God and become uncontested ruler.

Whenever human reflection arrives at a universal generality, either optimistic (pax Americana) or pessimistic (existential perplexity), the rough-hewn biblical accounts refuse to fit in. "Jesus thrown everything off balance," says Flannery O'Conner's Misfit (in "A Good Man Is Hard to Find"). That is indeed the role of the biblical Jesus.

The Bible as key to universal history precisely checks any hasty conclusion on how to dominate that history. The Bible allows no arrogance or elitism. It gives rather a long and hopeful journey called discipleship.

But is it true? The Bible invites us to follow its long and hopeful journey and see.

*October 1983*

# Are We True to the Bible?

MANFRED HOFFMANN

"Is the Bible True?" We hear this question again and again from the more discerning of our church folk. And closer home, it often fires back on us as it exposes, in the wear and tear of our ministerial vocation, the fundamental quandary of our call to be servants of the gospel. If God's revelation in Scripture is not right, the Christian faith is the greatest hoax, a supreme sham, a cruel joke. If it is right, then committing one's life to God in Christ is the ultimate truth.

So, for parishioners and clergy alike, this question is indeed so crucial that it touches the very roots of Christian existence; it is a matter of life and death. And although "experienced" pastors have a way with pat answers or evasive maneuvers to put anguished minds at ease, doubts keep lingering, on the part of the person who turns with a vital question to the professional-in-the-know expecting a definitive answer, and on the part of the official minister whose authority is to authenticate the truth and thus to confirm the faith. An easy way out, of course, is either to seek some alleged other source of truth or to take the Bible as the literally infallible word of God.

Those who turn away from the Christian truth, often not the worst ones, find themselves at the fringes of the congregation and eventually outside the fold. On the other hand, the fundamentalist believes the Scripture to be divinely inspired in all its facets, therefore factual on all accounts, the inerrant final word on problems ranging from biology, marriage and divorce, homosexuality, race relations, the status of women, and economical, social, and political issues, to the future of the world, war and peace, and the kingdom to come. The strong believer uncompromisingly fastens upon God's revelation as the timeless truth, never to be altered in any way but to be literally applied in the same way to all times and circumstances. To regard the Bible as liable to changing times and different social conditions is sheer apostasy, the sin of relativizing the absolute truth.

However, many parts of the Bible are not only inconsistent with each other but also clearly at odds with the canon of modern scientific knowledge. In fact, the question, "Is the Bible true?" expresses both honesty and fear, the honesty of facing the modern predicament and the fear of relativizing the biblical truth. Together they spell a fundamental dilemma: to ignore modern life in favor of Scripture is in the long run as futile as to assert modern truth at the cost of biblical truth.

So what is the truth of the Bible? Is the Bible reliable at all? Can one believe it? Can it be shown to be true? The answer seems to depend on what is meant by truth, and on where the person stands who asks these questions.

If we are looking for a set of stated propositions and perennial doctrines, for the whole truth and nothing but the truth, then we ask for eternal verities, absolute security of knowledge, the certainty of a once-for-all possession rather than the assurance of faith in hope. Rigidity of conviction replaces the vulnerability of commitment. What comes as a gift from outside is claimed as a property. This claim, then, makes us exclude all those who don't have it, or won't have it the way we think they should have it—our way. Intolerance with its double face of presumptuous indifference and aggressive denouncements raises its ugly head.

Further, precisely by claiming universality and finality for its particular perspective, the illusion of possessing the truth fosters its own isolation and nourishes its own subjectivity. Its dialogue is bound to wind up in monologue. And its need for being imposed on other perspectives exactly shows its insecurity as to its confinement within its own limitations. Even more, we tend to project our particular, exclusive perspective of truth back onto the Bible from which we claim to have derived it in the first place. But this projection is really an imposition, because it is now *our* view of the truth that is returned to the Scripture.

Hence, the view becomes so narrow and the words so circumscribed that the Bible promises what we expect and answers to what we ask, rather than speaking on its own. The promise is predetermined by our expectation as is the answer by our question. The Scripture turns into our property; we have made it the dispenser of special favors for us.

The usurpation of truth from Scripture is more perilous the more its claim extends beyond the self to a communal, tribal, or national "we": a manifest destiny has declared *us* to be God's chosen people. The particular cultural, social, economic, and political setting within which the truth is experienced becomes the reason, and the Bible becomes the divine sanction for claiming uniqueness for what we are: this is *it!* Our experience of truth is the only true experience of truth, or at least better than others. We elevate our way of life into uniqueness as a way preferred and especially blessed by God.

Yet, for all of this, what we actually are doing is simply moving from our particularity to uniqueness to universality in order to justify who we are and to call "right" the way we live. Theologically speaking, this is self-justification and works-righteousness by success. However, it so happens that God's word in the Scripture keeps liberating itself from such human presumptuousness. By calling us out of the prison of our particularism, it reveals its true objectivity as truth, its universality, and finality.

God's truth is a liberating power for all who are bound, and it is a binding force for all who presume to be free. And it's not just words, but word in action and action in word. It binds our presumed freedom to impose our particular grasp of truth on others, and it frees us from suffering the oppression of alien claims on us. If anything, the biblical truth calls us to a reversal of question, standpoint, and attitude. It has a peculiar, paradoxical way of turning our question around by coming to us as a word from unexpected quarters, crossing as it does our habitual perception of reality.

The question is not: "Is the Bible true to our standards of truth?" The question is: "Are we true to the standpoint of the biblical truth, the crucified Christ who is the way, the truth, and the life?" This reversal of question and standpoint, traditionally called conversion, engenders a new attitude, the ministry of freeing the bound and binding oppressive freedom. Only in this way do we hear the biblical truth in its objectivity, universality, and finality.

How does this happen? Christ freed the oppressed by stepping into their place and taking their burden upon himself. So, also, Christ's word of truth: It addresses us by making us hear it from the place of persons bound by false claims, not merely imagining their plight but in solidarity under their burden to make them free. And precisely thereby we are freed from ourselves, from our limiting scope of experience and perspective, from the parochialism and regionalism of our presumed control over the truth. We are converted from legitimizing ourselves by the Scripture to recognizing that the Scripture legitimizes the standpoint of the oppressed and their move toward freedom. The "for me" of the biblical truth is not there for self-confirmation but is first of all a "for you" and a "for all," for the remission of sins.

The truth of the Scripture is against me as long as I take it for myself alone; it is "for me" as much as I submit to it as being given "for you" and "for all." As we are bound in our presumed freedom of particularity, we are called to free those who are bound by the exclusion of our or any particularity. When free agents hear that God in Christ sets the captives free, they hear the truth as slaves. When Americans hear that in Christ there is no East or West, they hear it from the other side. When men hear that in Christ there is neither male nor female, they hear it from the place of women. When I hear that God is no respecter of persons, I hear it from the standpoint of any person, however different from me.

*October 1983*

# The Trinity:
# A Doctrine to Be Used

## ARTHUR WAINWRIGHT

It is because the Christian doctrine of God did not make sense to people that theories about the Trinity came into existence. The root of the problem lies in the divinity of Christ. If Christ is God, and yet prays to God, how can God be one? Critics have often accused Christianity of believing in more than one God, and trinitarian theology makes an attempt to answer the question.

Much ink and large quantities of blood have been spilled over the doctrine of the Trinity, but in spite of all these sacrifices and endeavors it has never made complete sense. When it achieves clarity, it is manifestly inadequate. To speak of Father, Son, and Holy Spirit as three persons in a divine society makes sense, but unless this expanation is fenced about with numerous subtleties and qualifications, it is likely to give insufficient emphasis to the idea of divine unity. On the other hand, to speak of three functions of divinity or modes of divine revelation and activity can easily lead to the neglect of the idea of plurality in God.

Moreover, when attempts are made to distinguish the functions of the three persons of the Trinity, the varied nature of biblical teaching can easily be overlooked. If the persons are described as Creator, Redeemer, and Sanctifier, there is a tendency to forget that the Bible ascribes the functions of creation and sanctification to all three persons. Or if they are described as Creator, Reconciler, and Redeemer, some explanation needs to be given of the Bible's tendency to link the first two persons more clearly than the third with the work of redemption.

Another perennial problem is the difficulty of distinguishing between the indwelling Christ and the indwelling Spirit. The doctrine of the Trinity frustrates all attempts to state it in a manner that is both clear and adequate. Theologians have often demonstrated their skill at intellectual gymnastics, but none of them has cleared the crossbar in the trinitarian high jump.

Many people assume that, because the doctrine defies understanding, it should be thrown into the garbage can. But it deals with matters essential to the Christian revelation. The problem that gave rise to the doctrine is already present in the assertion of John's Gospel that in the beginning "the Word was with God and the Word was God" (1:1). The problem is also present when Thomas, free from doubt, greets Jesus as "My Lord and my God!" It is there in the accounts of the Spirit's descent on Jesus at his baptism and of Jesus' rejoicing in the Spirit when he prayed to God. Although these passages from the Bible do not present a systematic theology, they give expression to the beliefs and experience of early Christians.

Because the doctrine of the Trinity is not just the fruit of academic speculation but proceeds from faith and experience, its place is at the center, not at the fringe, of Christian thought and worship. Yet any discussion of it needs to recognize that it does not make complete sense to us and is not likely to do so. No doctrine framed by human minds is able to give an adequate explanation of the mystery of God. But fruitful insights can be gained from reflection on biblical teachings about Christ and the Spirit which gave rise to the doctrine of the Trinity; and fruitful insights can be gained from thinkers who have subsequently paid attention to the subject.

The appropriate way to use the doctrine is for reflection and discussion, not for enforcement. It is a great tragedy that ecclesiastical and civil authorities have tried to dragoon people into accepting what at best are imperfect formulations of truth about God. Trinitarian theology is more helpful as an invitation to think about God than as a test of theological orthodoxy. Above all, the doctrine gives expression to the distinctive content of Christian worship. The biblical language and imagery which underlie the doctrine have been linked with Christian devotion and liturgy since biblical times. Baptism, according to Matthew's Gospel (28:19), is in the name of the Father, and of the Son, and of the Holy Spirit. Paul's benediction to the Corinthians speaks of "the grace of the Lord Jesus Christ and the love of God and the communion of the Holy Spirit" (2 Cor. 13:14). The Book of Revelation contains doxologies to God and to the Lamb.

Before there was any theory about the Trinity, this language was used in worship and prayer, and such usage has continued and developed. In a hymn to the Trinity Isaac Watts wrote, "Where reason fails, with all her powers, there faith prevails and love adores." Millions of people who would have been bewildered by the perplexities of trinitarian theology have gladly used the language of the doctrine in their adoration of God. It is in the employment of trinitarian language that we can share in the worship offered by Christians in all ages. We have great freedom of interpretation. We are not bound, for example, when we speak of God as Father, to conclude that God is male. But we are also free to use the imagery of trinitarian devotion. If we cut ourselves off from this heritage, we cut ourselves off from teaching and experience central to Christian faith.

The doctrine of the Trinity may not make complete sense; at least it may not make complete sense to us. But the truth which it imperfectly approximates makes sense to God. It is therefore a wise procedure to reflect on the doctrine and to use it as a framework for worship. The Christian approach to God has been made possible by the work of Christ in his earthly life. It has become a reality through the power of God's indwelling presence, whether that presence is described as "Christ in us" or "the Spirit in us." When attention is focused on these aspects of the Trinity, the doctrine can be said, in the words of the old Congregational confession, to be "the foundation of all our communion with God."

*May 1984*

# The Trinity:
# A Mystery of Community

## WALTER LOWE

In the modern age, the doctrine of the Trinity may seem a scandal to those outside the church and a stumbling block to those within. From either perspective, many may be inclined to think that with this doctrine the theologians have finally gone too far. They have asked too much of Christian credulity. The complaint might go something like this: "In the modern world it is hard enough to believe in God at all. Surely this is too much—to ask a person to believe that God not only manages to exist, but contrives in some mysterious, unexplained fashion to be a 'triune' as well!"

The suspicion grows that the whole business is simply the lamentable result of theology's having got mixed up with Greek metaphysics. And so we may feel the urge to return to an earlier, less difficult time. "Ah, for the simplicity of the early faith, when the believer was just called to follow Jesus, unencumbered by the metaphysical inventions of the theologians!"

But was it really such a simple thing, that early faith? Perhaps we imagine too quickly that problems of belief are the special prerogative of our own times. We forget too easily what an incredible, implausible thing the faith is in *any* age. Consider, for example, the scandal which is caused to the Jews of Jesus' time that Jesus should dare to address the transcendent God, Creator of heaven and earth, as "Abba"—"Parent" or "Father." In our own time this familiar form of address has become so commonplace, so obstructed by sentimentalism, that we lose the awareness of the unspeakable distance it overcomes. But the Jews indeed knew better. They had waited long centuries for the Messiah. They had suffered much from history. They knew something of God's unfathomable remove. And the wisest of them knew too that on those occasions when God *is* close at hand, that nearness may be the source of trembling and fear. So they had within them the good sense to be shocked when this individual, Jesus, presumed to be on such familiar terms with the God of power and might.

Or consider another example, the earliest gatherings of the Christian community depicted in Acts. Consider the utter incredibility of their conviction that the one who was crucified had risen from the dead and was actually with them as they gathered to worship! They themselves were aware that it was implausible. They did not presume to speak of that incomprehensible presence of the risen Christ except insofar as they were supported by prayer and worship—insofar as they spoke "in the Spirit."

That is simply to say that the early Christians had the good sense to know that they had been drawn into a mystery, into something that surpassed their comprehension. To "comprehend" means literally "to grasp or seize." The early community knew they could not stand outside this reality to grasp or seize it. They could speak of it only from *within* the mystery—"in the Spirit." But the marvel is that within the Spirit they *were* empowered to speak: to speak the words of worship and proclamation. And it was that very empowerment which made of them a particular people, an "ecclesia." The very mystery which they could not comprehend had made of them a community.

And therein lay a clue to understanding the mystery, insofar as it could be understood. For what God gave, God gave from God's own being. The mystery had made of them a community because that mystery *is*, in its very being, a community. Indeed the two communities were in a real sense one: the little group of believers had been drawn into the community of the Godhead! It is this discovery, rather than any abstract notion of one-in-three and three-in-one, which gives us, as it gave the early Christians, a way into thinking about the Trinity.

Once we begin to look for it, we find this deeper notion of community throughout the New Testament. Again it is just a matter of getting beyond our modern optic: in this case our modern individualism. We tend to fixate upon the image of the isolated believer, and so we miss the fact that when Jesus speaks to the "Abba," it is not just the expression of an individual's faith. It is the witness to a relationship—a relationship which unfolds, in the course of the New Testament story, as being itself a community.

And it is because that divine community exists that we ourselves exist. Earlier, in the course of the history that generated the Hebrew Scriptures, the people of Israel had to think their way back from the experience of the Exodus to the recognition that the God who had delivered them from Egypt and made them to be a people was the same God who had delivered the creation itself from the primordial chaos and made the earth habitable. Creation echoed exodus: from the first things to the last, there was one God.

In a very similar fashion the church, too, had to think its way back. It did so through a process of worship and reflection which spanned several centuries. And like the Jews of an earlier time, the early Christians grew into a recognition that the reality which had constituted them as a peculiar community was a reality which reached back to the act of creation itself.

It is that reality, and that entire story, which we recall when we speak of the Trinity. And this perhaps is the essential point with which we may conclude. For it is indeed the entire story—from creation through redemption—which the doctrine of the Trinity is meant to recall. And it does this in more than simply arithmetic fashion: the doctrine of the Trinity is not simply a list of the principal players. Rather the doctrine recalls the story by recalling the reality *from* which the story springs, *by* which it is sustained, and *towards* which it relentlessly drives: the reality which we have sought to suggest by the frail word "community."

The pity, then, is not that this doctrine should be a mystery, but that this mystery should so often have been regarded in isolation. Little wonder if, uprooted from its essential relatedness, the doctrine should become a barren enigma: for everything it wishes to say has to do, precisely, with community and relation! The real issue, I have been trying to suggest, is not that the doctrine of the Trinity should contain so much mystery. The real issue is that the rest of our faith, when it is separated from the Trinity, should seem to contain so little.

*May 1984*

# Hal Lindsey's Gnostic Heresy

## THEODORE H. RUNYON

Gnosticism has been a persistent threat to Christian orthodoxy down through the history of the church. It was the first great heresy, and we see traces of the battle against it in the New Testament itself (cf. 1 Corinthians 11, Colossians 2, all of 1 John) as well as in the ancient church. Gnosticism claims to have a secret wisdom, an inside track, an arcane clue to the real nature of things. To possess this knowledge is to have power, to be in the know while others remain in ignorance, to be linked by means of this knowledge to the forces and powers which determine the way things are and shall be. Gnosticism's fundamental appeal is seen in something as simple as the child's taunting, "I know something you don't know," or something so sophisticated as the inner circle which has access to presidential decision-making.

Moreover, gnosticism is close enough to Christian faith to be mistaken for the genuine article by the untrained eye. This is what makes it so insidious. After all, Christianity claims to know some things which the world does not know. It claims to have a revelation which is transmitted "from faith to faith." It claims insight into the destiny of the world which is not available simply by reading secular sources of analysis. It claims to know the truth! How then can you differentiate between bogus claims and legitimate ones? How can you tell a gnostic when you see one?

Historically, gnosticism has been characterized by three consistent tendencies which run counter to the fullness of the Christian message. First and fundamentally, gnosticism lacks a positive doctrine of creation and is therefore marked by hatred of the world. For the gnostic the world has been so completely corrupted by human sin and dissipation that it is worthy only to be abandoned to destruction.

As a result it has, secondly, an escapist understanding of salvation. If finitude is by definition evil, salvation must be escape from the world rather than transformation of the world. The notion of the "rapture" is a variation on this theme, which at least has the virtue that God reaches down to rescue the individual. The tendency toward docetism is unmistakable. If the finite is evil, then the Savior could not really have participated in it. If the Scriptures are sacred, by definition they cannot be subject to the limitations of their humanity; they occupy a special position as the divinely wrought exception to the corruption of finitude.

And thirdly, the eschatological culmination is not the transformation of this world as was envisioned in Jewish apocalyptic and Jesus' preaching of the kingdom but, in consistency with the view of matter as evil, the annihilation of the material world followed by the reign of pure spirit. If the goal of the world is in any case destruction, it follows that it is pointless to waste time trying to reform or change it. One had best withdraw from it as much as possible, except to urge others to flee from it, until such a time as one is snatched up by a God who condemns the whole enterprise to destruction.

Hal Lindsey's view does not conform to this picture of gnosticism in every respect, but it is similar enough to give pause to sober Christians seeking their way through the competing claims to truth. In the first part of *The Late Great Planet Earth* he inveighs against "astrology, soothsayers, vibrations and spiritism," yet the methods Lindsey employs to ferret out the biblical messages resemble nothing so much as the methods used by those against whom he protests.

He reads the Scriptures like fortune cookies. Claiming that "prophecies can be pieced together to make a coherent picture, even though the pieces are scattered in small bits through the Old and New Testaments," he proceeds to carve the Scriptures up into pieces to find his message much as the ancient soothsayers split open the sacrificial animal and read the future out of the entrails. To read the Scriptures in such a way is possible only on the basis of the docetic presupposition mentioned above.

It is not so much the bits and pieces of Lindsey's prophecies about which I am concerned, however, but the string on which those bits and pieces are strung. That is what gives coherence to the whole enterprise, or at least guarantees its emotional impact. And what is that string? It appears to be a random assortment of the fears, anxieties, and prejudices of white, Anglo-Saxon Protestants. Lindsey rings the changes in a not too subtle manner.

First there is the Russian menace, predicted in Ezekiel 38, coming down from the north. And coming up from the south are the Cushites (blacks); while from the east emerges the Yellow Peril. True, you can't find the latter in Ezekiel, but Revelation 16:12 mentions the kings of the east (bits and pieces, you know). Are there any other fears, anxieties, and prejudices not yet covered? Yes, of course, the Roman Catholics. But Lindsey takes care of them with an exegesis of Revelation 17, which refers to the harlot Rome, who is going to form a coalition with the Russians, the Yellow Peril, and the Cushites. What began with the claim to be biblical prophecy turns out to be a string of familiar and tired prejudices paraded across the screen to the accompaniment of biblical quotations.

Now I would not want to be critical of Mr. Lindsey's use of Scripture, especially since he has already pronounced curses upon anyone who would question his interpretations. But I do wonder why people who ought to know better so readily buy into this sort of thing. And this is the pastoral question about which we must all be concerned. People buy into this because life around them is confusing; they can't put it together or make sense out of it. It just seems to be bits and pieces that don't fit into any coherent pattern. Lindsey comes along and shows them how you can take bits and pieces, put them together with deep-seated fears and anxieties, and come up with a coherent picture which not only fits rationally but packs a wallop emotionally.

Knowledge is power, power to make a disjointed world appear whole.

That's why gnosticism was so attractive in the first century, and that's why it is attractive again today. To know, to be in on the secret, is to have some power, some control over your life—because you know what is controlling everything. There is no genuine Christian *gnosis*. Christians do know who it is that as Creator and Lord undergirds and judges all of our existence. But the doctrine of the Incarnation, God's commitment in the flesh to the redemption of this world, ought to guard us against the wiles of those who are purveyors of a docetic Christ and docetic Scriptures.

*February 1977*

# "I Wish We'd All Been Ready"

JOEL KAILING

Some of us were standing outside of our Jesus People meeting house on a warm summer evening. My friend Dave approached me and pointed to the sky. "Look at those glorious clouds," he said, "I love cloudy days." It was a beautiful sight, but I wondered why such days should be so fascinating. He replied, "Because in Revelation 1:7 it says, 'Behold, he is coming with the clouds.'"

Along with the rise of the Jesus Movement in the early seventies, there also came a renewed interest in the Second Coming of Christ. Fed by popular books and songs like "I Wish We'd All Been Ready," this radical expectation became a distinguishing feature that has outlived most of the movement's other trappings. This has convinced some that the church ought to become more occupied with the end times. Yet, history reveals that practically every age has had its own last-days prophets or millennialists. None of them has ever had very far-reaching or long-lasting effects on either the Christian community or society in general.

The most recent type of this thinking can be distinguished as "premillennialism." Put briefly, this is the belief that things will continue to get worse for this world until Christ returns to destroy it and bring his kingdom. In popular thought there is a great deal of speculation over the nature and order of last events, such as the removal of believers from the earth (the Rapture) and the reign of the Antichrist (the Tribulation). The system can become increasingly complex depending on how one interprets difficult biblical passages, and perhaps on how imaginative one is.

Premillennialists were reacting to what they perceived as a total neglect of the Second Coming in modern theology. In actuality, the new positions did not deny the Parousia so much as reinterpret it beyond the recognition of older thinkers. To these people—the postmillennialists—human society was slowly progressing toward the kingdom. The earth will evolve toward perfection, and the Second Coming is a symbol of this progress. This view gained much popularity in the liberal eras of the past two centuries, partly because of great scientific and technological strides.

In recent years, however, a number of events have severely called the "humanist-progress" view into question. It was very difficult for a young person during the Vietnam war to see things as getting better and better. As a matter of fact, the doomsayers seemed to have all the facts on their side, considering war, ecology, and population problems. Suddenly the biblical concept that human beings are unable to save themselves became very real. An actual future return of Christ could very well be the answer to the world's dilemmas. Born of this potent insight, the new premillennialism developed an overwhelming force.

Problems with this idea arise when the worldview of the premillennialists is examined. Reacting against one extreme, they find themselves dangerously close to an equally bad position. When preoccupied so greatly with the end of things, the temptation is to consider every created, worldly thing as evil. This gives a highly negative worldview which goes beyond watching the world crumble to the position of desiring doom and secretly wishing to hasten it. The present world is past redemption, and any attempts to improve it are futile or even contrary to the will of God. If war in Israel is a sign, then it is greeted with joy instead of despair. If pollution is a sign, then it is almost sinful to stop it. The world is going to burn anyway, so let it, and the sooner the better. The only Christian mission is to rescue as many souls as possible before the end.

Premillennialism starts from a good critique, but it fails because the worldview it establishes cannot be maintained. In the first place, human nature is not built to live with such a total hatred of the physical world. Even the most confirmed pessimist must occasionally see a sunrise or a field of flowers and admit that there is beauty and goodness here. Secondly, the biblical position is to affirm the goodness of creation. Genesis and the Psalms are particularly clear on this point. Finally, to deny the worth of creation is somehow to deny the Incarnation as well. Jesus could not have been fully human unless redemption is possible for all that is human and material. This is why so many millennialist groups tend toward a docetic Christology, making the Christ something less than fully human.

It seems to me that the premillennialists are right in condemning the triumph-of-progress position. The world is in a mess that will never be solved by human effort alone, and all programs to do so will be hampered by the sin which is a part of every person. Yet, this does not excuse Christians from making social efforts. Indeed, we are commanded to do so until Jesus does return. At that time, he will fully restore the earth and complete the work of redemption which has already begun (as implied by Romans 8:18-25).

Until then, the Christian is living in a new time span and cannot get too mixed up in radical millennialism. Any overemphasis on the future neglects the fact that the kingdom of God is a present reality. It is already in our midst. As Christians, our task now is not to await or to build this kingdom, but to be worthy citizens of it.

*February 1977*

# Rethinking Hell and Heaven

DON E. SALIERS

We live in a time of apocalyptic and false apocalyptic. The popular imagination is filled with it, fired by films, fiction, and, recently, Jonathan Schell's book on what a nuclear holocaust will be like. At the same time, the religious imagination is confused. Christian preachers seem to offer little assistance to churchgoers who want to know what to believe about the "end time," and what to confess about heaven and hell.

While twentieth-century theology has rediscovered eschatology as a style of thinking, the preaching and teaching pastor is perplexed by a strange mixture of popular doctrine and superstition in the local church. Some cry for more "hell-fire" from the pulpit; others prefer the ease of a demythologized heaven and hell. The time is ripe for a reconsideration of these eschatological doctrines. What, then, can we say to a church whose ideas of hell are either an extension of Hal Lindsey, or politely psychologized, or even nonexistent? Here are six starting points:

1) Hell and heaven must be seen in light of the permanent crisis which the kingdom of God brings to the world.

2) Damnation has been a profound theme in contemporary literature which may help us construe the meaning of hell, and must not be confused with religious hucksterism of cheap apocalyptic.

3) Christians confess that Jesus Christ embraces damnation as well as death in his own "obedience unto death."

4) To hope for heaven is an appropriate Christian virtue and to fear hell an apt emotion, provided that heaven is not conceived as payment to the righteous, and running from hell as a program for salvation.

5) The powers of hell, damnation, and death are real but based upon the illusion of power. This is why we must call Satan the Self-Deceived as well as the Deceiver.

6) We profess belief in God, resurrection from the dead, and eternal life, and do *not* profess co-equal belief in Satan, damnation, and everlasting torment.

Let's look at each of these points in more depth.

1) If we are to make any sense out of heaven and hell once we have stopped trading snippets of Scripture as proof-texts, we must begin by showing the way in which these doctrines must be re-thought in light of Christian eschatology and contemporary culture. There is a two-fold emphasis in New Testament eschatology: a) the end of all things is at hand, and b) human history goes on—so live accordingly! This is the familiar "already/not yet" of the kingdom of God.

On the one hand, the church proclaims that the Word has become flesh and that judgment of the world is already present. The rule and reign of God has been initiated definitively in Jesus Christ, so the *crisis* in the world as we know it is radical and permanent. The judgment and sense of damnation we picture in various teachings about hell is in some manner already known in part, just as the kingdom and its fruits are known in part. Judgment infuses and permeates the way the Christian community must live and think and feel. Beatitude must also infuse and permeate the self-understanding and the life of the Christian community. Damnation and beatitude are the experiential basis of any rethinking of hell and heaven. The permanent crisis is not just in the church, but in the whole cosmos. What we believe about the consummation is already beginning to take place.

2) In much twentieth-century literature there are several expressions of damnation which may assist the Christian theological enterprise. In Camus' *The Stranger*, for example, we have an unforgettable expression of alienation. Here is a world of self-chosen aloneness, a detachment from every human contact. So far as modern people grasp this idea of aliena-tion, and its extension toward alienation from others, from work, from the sources of human responsibility, the concept of damnation is clarified. Paul Tillich has brought this forcefully to our attention.

A second literary image is "the condemned." Kafka's *The Trial* portrays a world in which every human enjoyment is invaded by the shadow of the executioner: the human predicament is that we are all condemned to death, without trial. This is powerfully expressed in light of racial condem-nation by the great black American novelist Richard Wright. Damnation has also been construed as unrelieved guilt. Evidence for this is widespread in fiction, but is more likely derived for us from the psychoanalyst's couch than from main-line Christianity.

But these images of alienation, condemnation, and infinite guilt are all part of what the Scripture means by being "cut off from the land of the living." If hell is pictured simply as a fate after death for reprobate souls, then our essential humanity is split asunder and God's justice is made to work its damage upon God's love. The question is not how many of us are going to hell and how many to heaven, but how much of the human enterprise is to be damned, cut off from the reality of God.

3) Here it is crucial to reassert our basic Christian claim: Jesus Christ embraces damnation and death. The character of damnation as *fate* is done away with. Destiny in God's grace replaces fate. Jesus Christ tasted alienation, unjust trial, condemnation, and guilt-bearing death. His redemptive power extends even to the realm of the dead. He knew temp-tation and was in solidarity with us, yet presented himself sinless as a liv-ing sacrifice of praise, obedience, and love. By the way, shouldn't those churches that do not say it reinstate "descended to the dead" (a liberal deletion) in the Apostles' Creed?

4) Heaven is thus what Jesus Christ opens the way for—non-separation filled with the intensity of God's being and glory. Hell is where and when God is not present and is precisely the absence of glory and grace—a

condition where no beatitude is possible. Picturing this as a place of eternal physical torment has a point, so far as the physical is a metaphor and figure of the spiritual. This is why hope for heaven is an appropriate Christian virtue, and fear of hell an understandable emotion. But idolatry and superstition are close at hand when we begin to think of heaven as a reward for righteousness, and fear of hell as a program to drive people to heaven. So easily God is made to condemn those whom we judge to be the unrighteous. Here we must see again what Jesus says and does with the sinners and the unrighteous! Running from hell can never be a program for salvation if the God of Jesus Christ is our focus. Neither heaven nor the title "Christian" is a merit badge.

The hope for heaven—to be part of the blessed community—need not be self-centered or based upon fear, precisely because it is already the direction in which human existence moves with Christ. Heaven is the blessed community of those who love and rejoice in God. It is not a fanciful mythological extra; rather, Christian life between the times does not make sense without it. For here and now we have a foretaste in the means of grace and works of mercy—on behalf of the whole world.

5) Yet the powers of hell are real. Christ comes preaching and healing, and the demons emerge. The demonic has become an industry within our century, and within living memory: the Nazi death camps and the systematic exterminations under Stalin, Idi Amin, and others. The litany goes on. But the Christian gospel, realistic about evil and the death-dealing principalities and powers, has a final word: even they will be brought to truth. Then even the most perduring enmity toward God will be shown for its self-deception. Judgment will come, though we know not the season and do well not to sell the gospel by predicting the time and the place ("Lo, here; lo there"). Consummation will come for each of us in the hour of our death, and will come to the whole world. The time of crisis is permanent because Christ has come and will come again. All things will be brought to the light.

Perhaps the most fearsome and most telling picture of Satan in hell is given to us by Dante in the *Divine Comedy*. The "Inferno" pictures him, a titanic figure, frozen in a lake of ice in the center of hell, frozen in impotency. Satan's power is finally to be conceived as a function of self-deception. He does not know his impotency and works only under the illusions which can be perpetuated among humankind. *Stultus maximus* is himself deceived.

6) Finally, I must remind us that we profess belief in God, the resurrection from the dead, and eternal life. We do not profess coequal belief in the devil, condemnation, and eternal torment. There is nothing in our baptismal creed about damnation, though Christ will surely "come to judge the living and the dead." Any speculation we sinners make about damnation beyond those modes we already know in this world does not have the same sanction as does our positive profession of faith in God. Our need to see others in hell is often the power of our own unresolved

need for vengeance. But to speak of God's saving grace and of heaven as the goal God has for the creatures certainly raises the issue of what it might be like to be *without* God forever, and that should be sobering enough! To the demythologizers and to the literalists I say, think again. Will God's love ultimately melt the lake of ice which God's justice appears to demand? That is a question worth living with.

*March 1983*

# Hell and the Early Church

## ROBERTA CHESNUT BONDI

"Hallelujah, praise the Lord; I'm saved!" Within a certain conservative religious tradition in America, this statement of salvation means, among other things, "I've been saved from sin, so I can go to heaven and be spared the fiery torments of hell God justly reserves for the sinner." To many people, the threat of eternal torment in a place of fire is a basic, fundamental truth that Christianity has always taught—and the only real reason most Christians are good. But is it true that such a teaching on hell has always been a part of what we believe? What did the church of the first few centuries think about hell?

In Old Testament times, of course, there was no hell at all in our sense of the term; people believed that all who died, good or bad, went to the same place, Sheol, or the grave. Even without fire, this was a terrifying place to our ancestors, a place of shadows and weakness and dust. Once you were there, you were there for good, unless you were summoned, perhaps, to give a ghostly oracle. In the intertestamental period, however, the idea of a special place of torment for the wicked arose, perhaps under Iranian influence, and we meet this idea in the New Testament in many places.

But the idea of hell was not firmly fixed in the mind of the early church. First, it was not hell so much as death that appeared fearsome to the people of the early Christian period. "The last enemy is death," we read in 1 Corinthians 15:26, and all those who followed concurred. Athanasius, for example, writing in the fourth century in *On the Incarnation of God the Word*, tells the story of human life from creation through the Fall to our own restoration in Christ, and in his telling of it, the emphasis falls upon the unnaturalness of death, which had not been part of God's original intent for the human race.

Whatever the first sin was, and there was no consensus among early writers, it was the fact of our fear of death and our resulting blindness to reality that turned us over to sin and the assault of the demons, who in *this* life could cause us misery as they tempt and delude us, always with our own permission. Satan, until the time of Christ, presided over death, and that was terrible enough without adding to it images of torture or fire. It was the work of Christ to break the stranglehold of death and restore to us the possibility of our former condition. That Christians died fearlessly was taken to be a convincing argument for the truth of Christianity all the way back to the earliest martyrs.

A brilliant theologian and biblical scholar of the third century, Origen of Alexandria, rejected the idea of a place of eternal punishment altogether. God created all souls out of love in order that they share in God's love and life forever. How, logically, then, is it possible that God's intent be thwarted? Looking at the biblical promise that the time will come when God will be all in all, Origen was convinced that all beings, including the devil, will ultimately be saved, and all will be restored to what God originally created. Life, as we know it on this planet, is meant to be educational, disciplining us to move toward our ultimate restoration in God. Origen was accused, probably rightly, of believing in reincarnation; what a person did not learn in this lifetime, that person would learn in the next.

Origen himself, not surprisingly, was a controversial figure; he was finally condemned by the second council of Constantinople in 553 for, among other things, his rejection of ultimate damnation for the wicked. Nevertheless, he was extremely influential for a very long time; indeed, that he was condemned so long after his death tells us far more about the strength of the sixth-century followers of his ideas than it does about him.

In the fourth century, Gregory of Nyssa, a perfectly orthodox major opponent of Arianism and a writer on the spiritual life, and Evagrius Ponticus, another extraordinarily important writer on the spiritual life for many centuries, were among Origen's followers. Gregory, like Origen, believed that in the end even the devil would be saved, but he also believed most people would have to go through a period of suffering after death. This suffering would be necessary to purify each person from the accretions of sin that covered over the image of God present in each of us. But suffering was not explained in terms of punishment, but rather as the necessary preparation for entering the presence of God. Furthermore, this purifying process did not have to follow death, but could be accomplished in this life by serious self-discipline coupled with God's gracious help.

Isaac of Nineveh, a later writer of the seventh century who was influenced by Evagrius Ponticus, in many ways did believe in hell, and yet the hell he visualized was not a fiery one either. Instead, he explains the suffering of the damned to be exactly like the kind of suffering we experience in this life when we know we have done an injury to a friend. Those who are damned love God, and it is by this love that they are tortured because of the very nature of love itself, and not because of some desire of God to punish the wicked or see that justice is avenged.

All in all, though the major tradition of the church in its first few centuries affirmed the reality of hell, there was little uniformity in what was believed about it. The affirmation of the early creeds is of life everlasting, not of eternal damnation. The spiritual writers of the period rarely talk about hell; more often their concern is to encourage the sinner who might be tempted to fall into despair because of actual sins or failed intentions, and thus become too disheartened to respond to God's never-failing forgiveness. Those who believe that the church has always adhered to the hell of fire and brimstone may learn of the real diversity of belief among early Christians on this subject with interest and, perhaps, relief.

*March 1983*

# Jesus Descended into Hell

EDWARD JEREMY MILLER

"He descended into hell." When was the last time you heard someone confess this article of the Apostles' Creed? But there it was, in the creed for centuries, inviting meditation and reflection. John Wesley deleted it from the Sunday Service he sent to America, thinking it not central enough to the biblical message. My own Catholic tradition retains it in the Apostles' Creed, but I have rarely heard preaching on it. However, writers such as Ratzinger, von Balthasar, and Rahner have helped me reclaim it as very important for my Christian living.

I had grown up with the idea that Jesus "descended into hell" to liberate the just of Israel (e.g., Abraham, Sarah, etc.) who were held back from entering the kingdom until Jesus entered as the firstborn of the dead. This idea, which found its way into my catechism books, came from St. Augustine and was further developed by Thomas Aquinas. "Hell," obviously, did not mean the place of the damned but some kind of shadowy existence, perhaps answering to the Hebrew word Sheol. The just of Israel, who indeed lived by faith as we read in the letter to Hebrews, were held back from immediately entering glory by the effects of Original Sin.

With all due respect to these two saintly doctors of theology, the idea ceased to make sense to me as I grew older. If it were true, I simply did not think much of it. Then I read Joseph Ratzinger's *Introduction to Christianity*. He mentioned some things about feeling the absence of God, things which touched me to the quick. When Jesus cried out, "My God, my God, why have you forsaken me?" his cry was not for himself but for his *Abba*. His cry stood against the reality of the world around him, for it could not help him. Do we still need to wonder what that prayer, in our hours of darkness, must mean? God's silence is part of Christian revelation, and Holy Saturday, standing between the cross and Easter, captures this liturgically.

The word "hell" was a bad translation for Sheol (in Greek, Hades), which meant a vague state after death, more non-being than being. That Jesus entered Sheol means that he died. But what is happening when someone enters the fate of death? The throb of Jesus' suffering was not the physical pain but the radical loneliness, the feeling of abandonment. What comes up for view is the abyss of human loneliness in general, how people can be alone in their inmost being. We try to overlay this loneliness by seeking company, playing music, drinking to excess; but there it is, something we have and something we fear. There is a great truth about us when we reflect on our inmost being. We cannot exist alone for long; we are made for company.

Let me take a simple example. Notice why a child is afraid of the dark. You may say to the child that there is no one lurking there in the room who will harm him or her, and you may give all the cogent reasons you wish. But the thing which calms the fear is the parental voice which says, "Don't worry; I am here with you. It's all right." I think a child's fear of the dark is an echo of the fear we have when we are brought into contact with the depths of our being.

Did you ever keep watch in a room with a dead person? There is nothing in the room which can harm us, and yet there is a scary feeling. The corpse causes us to feel the loneliness of our own existence, and how at the moment of death we too must let go of the hands of companions and step forward alone. And stepping forward alone goes against our deepest wishes. The fear which is special to a human being cannot be overcome by reason, but only by the presence of someone, especially by the presence of someone who loves us.

Now let me apply this to Jesus' "descent into Sheol." Suppose there were such a condition as a loneliness which could no longer be penetrated and warmed by the word of another. Suppose a state of abandonment were to arise into which another person could not reach, no matter how much this person loved you and did not wish to see you all alone. If there were abandonment into total isolation, into full loneliness and fright, then this is what theology and our religion call hell in the strict sense. It would be the situation in which the word "love," the experience of being loved, had no presence.

From this point of view it is understandable why there is only one Hebrew word for hell and death. Sheol. To go into death is to go into the possibility of loneliness and abandonment. No matter how much we believe in afterlife, the specter of this possibility must cross our minds from time to time. And it is into this situation that Jesus "descends." That is to say, our blessed Lord, in experiencing all that we do, experienced even this final moment and apprehension. There was no "mediator" who preceded him to soften the way. He entered it needing a trust far stronger than ours. But having entered into death, in this psychological way, and having found resurrected life in and through death, our Lord has permanently established in the realm of death the presence of a loving voice, a loving presence.

As we die, the voices of those at our bedside grow dim and trail off. But the faithful begin to hear the voice of the One who loves us from time everlasting and who says, "Come, beloved, to the place I have prepared for you." Where no other voice could reach, there was our Lord. Hell is thereby overcome, or, to be more accurate, death which was previously hell, is hell no longer. If we forget this doctrine of the faith, this article of the creed, we shortchange ourselves.

*March 1983*

# The Strange Faith Next Door

## JAMES F. HOPEWELL

"All our prisoners used to be Baptists," grumbled the assistant warden of a southern prison last month. "Now they hold the darnedest sort of belief: Rastafarian, Muslim, Buddhist...." Salt water no longer separates our nation from most of the world's faiths. Non-Christian religions now touch our neighbors, even our jailed American underclass. Today local churches confront an issue that not long ago was primarily a concern for foreign missionaries: what constitutes Christian witness to an active participant in another religion? When Zen fascinates your own relative, or the girl next door seeks Krishna Consciousness, we enter a ministry situation distinct from one in which all parties in the neighborhood held roughly the same worldview. Nowadays groups that persuasively offer quite different interpretations of life inhabit the same community in which our congregation resides.

What should we ministers do in this time of local pluralism? We are certainly not ordained to be grand viziers. In our call to ministry God does not appoint us overseers of society to stamp out heresy. The shocking cruelties of our own time—the Holocaust and religious conflict in many lands—convince us how mistaken are claims that an orthodoxy authorizes its faithful to judge the worth and survival of other types of belief. As God's people we are under judgment, not on top of it. We are servants, not magistrates.

But neither, therefore, are we called to be cheerleaders. A now more frequent attitude towards other religions casts us again in the role of judge, but one that gives a favorable verdict. In this posture we assess all faiths to be equally valid and worthy. The stock phrases, "It doesn't matter what you believe so long as you believe," and "All faiths are different ways up the same mountain," accompany this sort of judgment, and the person who utters such comments performs a kind of judgmental cheerleading that from the sidelines applauds all teams and plays.

Not only does the cheerleading stance again mistakenly assume some obligation of ministry to judge other faiths; it also tends to promote an outlook that in the end discredits the very religions it was attempting to validate. The outlook usually holds that the beliefs that distinguish one faith from another are to be counted their less essential phenomena, secondary in importance to qualities in the religions that show their common nature and permit their common efficacy. Ranking beliefs in this manner, however, obscures the perception of reality that believers themselves hold. Christians, for example, generally consider the existence of God to be crucial for their faith, while many Buddhists find God's existence ultimately irrelevant to theirs. To conclude that such radically different perceptions actually dissolve into a common world faith violates the core visions of both Buddhism and Christianity, and shows how fatuous the pose of cheerleading can be.

How can we address other religions without judging them? The Christian church has developed several other approaches that, while maintaining the church's conviction about the lordship of Jesus Christ, nevertheless attempt to avoid valuations of other faiths.

One approach is to consider the relation between Christianity and other religions to be paradoxical, that is, not reducible to a single condition that eliminates opposing states. The church celebrates several paradoxes, such as a Christ who is paradoxically both divine and human, or a God who is both three and one, or a people who are both saved and sinful. While these concepts are logical absurdities, we Christians find them mysteries that show the suspense at the heart of our gospel. The ultimacy of Christ's lordship, on the one hand, yet the sufficiency of other religions, on the other, are viewed by some to be a similar paradox. In communicating with persons of other faiths, we may acknowledge an ambiguity that seems often to accompany deep insights, in this instance the contradiction between the exclusive truth of our own faith, and the conceptual integrity of a religion that denies our creed.

Another approach recognizes an unknown Christ in all religions. Relying upon the revelation of Christ as the *logos* within creation, and, thus, in all human creativity, this view sees a ripening of all religious endeavors towards a final future expression in Christ. Participants in the various religions, of course, do not recognize Christ, but they are, by virtue of their piety, "anonymous Christians," the redeemed who choose no Christian name. In this understanding, each religion, including Christianity, is a preparation for the gospel that Christians have the momentary privilege of experiencing more fully. Christians enjoy no greater certainty nor higher status; they gratefully find themselves in a world of fellow seekers whose own cultures also prepare the way for the kingdom.

My own approach, while dependent upon those already mentioned, tries to avoid both the passivity that may accompany an understanding of paradox and also the patronizing that may afflict the treatment of non-Christian believers as anonymous Christians. Building upon an understanding of Christ's presence outside the gate (Hebrews 13:11-14), I find mission to non-Christians to be a response to the Christ who is manifested essentially in my encounter with them. Being outside the gate of any religious system, Christ draws the Christian towards him in an exodus that leaves behind the security and meaning of an orthodox religious "city." Hebrews reminds us that we live in no continuing city but seek the city that is to come.

In mission, therefore, I do not bring Christ to a new setting. Rather I meet the Christ who emerges in the encounter beyond the gate that enclosed my own faith formulas and presuppositions. In joining people of other faiths I witness Christ, but not the Christ that I supply. Christ is instead manifested to me in my insecure, ambiguous meeting with people of other faiths. The door bell rings and there on our stoop are the evangelists of a non-Christian faith. Our temptation is to close the door and protect the Christ we already know. But Christ is outside the gate. Neither our private possession nor that of our non-Christian neighbors, Christ is present in our honest dialogue with each other. In mission we find him; we do not bring him.

*December 1983*

# Encounter and Transformation

## THEODORE W. JENNINGS

How are we to understand the faith of folk whose traditions are so different from our own? Is the essence of other traditions something to be overcome through conversion? Are we to regard other faiths as alternative ways of worshiping the same God in different ways? I find neither of these approaches satisfactory. I believe it is helpful to see religious traditions as encountering one another not as fixed entities, but as historical processes in transformation. Moreover, it is useful to recognize that in this process of mutual transformation these traditions have a quite different relationship to one another. The relationship of Christianity to Judaism is by no means the same as its relationship to Islam. Quite different dynamics appear in our relationship to Hinduism and Buddhism.

From its very beginnings Christianity has been nourished by contact with other traditions. Its rootage in Judaism demonstrates this and prepares the way for other kinds of encounters. In the last century we have learned how much the language and lore of the Old Testament itself was drawn from the religious world of the ancient Near East—both by way of appropriation and transformation. The same is true of early Christianity. The language of liturgy, ethics, and theology is borrowed, appropriated, adapted from the religious and philosophical traditions of the Hellenistic world.

Christianity was thus nourished and shaped by its contact with mystery religions, gnosticism, stoicism, etc. In some cases these contacts have resulted in the appropriation of terminology and insights. In other cases these contacts have forced Christianity to sharpen its sense of distinctiveness—to clarify its peculiar identity. Usually the result of encounter has been an admixture of these two responses. The most important thing to learn from this history, I believe, is that Christianity should welcome the opportunity for contact with other traditions, expecting that these encounters will result in the creative transformation of our own understanding of faith. Christianity always betrays itself when it refuses the open and honest and hopeful dialogue.

In order to think more concretely about our dialogue with other religious traditions, it may be useful to be clear about the global situation. Roughly one-third of the world's population is at least nominally Christian. The next largest group is Islamic with about 16 percent of the world's population, followed by Hinduism (13%) and Buddhism (6%). Traditional or so-called primitive religionists are about as numerous as Buddhists, while nonreligious Marxists (there are also Christian and Islamic Marxists) are about as numerous as Moslems (Source: *The World Christian Encyclopedia*). The dramatic growth of Christianity in the Third World is more than offset by the loss of vigor (and membership) in Europe and North America. Against this global background let us consider particular cases.

**Judaism.** The Holocaust has forced Christianity to undertake a complete reappraisal of its relationship to Judaism. We cannot consider Judaism as simply "another religion." It is instead, as Paul makes clear in Romans, the root and trunk onto which Christianity is grafted. The continued existence of Judaism alongside Christianity is the concrete historical reminder that we owe our existence to another, that we are not the source of our own life and meaning. Anti-semitism is thus, as Barth suggested, the sin against the Holy Spirit.

From our encounter with Judaism, then, we are summoned to learn again and again to rely upon the promise and faithfulness of God which is the source of the faith of Judaism and therefore the basis of our hope and confidence as well.

**Islam.** Despite the fact that Islam is, after Christianity, the largest and most vigorous religious tradition on earth, it is curiously neglected by Christian theologians who generally prefer to talk about the more esoteric forms of Buddhism. The emergence and rapid growth of Islam is a sign of Christianity's failure to be good news for the poor. When Christianity retreated behind the walls of its dogma and liturgy and imperial privilege, Muhammed arose as a prophet calling for radical monotheism, the reign of justice, and the dignity of oppressed peoples. Christianity was obliterated from the map in that very part of the world in which it had first found a home.

Precisely where Christianity seemed most entrenched, most justly proud of its cultural and intellectual achievements, it proved most fragile and vulnerable. It survived only in the cultural, political, and intellectual backwater of Europe. And when Christianity began to emerge from the "Dark Ages," it did so by borrowing from Islam the intellectual tools for formulating its own faith. When in the last century Western Christendom returned to the Middle East and North Africa as the most potent intellectual and military power, it did so only in such a way as to reinforce the sense of Islam as the indomitable faith of the poor. Events in Iran are only the last episode in that encounter. The relationship of Christianity to Islam is thus a complex and disturbing one.

I believe that we have much to learn from Islam about ourselves and that this learning will entail for us a painful process of repentance. Only in that way will we learn what "good news" we have to address to our estranged sibling.

**Marxism.** Although not a religion, Marxism constitutes today (as Islam has since the Middle Ages) a militant challenge to Christianity. Like Islam, Marxism has arisen where Christianity has forgotten the poor and its own world-transforming hope. Where the confronting with Marxism is most intense—in Eastern Europe and Latin America—Christianity is faced with the necessity of recalling what it means to be good news for the poor and to join in the work of transforming the earth in anticipation of the reign of God. There are signs that when this occurs many Marxists are challenged to find in Christian faith a more firm rootage for hope and commitment and to become critical of the imperial and bureaucratic brutality encountered in officially Marxist societies.

Christians, Moslems, and Marxists, or nearly two-thirds of the population of our planet, have root in the prophetic traditions of Judaism. We have a common origin, a common hope for global transformation, a common zeal for conversion. We also have in common the capacity to destroy the earth in thermonuclear conflagration. What of the gentler traditions of the planet?

**Hinduism.** The resilience of Hinduism under the impact of militant Islam and Christianity (and Marxism) is one of the most astonishing features of modern religious history. The resilience is due to the fecundity, fluidity, and adaptability of Hinduism, to its permeation of every sphere of life, and to the perception of Christianity (and Islam) as intrusions of imperial powers destructive of the intricate balances of village and national life.

Yet already Christianity and Hinduism have been enriched by their encounter with one another as the striking figure of Gandhi most clearly attests. Certainly the Hindu tradition has been greatly enriched by Gandhi's opposition to untouchability, his commitment to nonviolence, his religious tolerance, his example of voluntary poverty. All of this is recognizable as an authentic expression of Hinduism as it is also recognizable as an authentic expression of Christianity.

It is too early to tell what may be the results of this encounter, but as Christians we are certainly entitled to hope for a reawakening of the vision of transforming love, of liberating nonviolence, of lifestyles of simplicity and dignity. And if the instrument for awakening in us and in Hinduism a taste for simplicity, for justice, for nonviolence should be (like Gandhi) a Hindu, should we suppose that this means a loss of Christian identity? Or should we instead welcome this as testifying to the presence and power of the Spirit of Jesus?

**Buddhism.** A religion in exile from its native India, Buddhism began as a reform movement within Hinduism. It exercises a peculiar fascination for Western Christians, especially in the form of Zen Buddhism. Both traditions have influenced one another in subtle ways. In "pure land" Buddhism, millions of Asians have encountered a gospel of redemptive love and grace, while many Christians have discovered in the meditative disciplines of Zen a way of reshaping their own traditions of contemplative prayer.

Christianity is most vital today where it is also being transformed by encounter with other religious traditions: Africa, Asia, Oceania. In North America and Europe we are often alarmed by the forms which Christianity takes in the former "mission" churches of Latin America, Africa, or India. When we become alarmed we speak of "syncretism." This is an appropriate issue when it is a question about the identity of the gospel. But we must be aware that the familiar forms of Christianity which we encounter in Europe and in the U.S. are also products of syncretism, in which the heart and center of Christian faith is sometimes lost in the midst of cultural accommodation.

We are never finished with the critical question about the identity of the gospel, but we are also entitled to celebrate the incarnational character of the gospel which takes on ever-renewed expression in new religious and cultural contexts. The creative transformation of Christianity in Asia, Africa, and Latin America demonstrates the vitality of the Jesus movement.

Accordingly, we should eagerly and confidently welcome the encounter with other religious traditions. But we should not expect that the only correct result of this encounter is the growth of Christianity at the expense of other traditions. For one thing, Christianity itself is transformed by this encounter. But most importantly we must beware of the temptation of identifying the church or Christendom with the reign of God for which we hope. It is our task to sow the seed of this hope in every culture. But we hope not for the triumph of the church (how empty such a triumph would be!) but for the triumph of God which abolishes all divisions and enmity. We live out that hope for reconciliation when in friendship, respect, and gratitude we welcome the other.

In our encounter with other religions we learn to clarify our hope, to purify our love, to enrich our faith. Perhaps we will learn again that we are called to be leaven and not the loaf. And perhaps also we will learn that the One in whom we hope is not the "God of the Christians" or the "God of the Church" but the One who promises justice and peace and joy for all creation.

*December 1983*

# V
# The Ordained Life

## Four Steps toward Ministerial Burn-Out

CHARLES V. GERKIN

The pastor I was going to see in the hospital had all the outward appearances of success in his ministry. He served one of the larger churches of his denomination. The church seemed to be prospering. His marriage seemed stable, if a bit squeezed by the demands of his work. His children were growing up and seemed to be avoiding the worst of the adolescent pitfalls of the time—drugs, irresponsible sex, and passive refusal of their potential. But he had been stricken in his office while meeting with some lay leaders of the congregation in a planning session. First appearances indicated a heart attack, but later diagnostic studies resulted in a diagnosis of "nervous exhaustion."

The man across from me in my seminary study looked well enough. His clothing and demeanor indicated that he, too, had known a measure of success. But he quietly shared with me that two months previously he had, after considerable prayer and reflection, resigned his pastorate and was now temporarily employed in a retail business. The purpose of his visit was to explore with me in retrospect what had happened and to consider what next steps might be taken either to reestablish himself in a meaningful ministry or to firm up his secular vocational goals.

The next pastor is somewhat younger than the first two. Five years out of seminary, he is serving a small congregation in a rural community on the fringe of a large metropolitan area. His church is equally divided between stalwart old-timers who have been the backbone of the community for years and a young, new group of families who have moved from the city into a new subdivision. Conflict has been present but contained, in part by the pastor's ability to bridge the gaps and evoke loyalty from both sides. But that has become burdensome. The time demands are not as great as are those for energy to keep the peace and keep things happening. Gradually, the pastor tells a group of his peers, he has found himself backing off from the effort. He fishes more, spends more time in his study, and no longer looks forward to conference and the annual possibility of promotion. Things seem stagnant.

Though situations in the lives of pastors such as these have undoubtedly been occurring for many years, it was not until the midseventies that these and related problems became so pervasive in the helping professions as to warrant a special name: burn-out. Now recognized as a major occupational hazard in all professions that involve human services, the symptoms may be as varied as a real or quasi-heart attack, the sudden impulse to change vocations, a quiet decision to do more fishing and less ministry, or the eruption of marital conflict. Divorce, alcoholism, and more or less complete physical breakdowns are among the more serious results that occur with some frequency.

The question as to whether burn-out occurs more frequently in the helping professions deserves more empirical research. I suspect that it occurs in many occupations in which the rewards are few or ambiguous, the frustrations great, and the evidence of accomplishment hard to measure. But there do seem to be special problems in the helping professions that can lead to burn-out if they are not recognized and given response both by the individual and by the systems in which human service is offered. Jerry Edelwich and Archie Brodsky in their book *Burn-Out: Stages of Disillusionment in the Helping Professions* (New York: Human Sciences Press, 1980), following the current trend to develop stage theories in all human processes, sort out four stages in the typical process of moving toward burn-out.

The authors speak of the common entry into a helping vocation with great enthusiasm and desire to be of service to one's fellow human beings. This enthusiasm is often of a naive sort, untempered by awareness of the intractable, stubborn nature of the human problems to be addressed. Most pastors can remember feelings of that variety. Preaching and pastoral care looked like great opportunities to change the lives of literally dozens if not hundreds of people. The enthusiastic stage involves the expending of much energy and creative effort. If even minimal results are forthcoming, there may be enough rewards to sustain the novice in the vocation until more sober and realistic expectations can take form. But for few are the results achieved commensurate with the expectations and the effort. In ministry that problem is greatly complicated by the intangible nature of the stuff of faith and commitment with which we work.

The second stage on the way to burn-out Edelwich and Brodsky describe as stagnation, though they acknowledge that this stage is somewhat interchangeable with the third stage, frustration. Who in ministry has not felt both these conditions? Initial enthusiasm, even when accompanied by deep personal commitment to serve God and God's people wherever and whenever one is sent or called, can carry one only so far. The same old resistances to change, the same old stereotypical caricatures of what living in faith means, the same old demands for ministry wish-fulfillment appear again and again. One must find a reasonable distance from the dailiness of these realities that confront ministry.

If one's personality tendencies are more overtly aggressive, one can easily become preoccupied with all those forces, personal and systemic, that frustrate ministry. The limited yardstick the ecclesiastical system seems to use to measure results in ministry, the lack of an adequate support system—personally or institutionally constructed, and the growing awareness of the pervasiveness of human sin and resistance to the gospel can combine to create enormous frustration. Particularly is this the case when these conditions are rubbed against the week-to-week vulnerability involved in making one's living by seeking to help persons in need and by preaching the gospel.

The fourth stage Edelwich and Brodsky designate as apathy, though they recognize that intervention to change the course of the process can occur at any of the earlier stages. Apathy may be recognized in those who have either so distanced themselves emotionally from the vocation as to be effectively disengaged, or fallen into an apathetic routine practice of the vocation that has settled for stereotypes. Interventions may be either creative or destructive, moves toward change of self or situation that cope with burn-out or moves that sidetrack the self's engagement of the issues of the vocation.

Viewed sociologically, the apparent increase in the phenomenon of burn-out in the helping professions can be seen as a symptom of larger issues and movements of our time. It is perhaps to be expected that the seventies, which have gained the label of the "me decade," in which the human desire for self-gratification and self-actualization gained ascendence, also produced a rise in burn-out among those who chose vocations that are altruistic and self-giving at their core. We who have chosen those vocations are not, of course, immune to the mood of the times. We, too, harbor our heightened desire for self-fulfillment. So the lower pay, the reduced rewards of success, and the limits on what we can do tend to look less tolerable in such a time as that which our society is now passing through.

Viewed theologically, the burn-out problem takes on both greater complexity and, hopefully, greater possibility of being overcome. "He [or she] who would be the greatest among you would be the servant of all," the biblical injunction reads, which certainly states a paradox—the greatest servant. Taken at face value, it seems both to bless our desire for achievement and to reinforce our motivations for service. Therein lies the tension in any ministering vocation. How can we both achieve and serve?

At the very least, on the human level this biblical view means that it behooves us to look in the direction of both achievement and service in our ministry if we are to avoid burn-out. One side of the solution of the problem lies with a continuing process of developing our skills and deepening our understanding of the issues of our vocation. In that we should and can turn toward greatness and avoid stagnation, frustration, and apathy. The other side involves us in continuing examination of our deepest motivations, the sources of our most profound satisfactions in ministry. Are those to be found in our servanthood, or have we been entrapped into the self-orientation of our time?

Reflection on clergy burn-out, however, confronts us with the inadequacy of our penchant for individualistic resolutions of the problems of the human condition, whether psychological or theological. Much as we may need individually to hone our skills and review our motivations for ministry, the problem in its largest dimensions cannot be addressed by simply an individualistic approach. The corporate systems we have constructed in congregational life—the deployment, evaluation, and support of ministry and ministers—come under judgment as contributing to situations that consume ministerial motivations and burn them into ashes or allow them to grow cold and dead. Better ways must be found both to use and to renew ministers in ways that make full and productive use of their talents and their desire to be of service. Tired, burned-out clergy are all too often the result rather than the cause of tired, outworn structures for getting the work of the church accomplished in a changing world.

At a deeper level, theological reflection on the problem of vocational burn-out would remind us that the gospel we are called to share is that we and our colleagues are not saved either by our achievement of greatness or by our service, but by the grace of God. God's incarnate presence both in our service and in those events and relationships that make up the context of our ministry is the power upon which we finally can depend. The mystery of that power is that it gathers to itself both the weakness and failure of the cross and the hope and promise of the final achievement of that kingdom in which all God's people will both serve and be served. The experience of being "burned out" can be for some an experience of crucifixion. As with the Good Friday cross, the experience may be one of feeling abandoned by God. But, as with all crosses, there remains the hope of resurrection into new life, new service, new being.

*Spring 1981*

# The Lonely Minister

JAMES F. HOPEWELL

A rude shock at mid-career may be our recognition that we are lonely. We then look around us and count few comrades who appreciate and understand what we personally transact in ministry. Both pastors and professors report their dismay at being loners. We seem to carry around in our own work a subtle filter, through which flows necessary and minor talk with other ministers, but which dampens moves from either side toward common meaning. In an ocean of talk, we are often solitary swimmers.

Swimming alone in that sea now seems dangerous. "It is the Year of the Shark," one pastor wryly observed last month, dealing with the shadowy, malignant forces that menace the minister minding his or her own business. From one direction our isolation may attract that maw of meaninglessness which devoured the faith and jobs of so many ministers in the last decade. Yet the very escape from such death may rather drive us deep into the jaws of Leviathan—the big Church System—which slowly chews and digests its way through countless functionaries. It is a bad time to be alone.

Proposals made by our generation of ministers to the issue of professional loneliness are modest, but real enough to gain wider testing. Several are intriguing, in that they require no big apparatus and can be advanced by as few as two ministers making covenant with each other. Talking about our personal loneliness with other ministers is the point of one of these proposals. At first such talk seems distasteful and somehow un-Christian and unprofessional, because our times picture the faithful minister as a rugged individual to whom God has given a bulletproof temperament. A different display of faith, however, occurs in the Bible. "I found no friend at my side," cries the faithful minister of the Psalms, "no one comes to rescue me." Faith can in fact generate the power and reason to confess one's isolation.

Another proposal deals with the manner in which we talk about our vocation. We now profess very little about our profession; when talking about ministry with ministers we rather slide into a discussion of its activities. Anecdotes and observations about activities (programs, progress, and problems) are actually a very thin basis for comradeship. They often merely shield the actor or provoke a can-you-top-this response. What would more likely connect our profession is our professing—our surprisingly rich and personal, yet underused, witness to what ministry is. That unique mix of biography and heritage and call which creates the meaning of our ministry is seldom shared in our talk with ministers, to our mutual loss and estrangement.

The most radical proposal takes ministry at its word and says, do it! When ministers gather together there is an almost automatic assumption that this gathering constitutes a producing unit for ministry rather than a consuming unit. My first discovery of this peculiarity—and perhaps yours as well—was as a seminary student. Seminary was seen as a place not where ministry occurred, but where ministry was somehow mysteriously produced for export. Later meetings of clergy tend only to reinforce this weird, alienating model of corporate behavior. How delightful it is when ministers finally discover that they can minister to each other and not just to the public at large!

Confessing, professing, and ministering are classic yet strangely new responses to our loneliness.

*December 1975*

# Keeping the Vision of God's Whole Creation

## SUSAN HENRY-CROWE

As I complete five years in parish ministry, my reflections come out of two years spent in two rural churches and three years spent in two "textile" churches in South Carolina. There is joy in my recollection, as well as a sense of loneliness and struggle. During these five years, the primary source of my strength has come from a deepening commitment to the Christian ministry in the United Methodist church. That commitment has come with a stronger understanding of my theological purpose. In some ways, it combines an affirmation of my biblical and theological heritage, but in other ways it grows out of my search for meaning in ultimate things.

Out of a deep sense of call, a wrestling with my place in ministry and in the church, my need of affirmation and fear of rejection, the little-known prophet Habakkuk has held special significance for me in recent seasons. The Lord offers Habakkuk courage in the face of meaninglessness, doubt, fear, and tiredness. The Lord answers Habakkuk's despairing cry with these words: "Write down the vision; make it plain upon the tablets so he [or she] may run who reads it. For still the vision awaits its time; it hastens to the end—it will not lie. If it seems slow, wait for it; it will surely come, it will not delay" (Habakkuk 2:2-3).

The vision is of God's whole creation—or God's kingdom. The vision is a vision of the fulfillment of God's creation, in God's time. A vision is what is to be—a just world, a righteous place, a community that seeks to do justice and love kindness (Micah 6:8), a people who turn their swords to plowshares to feed the hungry of the earth, a place and a time in which the meek inherit the earth and the peacemakers and the poor are blessed. And yet we can only see glimpses of the New Age—the fulfillment of creation. Our task is to keep the vision, the dream, alive. Our task is to be faithful.

Faithfulness is our willingness (even though angry, despairing, and tempted to let go) to wait for the vision. As the writer of Hebrews reminds us, "Faith is the assurance of things hoped for, the conviction of things not seen" (Hebrews 11:1). Laying hold of what I understand to be the vision of God's whole creation helps to keep the dream alive and gives my being in ministry integrity. If I am to take seriously God's call to ministry, it is increasingly important to remember for what purpose I am called. I am called to be a co-worker in the vineyard. I am not called to save or redeem the world (that has been done for us). I am called to make manifest God's love in me and bear witness to that in a hostile, cruel, un-just, and broken world. This sense of purposefulness has been central in my ability to live, and work, and survive in the parish.

Keeping some perspective about one's worth and contribution to God's creation is also crucial to survival. The knowledge of belonging to and being cared for by God and having that loving relationship expressed in relationships with others gives me a sense of self-knowledge and self-worth that keeps me from falling into despair when those around me are resisting (simply because I am a woman), fighting, or ignoring me and my gifts, graces, and insights. Acknowledging my own finitude and morality, on the other hand, keeps me aware that my contribution is distinctive but not ultimate. When these two perspectives are balanced there is freedom to be myself in the parish, without giving myself over to my role as minister but with authority enough to be a pastor without having to be a messiah. The ability to survive in the parish comes with being able to understand the theological nature and purpose of my life. Finally, God decides whether or not my ministry is worthwhile; I have only to be faithful to myself and to my call and task as I understand them.

For me as a woman, my survival is dependent upon having brothers and sisters who give me care and support. These are the ones with whom I am free, open, angry, disappointed, and despairing. These are the ones who enable me to keep the "vision," and when I cannot, who keep it for me until I can. Families do this at times but should never be expected to be one's sole support. Clergy sisters most often do this—partly because their journey and struggle have been similar enough that I rarely have to explain the joys, the fears, the rejection, or the set-apartness. Ministers and other professional colleagues do this. Occasionally, there are a few friends in the parish who can share my joys and griefs, but it is usually too much for most of my parishioners. While the task of ministry is a weighty matter, relationships beyond the life of the parish are not only needed for survival but significant for my own life. The last pragmatic word is humor. Many times being able to take lightly a light matter or take humorously a heavier but not ultimate matter has kept my time in the parish enjoyable, as well as tolerable.

In conclusion, the concrete things that make survival possible are sisters and brothers who sojourn with me in life and in ministry. We are bound together in ministry—but not bound by it—struggling to find meaning and have integrity while not losing ourselves and our mission in ministry; there is a time and season for keeping the faith and holding the vision of a whole creation. To keep the faith is finally to believe in the substantive reality of the gospel. To be faithful is to respond by keeping the "vision" and holding on to the dream of God's whole creation. And it is at last knowing that as the writer to the Hebrews soberly but faithfully knew, "These died in the faith—not having received what was promised, but having seen it and greeted it from afar and having acknowledged they were strangers and exiles on earth" (11:13).

*Spring 1981*

# Religion: The Opium of Ministry

JAMES F. HOPEWELL

All of us ministers work small deceits in what we do. The promise of closer union between God and people prods us on. Satan seduces every minister since Christ with modes that seem effective ways of ministry. Jesus saw their peril. He rejected the mode of magic, which for the Messiah meant changing stones to bread and surviving a fall from the parapet. He dismissed also the mode of religion, magic's strange counterpart, which promised the delivery of all nations as his property.

Had not Satan himself so openly offered these gifts, we ministers might be troubled by Christ's rejection of them. They seem such splendid means of binding folk to God. But Jesus blew Satan's cover, so the latter is more discreet today. Concealing his hand he pushes small, attractive magic and religion temptations upon us neighborhood ministers, and we gobble them up like pills. And like drugs these deaden our discipleship.

Magic is the less frequent temptation. Because people are today more skeptical, our forays into magic are less pronounced than in other times. We are held to little postures which suggest that through our call and ordination we become sacred heroes or gurus that dispense blessings from our person. Often our congregations abet us in our desire to be a little bit superhuman—not much, but enough to provide some mystical energy or ethos for churchly occasions.

Far more prevalent than magic, however, has been the seduction for us to engage in religion. Religion is that possibility of dealing with the beliefs and behaviors of faithful people without being personally claimed in the faith they express. Religion is the illusion that grace and human response are an objective reality without subjective consequences. Religion for the minister is the commodity that can be concocted, the system that can be analyzed, the condition that—if one is skillful—can be delivered in teaching, worship, and pastoring. How devilish the tempter is! By making us feel that we are purveyors of religion he leads us away from personal faith into any number of works that supposedly deal with another's religion: critiquing the religion of the New Testament, for example, or modifying the religion of a congregation through preaching. And our own faith withers.

We live, says Paul, at a time of two aeons, the old and the new. The business of ministry is to mark their juncture in personal and corporate life. To forget the old aeon is the mistake of magic; to forget the new is the illusion of religion. To do either is a sweet and deadly temptation.

*April 1976*

# Young Woman Set Apart

TONI WHITE

I write about ordination from the viewpoint of a parish minister. I also write as one who has long struggled with the issues of professional ministry and ministerial direction, as well as of ordination. Unlike Abraham who was called and responded without question, I have been more like Jacob, wrestling with and questioning that call, or perhaps most like Sara, who laughed. I was not laughing, however, at the service of ordination when I received Deacon's Orders in 1972. The title of the sermon at that service was "Now That I Have Become a Man." As one of two women in that group of ordinands, I was quite sure that the moment of the laying on of hands would not symbolize that I had reached manhood. I was not equally sure what it did mean.

I knew that I was making a public statement about a personal commitment: that from a variety of professional options, I was choosing a relationship to the institutional church as a way of living out a personal faith response. The church, in turn, conferred upon me "authority" to perform certain functions and reminded me that I was "set apart." It is the understanding of being "set apart" that has disturbed me most about ordination. Too frequently, it seems that clergy, and sometimes laity, interpret that distinction as being "set above," in terms of superior status, or as "set over against" in relation to the laity. There is such a danger here of losing sight of the servant quality of ministry, and of confusing "special function" with "special privilege."

As a parish minister with specific responsibilities within the life of a particular community of faith, I believe that, because of my ordination, I have been set apart for special function. That function involves, at one level, the historic need of human communities for designated religious leaders: persons who are responsible for the tangible enactment of the intangible and mysterious relationship of the people and their deity and who serve as spokespersons for the religious community in the context of the larger, secular community.

That function is legitimate as long as religious leaders retain historical perspective and do not fall into the ego trap of believing that they are more holy, more spiritual (i.e., superior) than the people they serve and represent. In my own congregation there are many saints who are older, wiser, and more deeply dedicated than I. Compared to them I am a babe in the faith. They know it and I know it. But because of the function for which I was set apart at ordination, I serve as a religious leader in our community of faith in a way that is different from their own service.

At another level, being set apart for function is directly related to the concept of "many gifts, one Spirit." My call to and choice of ministry as a profession has a lot to do with what I do well and what I like to do. It is believing that my gifts and skills find best expression and use in the context of professional ministry, although that ministry may take many forms. Having tried several of those forms (rural parish, hospital chaplaincy, urban parish) and having explored secular forms of ministry, I have been increasingly surprised to find that professional parish ministry seems to be where I "belong" in terms of vocation. That realization enables me to give strong affirmation to those who use their "gifts of the Spirit" in vocations not directly related to the institutional church. Their work is ministry no less than mine; the difference lies in form and content, not value.

Ordination also raises the issue of professional credibility. In that sense it is for me a practical rather than a theological consideration. I have been asked so often, "Are you *really* a minister?" (People do not generally expect a minister to be a 5'2" female in a dress). "Do you preach and marry and bury and all that stuff?" they usually add. I don't get angry at the questions any more; I simply answer "Yes, I am an ordained United Methodist minister."

The fact that I am ordained gives public credence to what I already know about myself. To people who have difficulty matching my person to their image of my profession, it says that I have the "right" to do what I do. Without the professional credibility that comes with fulfilling ordination requirements, some folks could not accept my claim to be a minister of the gospel of Jesus Christ. Since their acceptance of my authority bears direct relation to the quality and effectiveness of my ministry, ordination becomes important as a public statement as well as a private one. While I retain many questions about ordination, and about the role of the ordained minister, at this point in my life it is the means by which I can be about my Lord's business and my own.

*March 1978*

# Ordination: Two Understandings

MANFRED HOFFMANN

It is not surprising that the Methodist church finds herself in a bind concerning her official view of ministry, for her structure and theology strain in different directions. Methodism appears as a body with a Catholic structure of the threefold ministry, but seems animated with a soul at home in a Protestant theology of the common priesthood of all believers. And, were this not enough ground for uneasiness, the inability of most students and many clergy to articulate a distinctly Methodist theory of ministry gives cause to suspect that the problem is a major one.

This dilemma comes to its sharpest focus in the prevailing concept and practice of ordination; it is not simply a quandary students are exposed to when preparing for their professional assessment in seminary, or that conference boards face when interviewing candidates for ministry. It is a problem that can be traced back to the multiple, perhaps irreconcilable, roots of the Methodist tradition.

As in other aspects of his theology, Wesley drew in his understanding of ministry upon an ecumenical variety of theological stances which were in their original setting at odds with each other: the (Anglo-) Catholic, the (Lutheran and Calvinist-Puritan) Protestant, and the Free Church concepts of ministry. Of course, in the early stages of Methodism, when the enthusiasm of the rapidly expanding movement discouraged thorough theological reflection, this synthesis worked and the joints between disparate elements held fast. Subsequent generations, however, found themselves with the task of analyzing and tracing these components as the couplings became brittle under the influence of time and different historical conditions. The seams threatened to come apart.

Limited space allows only a most general pointing to an obvious disparity, i.e., that of the difference between a Catholic and Protestant understanding of ministry and ordination. Briefly and to the point, at the risk of typecasting: In the Catholic concept of ministry a special infused status of the clergy determines their particular function; whereas in the Protestant concept, a special delegated function determines a particular status. This implies that a Catholic priest is seen more in terms of his representative status within an institutional, highly organized juridical structure, while the Protestant minister is more understood as a particular member of the communion of believers who is called to a public and professional function within and out of this body of the faithful.

The distinction between the two may be a matter of an emphasis in Catholicism on the exclusivity of the priesthood (although a part of the community) and in Protestantism on the inclusiveness of the ministry (although set apart within the community). The Catholic priest represents and reflects—if not embodies—the divine to his parishioners while advocating them to the divine. The Protestant pastor, on the other hand, acts as a member of the congregation, even while functioning in a particular way as a special, visible, and available minister.

Thus the difference between an official representative of the Church Universal and a set-apart shepherd of a single congregation, between centralism and independence, special status and entrusted function, exclusive performance of cultic acts and leading communal worship, between authority and service, a separate spiritual class and a commonality of faith, between tradition and freedom: all of these are implications of a bifurcation which, come to think of it, indicates a dialectic already inherent at the inception of Christianity. Certainly, neither of the two sides intends to lose sight of its counterpart. Yet an emphasis on one tends to de-emphasize the other. So the Methodist dilemma is basically an ecumenical dilemma.

Living out her Catholic roots, the Methodist church affirms the value of tradition, of hierarchy, of conformity, central government, and theological absoluteness. But living out of her Protestant heritage, she also upholds the worth of novelty, democracy, individuality, self-determination, and open questioning. These disparate elements are ones which Methodism has historically sought to hold together.

Catholic ordination is thought to be a sacrament which distinguishes the clergy from the layfolk. In his ordination the priest receives the sacerdotal authority from the hands of the bishops in the apostolic succession. An indelible character conferred by ordination warrants a special spiritual quality never to be lost. By contrast, the Protestant minister is called into a public function and receives the authority of office from the believers to whom he or she is responsible. This delegating commission is made visible in the ordination, which is not a sacrament and therefore does not spiritually distinguish the minister from the laypeople. The people entrust their priestly authority to a chosen and trained person for an official function, while themselves being called to minister in their own stations and vocations.

Methodist ordination is informed by this double heritage; to trace and clarify it is the task of the church historian. Such analysis does not yet provide clear answers to the problem. However, to recognize the problem clearly is already a good step toward an eventual solution.

*March 1978*

# Perversions of the Pastoral Call

## JAMES F. HOPEWELL

A sense of ministry includes the sense of when and when not to perform religious acts. By trial and error, seasoned pastors learn the difference between an appropriate gesture of faith and one that is inappropriate.

Knowing when and when not to pray or witness marks the difference between a graceful pastoral call that blesses its participants, and a perverse call that compromises their integrity. We all have our horror stories about hospital patients who have been turned off and put down by facile and frequent use of prayer or talk about faith. Conversely, we know about bedside meetings in which our silence in Christian witness was just as perverse. Gaining a sense of occasion is an essential yet elusive development in good ministry.

I have recently gained some insight into why this "sense of occasion" is so important by reading Bruce Reed's excellent book *The Dynamics of Religion* (London: Darton, Longman and Todd, 1978). In this book Reed argues, with the aid of a number of psychological studies, for the bimodal consciousness of the human being. According to a theory of bimodal consciousness, there are two types of mental activities that alternately dominate our thinking and outlook. One type is rational, analytic, and oriented in action towards our workaday world. The other type of mental activity is intuitive, creative, and given more to our imagination and fantasy.

Reed contends that the religious process that people follow is fundamentally an oscillation between these two modes of mental activity. In the workaday, rational mode, persons are primarily dependent upon their colleagues and common-sense data for their life. Their dependence, however, shifts to that which is beyond themselves in the more intuitive mode, and it is here that they gain meaning for existence from the symbols of their faith. A functional religious process is one that regulates oscillation between the two modes so that both depths of meaning and everyday work serve the welfare of the whole community.

Reed spends the latter part of his book demonstrating how ministry serves as a threshold permitting access to the next small part of this oscillation process. Various acts of ministry gain their relevance only at different parts of the cycle. Witnessing the good news of salvation, for example, is most appropriate at that point where a person, frustrated and unconvinced by the workaday world, turns to gain fresh meaning in imaginal activity. Ministry to persons already deep into that portion of their oscillation process where dependence upon God is dominant, however, is a more symbolic ministry of ritual and the preached word. Ministry has equally the task of assisting persons in their return to the workaday world in a refreshed and unanxious state, so that they may once again resume lives that directly benefit the community in which they live.

Reed's theory of oscillation between these two modes helps me to appreciate more fully why certain religious acts sometimes seem appropriate when I call upon a parishioner, and at other times do not. I must try to understand as best as possible where my brother or sister is "located" in his or her own intricate cycle of consciousness. If I am to be, in my presence and person, a threshold assisting that person in moving to the next part of his or her process, I need to understand just where that person in fact is struggling. Prayer, or witness, or communion, or a discussion about the news and the perplexities of life may be equally appropriate or inappropriate depending upon where the person is.

There are at least three perversions of ministry in a pastoral call. These are the errors of fanaticism, magic, and routinization.

Fanaticism is the perversion of clinging to the *fanum*, which is the Latin word for the structure that separates the sacred and profane, as does the altar rail in many churches. The fanatic is a person in ministry who always wants to force persons to the altar rail, no matter where they are in their own religious process. The fanatic is always concerned about whether or not persons are turning from the workaday world to the particular brand of religious symbols he or she fanatically espouses. This perversion is one that does not acknowledge that a human being proceeds religiously through many phases of dependence and perception other than the one phase seen by the fanatic.

Magic is another perversion. It assumes that the symbols employed at the deepest part of the imaginal, intuitive sphere are equally valid no matter where a person is in his or her religious cycle. Hence a pastor may employ prayer as magic when neither the pastor nor the patient is at a point of deep dependence, but instead when the pastor wishes some sort of sacred conclusion to an otherwise secular meeting. How many of us have ended a session with a parishioner with prayer, not because our religious cycles required it but because we wanted to get out of the room? Such prayer is magic, and it is a perversion of a pastoral call.

But we are just as likely to be guilty of perversion in what we may call routinization. In this state we merely talk with our patient about the weather, sports, their illness and the like, without seeing in our meeting a threshold in which that patient is actually turning deeper towards meaning and towards dependence upon God. Here we fail people, not by magic or fanaticism, but by our inattention to the possibility of a spiritual encounter.

Where are my brothers or my sisters when I call upon them? At what state are they in their journey, and can our meeting be a threshold that enables them to proceed onward?

*Fall 1980*

# Therapy and the Homiletic Process

## CHARLES D. HACKETT

Harry Emerson Fosdick used to speak of preaching as pastoral counseling on a large scale. In our time of great sophistication and variety in counseling and psychotherapies, such a definition seems naive. Nevertheless, every pastor senses some truth in Fosdick's aphorism. There is an innate connection between pastoral counseling and preaching. In the short piece that follows I would like to suggest a paradigm for this connection.

Virtually all counseling styles have in common a certain trajectory of progress. When a client or patient comes to a counselor, there is an initial period of mutual learning about this person who has come for help: the perceived difficulty, the symptoms, the family situation, the work and social situation, and the history. The counselor also notes matters such as this new person's affect (depressed? euphoric? etc.), his or her mannerisms, the way the person thinks and speaks. At the same time, the client is learning about the therapist. Usually what he or she learns is not personal information but more important things: Does this person listen? Is he or she kind? Does the counselor attend to me? Most of all, does this person to whom I have come with some pain seem to understand? Can I trust the therapist? Does he or she seem able to accept me? In other words, a basic partnership or alliance is being formed. The alliance hinges upon the client's perception that the counselor is empathic.

Empathy is a much-discussed word in clinical circles today, largely due to the work of the late Chicago psychoanalyst Heinz Kohut who made empathy the major therapeutic tool in working with people in our time. Empathy is, in short, the ability to identify the feelings of someone else by identifying in oneself feelings which are similar enough that the client knows that he or she is not alone and is being responded to at the emotional level in an appropriate and accepting way. The key to the concept of empathy is the belief that while no two human beings ever share the same life experiences, yet we are all similar enough emotionally that it is possible imaginatively to put oneself in the psychological frame of reference of another and, indeed, accompany that person wherever his or her thoughts and feelings lead. The need to be empathically understood is the beginning of any fruitful therapy.

Once an empathic alliance is begun, a second phase of work can be identified: clarification. How does the client understand him or herself in the world? Is he or she, for instance, a helpless victim? A basically worthless person who gets by by fooling others? An unappreciated genius? On the basis of the counselor's empathic acceptance, the client is able to articulate his or her basic way of seeing the world, of making sense out of reality.

Usually the therapist and client work together to identify the basic hermeneutic assumptions which the client uses to make sense out of life. Thus a person whose father was emotionally distant and whose mother was depressed and unresponsive may develop, as a means of survival, a view of the world as uncaring. Such a person may experience intense, chronic loneliness and emptiness, but will have survived by assuming that the world is so constructed that everyone must just get along without being close to anyone, because if people try to be intimate they will be disappointed. The pain of disappointment is greater than the pain of loneliness, so such a person may seek to make a virtue out of loneliness and to some extent succeed. The person may even take a grim pleasure in surviving in a world perceived as hostile and uncaring.

The third step is for the client to be able to sense that his or her habitual way of making sense out of reality, while it may have been necessary at an earlier point in life, is not necessary now. At this point, the client can imagine that the world is different from the way it was formerly perceived. Sometimes this therapeutic gain can come simply from the empathic presence of the counselor (i.e., "If I am living in a world where no one cares or understands, why does this person seem both to care and understand?"). Sometimes it comes through a recognition of a dissimilarity between what a person consciously believes and unconsciously assumes (i.e., "I have learned that the world is not hostile, and yet I always act as if it were!"). Sometimes it comes through a recognition that the world as it is, is not as it seemed in childhood (i.e., "My mother and father *were* cold and uncaring and so I had to protect myself; but as I think about it, my spouse is not like that. Perhaps I can risk some of the closeness I long for.").

In virtually all instances, however, the three-part movement of 1) establishing an empathic alliance, 2) clarifying an operative hermeneutic, and 3) considering an alternative hermeneutic, constitutes the trajectory of therapeutic progress. In this light, it is possible to make some correlations with preaching.

To begin with, the gospel is a hermeneutic. It is an understanding of reality in which the realities of suffering, sin, and death are taken with utmost seriousness but in which, at the same time, the ultimate victory of life, joy, and love is central. The exact ways in which these elements interplay with one another through the symbols of the faith vary from theology to theology, but the dialectic of real and present sin represented by the cross and the hope of love's triumph represented in the resurrection are at the heart of the Christian proclamation.

In a very real sense, we are, all of us, "clients" because our hermenutics are all distorted by our efforts to make sense out of a sinful world which inevitably treats all of us ungently and many of us terribly. We are born into a world which is sinful beyond the control or final remedy of human beings. Such a world does not make life, love, joy, and hope easy to find in the fabric of human existence. When they are spoken of, often it is in a kind of unrealistic way as if they were magic ideas by which we could protect ourselves from the reality of suffering and death. Such a use of hope is what a psychologist might call a "defense," a pretending about reality.

What, then, can we say of preaching and its connection with counseling? I am suggesting that a sermon can be seen as following the same essential trajectory as a therapeutic gain. In the first phase, the preacher's task is to establish an empathic alliance. Here the job is to so articulate reality as it is experienced by those in the congregation that they will say, in effect, "Yes, that is how it is . . . that preacher really understands."

The second phase involves articulating reality as it is presented biblically or theologically in terms of the human experience of sin, suffering, and death. Whether this is an exposition of a text like Romans 8:15ff. ("I do not understand my own actions, for I do not do what I want, but do everything I hate...."), or a description of Job's unwarranted suffering, or of Jesus' desolation and powerlessness on the cross, the material of our tradition does articulate the human situation in such a way that a person hearing a sermon might say: "Yes, not only does the preacher seem to be human, but people of the Bible—Paul, Job, Jesus—are like me."

The third phase is the articulation of the gospel in the context of the first two phases. Here the gospel of life and hope must be preached as integral to the portion of the tradition which "connected" to the congregation in phase two, so that the new hermeneutic offered by the gospel might result in a shift in the hermeneutic of the congregation. An example of such a sermon, in outline, might be:

I. We often feel helpless, disappointed, and frightened by what life gives us: recession, sickness, etc.

II. The disciples, and Jesus himself, apparently moved from high hopes to disappointment from Palm Sunday to Good Friday when they were overwhelmed by helplessness and fear when Jesus died.

III. Yet, some days later, these same disciples were transformed—proclaiming that Jesus had been raised and that God had won over sin and death and that we no longer needed to fear.

In this sermon, a fourth or "concluding" section is intentionally omitted. A therapist cannot "tell" a client how he or she ought to feel, but can only offer an alternative hermeneutic; a preacher cannot tell a congregation exactly how to see the world. The gospel is a revolutionary and saving hermeneutic, and the preacher's task, not unlike the therapist's, is to clear the way for the inherent power of God's spirit in each person, to move us toward an acceptance of the reality of love and life as ultimate reality.

*May 1983*

# Trends in Contemporary Preaching

GORDON G. THOMPSON

Of particular interest to persons interested in homiletics are the types of sermons that characterize contemporary preaching. Homiletics is a science as well as an art. We have a tradition as well as a significant body of literature which makes possible a critical analysis of modern preaching.

Any evaluation of preaching in the modern era would naturally concern itself with homiletical process. One aspect of homiletical process is the typicalities of sermons that are representative of preaching today.

Recently, I have been engaged in a research project that involves a study of the theological content, homiletical process, style, and delivery of the sermons of "The Protestant Hour." A collection of 1,700 sermons from a period of thirty-eight years, these sermons were broadcast in every region of the United States and overseas to a total listening audience of ten million persons. Ecumenical in character, all the sermons, except for a few, were contributed by selected representatives of the following denominations: Episcopal, Presbyterian U.S. and Presbyterian U.S.A., Lutheran, and United Methodist.

It seemed appropriate to assume that these sermons are typical of the preaching in the mainline denominations in the United States since 1945. For an in-depth investigation, a sample of these sermons was scientifically drawn. Included in the sample appear such well-known preachers as Edmund A. Stiemle, John A. Redhead, Robert E. Goodrich, and Theodore P. Ferris. Some mentors of mine are in the sample: Arthur J. Moore, John Owen Smith, and Wyatt Aiken Smart.

An intense study of such a broad spectrum of contemporary preaching calls for more extensive interpretation than is possible in this brief report. Even so, in this brief space it is possible to provide an insight into the typicalities of contemporary preaching.

Using several major classifications I did an analysis of the sermons by denomination and three historical periods: 1945-59, 1960-69, 1970-79. Topical preaching was a prevalent model throughout the last thirty-eight years. In a topical sermon the central truth of the sermon expresses an idea that is independent of the text and, if a text is cited, the text serves only as a resource for the topic, not the source of the sermon. The most popular period for topical preaching was 1945-59. Forty-one percent of the sermons were topical. A diminishing interest in topical preaching appeared in the later periods of 1960-69 and 1970-79. During these later periods, the percentage of topical sermons was twenty-nine.

Doctrinal sermons, while not a popular type, were evenly used in all three historical periods: thirteen percent of the total sermons preached in 1945-59, ten percent in 1960-69, and seventeen percent in 1970-79. A doctrinal sermon expresses the central truth of the sermon through a creedal affirmation or some other statement of Christian doctrine such as salvation, the covenant, incarnation.

By far the most popular type of sermon in each historical period was the textual-thematic sermon. In a textual-thematic sermon the central thought of the sermon and the central truth of the text are the same; there are continuing connections between the theme of the sermon and the theme of the text. This type of sermon dominates the entire series, averaging forty-five percent of the total number of sermons preached.

Expository preaching did not fare well as a type of sermon in "The

Protestant Hour." An expository sermon reproduces in contemporary language the content and form of the text with an application to an analogous situation. In this type of preaching the text is the source of the central truth and form of the sermon. In 1945-59, three percent of the sermons were expository; in 1960-69, ten percent; and in 1970-79, seven percent.

In addition to classifying the sermons, I also evaluated the forms of proclamation. In classical forms of proclamation a sermon discloses a viewpoint concerning the character of God. Of course, any sermon may well express more than one aspect of divine revelation. However, usually there is one dominant theological motif. For instance, the evangelical sermon shows God as Redeemer. Aimed at the unbaptized, it invites persons to receive Jesus Christ as Savior and Lord and enter the kingdom of God. Eight percent of all the sermons from 1945 to 1979 were evangelical.

Pastoral preaching, which shows God as the Shepherd who knows and cares for the individual, relates the gospel to the problems and concerns of persons in their everyday existence. There has been an increase in this kind of preaching. In 1945-59 pastoral concern was dominant in eleven percent of the sermons; in 1960-69, thirteen percent; and in 1970-79, seventeen percent.

Prophetic preaching increased in frequency with each historical period. Contrasting the norms of the kingdom of God with the prevailing loyalties of people, the prophetic sermon shows God as Lord of history and the church. In the light of divine promise and judgment, the prophetic sermon speaks to the larger community concerning issues of racism, sexism, classism, nuclear power, ecology, war, etc. In 1945-59 prophetic concern was the dominant note in seven percent of the sermons; in 1960-69, ten percent; and in 1970-79, twelve percent.

Ethical implications of the covenant relationship between God and believers were seldom a predominant emphasis of the sermons. Overall, only two percent would qualify as sermons in which the primary concern focused on ethical decisions and moral responsibility.

One form of proclamation that did not appear in the series was the pastoral-liturgical sermon in which the preacher offers the sermon to God, not directly to the people. Although there is a sense in which every sermon is a prayer offered to God, there were no sermons that would be heard as an act of communication with God instead of the people.

The most prominent form of proclamation in all of the decades was that of the teaching sermon. This kind of sermon shows God as the source of truth, builds up the Body of Christ, increases understanding, and deepens commitment. For the baptized, it equips persons for their Christian vocation. This form of proclamation averaged sixty percent for the four decades.

Several questions are emerging from this study. It is not surprising that there is a heavy emphasis on preaching as teaching. This model is constantly presented to seminarians by professors of theology. However, why aren't there more expository sermons? Has modern biblical criticism been seen as a threat rather than an ally? Do the seminaries do an adequate job of teaching biblical exegesis? Where are the prophets? Have ministers not heard the call of the prophet? Have they been equipped with the competencies and imagination to do prophetic preaching? In an era when persons are aware of their need for ethical guidance, why are there so few sermons helping people with ethical decisions?

Of course, one obvious reason for the absence of prophetic sermons in this series is an absence of minority preaching on "The Protestant Hour." Few women or black preachers have appeared on the program. Some of the most effective prophetic preaching in the past four decades has been done by black preachers. An exciting collection of sermons is a book by women preachers entitled *Spinning a Sacred Yarn*. Other books in the area of homiletics include the following: *Telling Truth: The Foolishness of Preaching in a Real World*, James Armstrong; *The Prophetic Imagination*, Walter Brueggemann; *As One Without Authority* and *Overhearing the Gospel*, Fred B. Craddock; *Liberation Preaching*, Justo and Catherine Gonzalez; *The Black Preacher in America*, Charles V. Hamilton; *Preaching to Suburban Captives*, Alvin C. Porteous; *How Shall They Preach?* Gardner C. Taylor; and *Preaching in a New Key*, Clement Welsh.

*May 1983*

# Called to Administer

JAMES T. LANEY

According to surveys, ministers spend more time in administrative work and enjoy it less than other aspects of their ministry. The amount of time taken up by such duties might be reduced by conscious adoption of methods of more effective administration. Seminaries and continuing education programs need to assist us in addressing this concretely.

Possibly more serious than how to administer well is the distaste many ministers have for administration. It seems contrary to the very spirit of ministry. It involves the responsibility of setting limits and goals and exercising supervision. It centers more on programs than persons, and it invariably deals with money.

An examination of the terms "to administer" and "to minister" can be instructive. The former is transitive and takes a direct object. One "administers" something, implying action upon it to direct or shape it. But one "ministers" to people. This means taking a stance toward or relating to in a certain manner but not in power to act upon or direct. In other words, in the art of ministering, people are addressed as before God in their freedom; in administration, people are dealt with in roles which bind and direct.

In a way, Luther's well-known distinction between the law and the gospel helps us here. For Luther these two were related but always in tension. The law without the gospel meant harshness, legalism, and impersonalization. The gospel without law meant indulgence, lack of discipline, and sentimentality. The one gives form and structure and helps point to hard reality. The other conveys affirmation, favor, and understanding. Our modern parallel to Luther's classic distinction is our own tension between administration and ministry. We need to see administration in terms of its necessary relationship to the gospel, as the implementation of the law.

In other words, we need to see it theologically. In a society that has become excessively bureaucratized, the church can witness to a more humanized structure and administration, which structure and administration help us all from falling into narcissism and privatization. The split between administration and ministry in the church has often meant that we have been guilty of programming through structures which have not carried the spirit of the gospel, while at the same time the gospel becomes sentimentalized, a sop to a harsh world.

Possibly our most urgent task to the church today is a theological understanding of administration and ministry. Such an approach would help many of us in our frustrations over the depersonalizing aspects of life, while at the same time give fiber and content to our ministry of the gospel as well.

*June 1977*

# Work Smarter, Not Harder

DAN W. DUNN

The field of time management is experiencing heightened importance in the 1980s, and appropriately so. Time is a central component of our stewardship. Unfortunately, few pastors concentrate on being trustworthy stewards of their time. Stewardship of time as a gift from God, then, must be the fundamental theological foundation for time management. The etymological foundation for time management is simple: it is time *management*, not time saving. We all have been granted the same amount of time. Thus, we cannot "save" time. We can manage it. Since we really cannot save time, the point is not to do things "faster." While this helps in some instances, it more often causes critical errors in judgment and action. The key is *doing the right things*. It is true: effective pastors work smarter, not harder.

Setting specific, concrete objectives is the best way to do the right things. According to Merrill E. and Donna N. Douglass, there are six criteria for setting objectives: they must be your own, they must be written, they should be realistic and attainable, they should be specific and measurable, they should have time schedules, and they should be compatible with other objectives (*Manage Your Time, Manage Your Work, Manage Yourself*). For pastors and churches a seventh criterion is important: the objective should be related to ministry and mission in the church and community. A central theme of the New Testament is mission. Objectives should focus on delivering concrete help to human hurts and hopes in the community.

In addition, there are four specific aspects of time management which are especially pertinent to pastoral work. The first is *closure*. Pastors often prefer activities which guarantee quick closure, but closure can trap us. Because we want that sense of having it "finished," we spend all our time writing letters, filling out forms, and straightening the files. This is why setting objectives is vital. With set objectives, you know which activities will work toward the accomplishment of those objectives, and which will not. Don't waste your time on the latter.

Objectives are also the key to our second point: *meetings*. Meetings should be understood as opportunities to make decisions, not just have discussions. Those decisions must relate to the objectives which have been set by the pastor and church. Praeto's Principle states that 20 percent of your work will yield 80 percent of your results. Meetings are called only to make decisions about that 20 percent.

*Delegation* is the third pertinent point for pastors. This is for two reasons. One, the pastor and/or committee will not have time to call a meeting for every small decision to be made (the non-20 percent decisions). Two, and more importantly, delegation is a central expression of the theological concept of trust. Pastors must learn to trust others' abilities to make wise and appropriate decisions. The key to effective delegation is granting the person both the responsibility and the authority for the decision to be made.

Finally, *emergencies* are a critical part of the pastor's time management. To avoid the potentially devastating effect of emergencies, simply place emergency time in your schedule. For example, if you calculate that most of your emergencies take no more than 2 hours, then 2 or 3 days a week, schedule a 2-hour block of emergency time. If an emergency occurs at 9 a.m., and your emergency time is 2-4 p.m., simply move the 9-11 a.m. schedule items to the 2-4 p.m. block. Of course there are some things which cannot be easily moved, but many items can be. If used properly, this tool can aid enormously with management of time.

For the pastor of the 1980s and 1990s, time management will be a must. It is crucial that the pastor's time management be based on solid biblical understandings of stewardship and mission, and a good working knowledge of how to set and reach specific, concrete objectives.

*May 1982*

# Going to Goshen

NOLAN B. HARMON

The Methodist system of making appointments has changed radically from the way it was in the old days. Up until the third decade of this century Methodist ministers never knew their appointments until the bishop read them out just before conference adjourned. Thus the "reading of the appointments" by the bishop was always a time of tension and surprise, often accompanied by great disappointment.

My own experience illustrates. I joined the old Baltimore Conference of the Methodist Episcopal Church, South, after I found myself pitched off in Washington city at the close of the First World War. I had been led to believe that I would be given a pretty good young minister's appointment, as I had been an Army chaplain and had preached around the city quite a bit. Imagine my surprise, then, to hear the bishop read out routinely: "Goshen: N. B. Harmon." Just like that.

"Where in the world is that?" I asked an older minister.

"Land O' Goshen," he laughed. "It's up in Maryland. They'll give you plenty to eat!" But food was the last thing I was looking for after that disappointing assignment. Then and there I resolved that I would find out where I was to be sent, if at all possible. And long after, in my own administration, I was careful to see that every preacher knew of his appointment ahead of time if this could possibly be worked out.

I must admit that "Old Goshen" was not too bad when I got there about a month later. They were fine cultured people, the ones left, for the lines of travel had changed and Goshen was pretty well isolated. The original building there was thought to have been built by Robert Strawbridge himself, and the body of Ignacius Pigman, voted his orders at the Christmas Conference, was said to be buried under its pulpit.

Since that time the so-called "open cabinet" has come into being; that is, making appointments known ahead of time. But no cabinet can do its appointment making in the open, for all the faults and failures, coupled with the doubts and fears that are had regarding every minister and every place, have to be frankly discussed when the slate is being made. But every bishop insists, and must insist, that what is said in confidence in the cabinet must never be repeated outside.

The years have brought changes in appointment making. Earlier in the century a time-tenure was fixed so that the bishop could not hold a person longer than four years in any one place. This tenure has been lifted within late years except with the district superintendency, which is limited to a six-year term. The bishop must read appointments to the cabinet before reading them to the conference. Also, and best of all, it is now provided that every minister shall be "consulted" about his or her appointment before the actual assignments are made. But what is "consultation"? Bishop Costen J. Harrell once held that posting the appointments on a bulletin board at conference ahead of their actual reading constituted consultation. But the Judicial Council knocked his ruling down, as I am sure they should have, for there must be a give and take in this business.

It helps greatly in the making of appointments if the bishop and district superintendents know where each appointee would like to go. Bishop Paul Garber once got out to all the Virginia Conference preachers a questionnaire asking them to indicate their first, second, and third choices for the year ahead. Such replies and wishes can be very helpful if it is clearly understood that telling where one *wants* to go does not mean one *can* or *will* go there. What if everyone asked to go to First Church, Metropolis?

What ought to be understood is that bishops and district superintendents are very anxious to get the best possible ministers to fill their appointments. No football coach was ever more eager to get winning athletes on the team than the district superintendents are to get their pulpits filled by first-class ministers. They may vie with each other to secure the best persons for their respective districts and have many private give-and-take conversations, even heated exchanges in front of the cabinet, to get whom they want. Nor will they let any of their preachers be moved to another district unless they feel the move is a helpful or at least a fair one. I have seen hardened conference veterans shed tears in the cabinet when they were dealt some great disappointment about a preacher or place for which they had made a great fight.

I remember one amusing incident in appointment making from North Carolina. A minister who had done good work was up for a move that would better him, but he said that he had a son who was turning out to be a crack football player on his high school team, and he wanted to be sent to a town or city that had a good team so his son could keep up his playing and maybe earn a college scholarship. Two of the superintendents subsequently got into a big argument over which town had the best football team! I said, "Well, I've heard every other reason for making appointments but never on what sort of football team a place had!" The sequel to the story is that the man evidently got to a town that filled the bill, for the lad in question did become a football star in college later on.

My own custom in making appointments was to hold everything in abeyance until after Easter when I would call the cabinet together. Each of us was furnished with a cabinet worksheet, a list of all conference appointments with their pastors for the year that was closing. A blank space was left for the writing in of new names. The promised salary was put opposite each appointment. In beginning the appointment making, a fair bishop will announce the appointments of the cabinet members first of all. Usually district superintendents are kept on if the term allows; if not, those are asked to retire from the room while the bishop and the cabinet consider where they may be stationed. That being fixed, they are called back in and told of their appointments at once, so that they can then help the others in making up the slate.

Each district superintendent is usually asked to read down his or her list of charges and indicate where a move or a reappointment is recommended. When all recommendations are in, the serious work begins, with all sorts of give and take called for in a big conference. First cleared is the matter of moves within separate districts. But the big work is crossing all district lines for making up the final list. A good way to start is to begin with "open" charges, or those vacated by retirement or death of the incumbent. A chain of appointments can be built by filling first the vacancy and then filling each appointment that has its incumbent moved up in the chain. Sometimes there is a swap between two ministers who thus exchange their charges for the new year. Swaps, however, are not always popular, for neither one feels that he or she has really moved "up."

And then there is the matter of releasing the appointments ahead of time. Everyone applauds bishops who can do this ahead of time, but a risk is run. If a congregation says heatedly that they will not accept the person chosen for them, can bishops afford to yield and make a change? If they do, they greatly offend some other charge where the rejected person must be placed. So unless bishops are sure they can make every appointment stick, they had better not sing out ahead of time what the appointments will be. "In this business of making appointments," Bishop Charles Selecman said, "you have to be as wise as serpents and as harmless as doves. And, brethren, you will need about two pounds of serpents for every ounce of doves in your make-up to make this business work out right!"

I am convinced that our system is the best way to fill all the churches all the time. Sure we make mistakes, in nearly every slate of appointments, but these can be remedied at the end of the year. In a "called system" mistakes cannot be remedied without turning out the minister, splitting the church, and losing traction while a committee hunts around uneasily for a new minister. The faults of our system are open for everyone to see, and are always played up by those disappointed in where they are to go. The faults of the "called system" can't be played up; a dispossessed minister can't go around saying "Nobody wants me!" If he did he never would be wanted.

But with us! When we get a poor appointment we stand on the corner and tell the world how we have been mistreated, not forgetting to mention the bishop, the district superintendent, and calling down the wrath of heaven on the whole appointive system. It sounds as if we are coming to pieces, but we are not. We blow off steam that way, and if we have any sense we are glad that the church is seeing to it that we have a job the rest of our lives, with a roof over our heads and people to love. Sure we grumble a lot, but so do all good soldiers. But good soldiers for all their grumbling *fight*, and good preachers for all their grumbling *go*, and that's the way it should be.

*June 1978*

# Justice for Pastors

ROBIN W. LOVIN

In 1850 the *Discipline* of the Methodist Episcopal Church provided that "The annual allowance of the married traveling, supernumerary, and superannuated preachers, shall be two hundred dollars, and their traveling expenses." I do not know whether justice—that process that Aristotle defines as "rendering each man his due"—was any more complete in the itinerant system of 1850 than it is today. I am pretty sure it was simpler.

Today, rendering each "traveling preacher" his or her due entails a complicated matching of experience to salary, abilities to expectations, family size to parsonage size, spouse's occupation to geographic location, and so on. Small wonder, then, that today's itinerants rarely survive the appointive process unscathed. We come out wondering not only whether we want what we got, but whether we got what we deserve, whether the cabinet has given us our due. As the number and variety of factors that make an appointment "good" or "bad" increase, the complexity of the cabinet's deliberations and the possibilities for dissatisfaction rise proportionately.

At the risk of only making matters worse, I want to suggest that the problem of justice in the appointive system is not that the process has become too complicated, but that it is not yet complicated enough. We have taken a matter that is fundamentally a covenant for ministry between all the pastors and the whole church and turned it into a negotiation between each pastor and his or her immediate superiors for salary and fringe benefits. In such a case, indeed, "causes of stumbling are bound to arise."

Justice in the appointive process will not be achieved by fine-tuning the salary-to-experience schedule or standardizing the requirements for parsonage furnishings. Justice depends on a renewal of the covenant on which the itinerant system rests. What is due to us and what is required from us are not matters of individual goals. Justice depends on a commitment by each part of the ministry of the whole church, allocating our talents and resources to insure that the word will be heard and Christ's presence will be felt wherever the United Methodist church may be. Justice determined by that covenant makes new demands and requires new styles of participation by all—pastors, congregations, and cabinets.

What is due to each pastor in the appointive covenant is a careful and honest appraisal of gifts and performance, and a field for ministry that matches those particular skills and accomplishments. A measure of comfort and security for the pastor and family are necessary, but secondary, considerations; the first priority is to insure that pastoral talents are not squandered in inappropriate assignments while genuine needs of the church elsewhere go unmet. (Incidentally, this accountability of one's gifts in relation to one's work applies to those of us who serve special appointments as well. Can we give an account of our ministry that justifies our ordination? Are we ever asked to do so?)

A covenantal acceptance of appointment demands much of the pastor, but it also carries the implication that his or her first claim against the cabinet is not a salary level or a certain size of congregation. The first thing due to the pastor is a measure of satisfaction that the appointment genuinely fits the person.

This covenantal itineracy cannot exist without a major change in the role of the local congregation. The United Methodist church too often denies its laity a mature and responsible role in the choice of their pastor. In turn, congregations who are treated like children develop childish expectations: their pastor must be perfect, must know their needs before they do, must appeal to every group equally. Congregations that are not required to specify what they want, specifically, from pastoral leadership feel free to demand everything. No cabinet can hope to perform the covenant-sustaining task of matching pastors to congregations unless the congregations are drawn into a mature and active role in defining requirements and evaluating performance of pastoral leadership.

Rendering each pastor and each congregation what is due becomes an infinitely complex task if we take the itineracy covenant seriously. Here, as nowhere else in the life of the church, haste makes waste. The minimal "consultation" the *Discipline* requires frays episcopal nerves annually from January to June. A covenantal consultation probably cannot be done at all in that time frame. Here we have much to learn from the Methodists of Great Britain, who draw the lay people of their circuits into a more active role in the choice of their pastors, and who often move to define needs and line up new pastoral leadership a year or more before the change is effected.

Participation in a covenant means learning to see things whole. When that whole is the complex reality of ministry in the United Methodist church, covenant justice is a demanding task. Settling for less is easier and quicker, but over the long run, it is less satisfying. And, as is usually the case when we settle for less than justice, it is also wrong.

*June 1978*

# When Should a Minister Move?

## J. MICHAEL RIPSKI

Having served for over three years as an associate minister in my present appointment, I have been faced with the decision to stay or move. Though I have elected to stay, in the process of making the decision I was forced to consider some of the pros and cons of being an "itinerant" minister.

In addition to this existential reckoning with itineracy, I have been given cause to reconsider the itineracy for another reason. At present my conference, the Memphis Annual Conference, and the Tennessee Conference are contemplating merger. A fellow minister has suggested that a strong argument for merger can be based on the fact that we belong to an itinerant ministry. His point was that ministers too often spend their whole ministry in a relatively small geographical locale. Thus, merger of the two annual conferences would encourage moving out of an area with which one has become increasingly too comfortable and complacent.

My existential perspective and the argument for merger lift up two different aspects of itineracy. One is temporal: When should a minister move? How often should one move? The other is spatial: How close to "home" is too close for one's ministry to be effective? I recognize that one cannot generalize about United Methodist clergy. Because we ministers reflect the pluralistic nature of our church, what is true for one segment of the clergy will not be true for another. For this reason, I will present what I believe to be traditional arguments for itineracy. Then I want to raise some questions which, although possibly not applicable to all ministers, will be appropriate for a portion of United Methodist clergy who previously have been expected to accommodate the traditional view.

Yes, we ministers do discover after several years in an appointment that our energy is depleted, our spirit is sagging, and our motivation is exhausted. What we were very excited about doing upon our appointment we have either accomplished or resigned ourselves to the fact that we will not be able to accomplish. Instead of wallowing in frustration over the undone, or attempting to get psyched up for a repeat performance of past achievements, we conclude, "It is time to move."

Yes, we ministers do tend to become complacent and too comfortable when serving an area that has been or has become "home." Our inclination, as with most human beings, is to want to sink roots and claim a particular geographical and social area as our own. It's nice to know your druggist, doctor, car mechanic, and barber or hair stylist on a personal basis. It is also nice to have the kids situated in a school that they and their parents like. But we admit that in order to maintain this sense of well-being, we sometimes pay the price of avoiding the conflict which inevitably comes with prophetic preaching, pastoral care, and community involvement. The itineracy makes it possible for us to minister outside our "backyard" where emotional ties are so strong and so inhibiting. It also permits us a safety valve should an appointment completely reject the kind of ministry we have to offer.

To these traditional arguments for the itineracy I would like to pose several questions. First, is not itineracy, *as it exists today*, based as much on appointment "ladder climbing" as it is upon the above-mentioned arguments? It is amazing how the Spirit works to bring about a concurrent feeling of "I've done all I can do here" and "It's time for a challenge," i.e., a bigger church with a bigger salary. If we are honest, it seems to me that our present itinerant ministry is based upon a combination of ambiguous motives, some of which are respectable and some of which are not so respectable. Have you ever wondered why those ministers who hold the biggest appointments across Methodism seem to be less itinerant than those in smaller appointments?

Secondly, to what degree is the itineracy used as an escape? From my own experience upon entering an appointment I know how I "hit the ground running." However, I must admit that a lot of my "running" had to do with ministries that proved my value as a minister. Things were undertaken that produced immediate and obvious sorts of results. Usually those issues and problems which require long-term and potentially risky attention are avoided. In this way, ministers never get around to dealing with the difficult and complex personal and organizational sins which afflict a congregation and its community.

Thirdly, especially in our highly mobile society, could not ministers be an example for what it means to claim a community as home and participate responsibly in its life? The itinerant minister is oriented to think just as most others who view themselves as in transition. "You are only going to reside (not 'live') in this place for a brief time, so why go to the trouble of getting to know it in a way that will thrust you into caring for it?" After three years in my present appointment, I am just now beginning to understand the "principalities and powers" at work in my community. More importantly, it has taken this long to make the necessary contacts and form the necessary alliances to respond to the community's needs. Could it be that today there is a real ministry in staying put in one's community or city long enough to be able to minister to that community as well as to one's church?

At this point, I note that my questions reflect a different reading of the demographic scene today. They also reflect a theology and theory of ministry that contain an imperative which carries the minister out of the church office and the church's membership into "the highways and hedges." Even if one were not motivated theologically to move outside the church, one would be motivated practically. Ministers cannot give pastoral care today without bumping up against the evils that exist in culture and society.

Granted, there are positive arguments for an itinerant ministry. But due to an understanding of ministry which includes more than preaching and more than pastoral care, there are arguments for a redefinition of what itineracy means for our day. It may be that we will be itinerant ministers not because we move a lot, but because where we stay, we stay as persons *in* that appointment but not *of* that appointment. We may claim it as home and become a responsible member of its community, but we never turn a deaf ear to God's call. We never lose sight of God's kingdom.

*June 1978*

# Future for the Ministry

## JIM L. WAITS

A return to the roots of Methodism in America provides perspective on ministry today—and on its future. The beginnings of Methodism reveal a simpler day, and a less complex church life than we know. It was a less ambiguous culture and a more authoritative ministry: a culture in which the minister was without peer, and the impact of his views and his proclamation of the Word was impressive in its effect.

One must not romanticize those early Methodist clerics, but it is the case that the minister of late 18th- and early 19th-century America was a central actor in life and society. His passion and his unmistakable commitment gave him a prominence we today only yearn for. The visit of the circuit rider was an event in that society, and the effect was inescapable. But the frontier is gone, and we have not adapted the effective practices of that day to the infinitely more complex society in which we now minister.

Today the church has a cluster of questions about the structure of ministry which it will be important to address, questions of itineracy, connectionalism, ordination, consultation, and the authority of the episcopacy. Equally important is an emerging set of questions about the character, identity, and standing of the minister in contemporary culture: questions which extend beyond Methodism to the very place and function of religion today.

Our attempts to deal with institutional structures of ministry in recent years have been less successful than our new approaches to the education and formation of the ministry. The consequence is that we have created expectations among ministers that our structures have been unable adequately to accommodate.

- The impact of a new image of the minister as professional (with certain rights and boundaries to his or her work) departs radically from older institutional understandings, and has required adjustments in the concept of what the minister is and does.

- The transition to a modern, technological society, increasingly secular and nonparochial, has undermined the authority and base of the minister in the community.

- New conversations about the nature of ordination and the new democratization of the church and its policy have had a more radical effect on the nature of ministry than we know.

All these factors have caused a diffusion of the identity and role of the minister, in contrast to that of the 18th and 19th centuries. The unhappy result is that in a time when society itself needs focus and a sense of coherence, its principal religious agency is ill-equipped to provide it. In the face of the steady erosion of religious authority and an indecisive image of ministry, we must urgently ask: What do we do within Methodism—institutionally and personally—to insure a forceful identity for church and religious life?

Here are some things we do *not* do: First, *we do not divide the orders of ordained ministry*, further diluting the image and authority of the clergy. While we must be understanding of the yearning of persons in diaconal ministries for a place in the professional life of the church, we must not sacrifice (in this society) a distinctive role and unmistakable authority for the ordained minister of the gospel.

Second, *we do not further weaken the historic itineracy system* by so insisting on our own ministerial prerogatives that we substitute a congregational method of pastoral deployment. Part of the historic genius of Methodism, still relevant today, is its capacity to assign traveling preachers to their places of service, and to appoint them where urgent need and the claims of the gospel require. To be sure, we must find new and sophisticated ways to adapt that historic system to the requirements of our day, but we will lose much, from a missional standpoint, if we allow that system fundamentally to be undermined.

Third, *we do not dilute the authority of the episcopacy* and settle for a middle-management executive whose work is merely funding and personnel administration. There is an abundance of roles—spiritual, educational, and priestly—that we must accord to our episcopal leadership if Methodism is to function prophetically in our world. And we must expect these leaders to be our most articulate advocates in shaping the religious values of our society.

Now let me speak of things we *can* do to strengthen the ministry and its impact on the society: First, *I believe in the itinerant system of Methodism*. But those of you who have lived with it closer than I, know that it is not above abuse and inefficiency. The church must find ways to incorporate into its system of ministerial deployment new and sophisticated methods of personnel management that are operative in the world today. It is time for us to undertake a careful analysis of the appointive system and its procedures, with a view to making it a more humane and missionally effective approach. We must seek methods to insure a genuine open itineracy, with the strategic assignment of those in specialized ministries. There is a world of technology and human-development theory that could assist us, yet we continue to act in appointive structures with the often outmoded means of an earlier day.

Second, *we must enhance the overall competency of the ministry*. Recent General Conferences have called attention to the importance of continuing education, but this emphasis has yet to achieve the status of a serious ongoing priority in our professional practice. The world in which we function is increasingly specialized and competent. If we are to influence that world for religious purpose, we must implement new and rigorous standards of continuing education and professional evaluation to equip us for that role. What we need in our day is a learned ministry, and that will not come by trading on simple piety and a winsome personality.

Third, *we must become more inclusive of lay ministries in the church.* While this does not warrant a newly ordained order as recommended in the Board of Higher Education and Ministry proposal, it does require that we give thoughtful place to lay professionals and openly invite all believers to the authentic ministry of the laity. We neglect an essential tradition of early Methodism when we assign the laity a subordinate place in the life and ministry of the church.

Fourth, *we must free the episcopal office for genuine superintendency of the life of the church:* for the overseeing of the quality of its ministry; for the work of mission, of teaching, and of evangelism; and for the advocacy of justice. We must find ways to give the leadership of the church prominence in our communities, so that these leaders become persuasive communicators and influential advocates for the ultimate values the church espouses for the world.

The purpose of all this is a ministry that is effectively deployed and enjoys high morale and commitment so that it may be about the task of evangelizing and changing this world. And this leads me to a final set of issues related to the future of the ministry: the identity and character of the minister. No revision of structures, no rearrangement of our procedures, no ecclesiology will substitute for the quality of person who bears the ministerial office. Surely it was the person and character of the circuit rider as well as the organizational adaptability of the church that accounted for the success of early Methodism.

We get so preoccupied with institutional things. But if we are truly about the evangelization of the world, we must find priority over our bureaucratic instincts. Covenant must find ascendency. In our life together, over and over we need to remind each other that we are charged with essential things. Religious professionals are often too enamored of the preoccupations of secular society. We fail to see the effectiveness of a clear religious identity and the yearning of hollow secularism for something to fill the void of contemporary life. Instead we are intimidated by the power and presumed satisfactions of the secular authorities. We need to believe more firmly that religion has a place in contemporary life! And the future of the ministry lies with those who have clarity in person and character about such matters.

One thing we surely claim from the tradition of the circuit riders and our forebears in early Methodism: an unashamed religious piety. We may think theirs an odd history to instruct us in this modern day—and few of us would want to go back to it. But as an early historian of Methodism wrote in 1867 of the itineracy: "Its roll is glorious with heroes and martyrs. What clerics since the apostolic age ever traveled and labored like these?

What public persons ever sacrificed equally with them the ordinary comforts of life?" (Abel Stevens, *A Compendious History of American Methodism*). What greater company could we find, what better tradition by which to measure faithfulness to our calling in our time?

*March 1984*

# Appendix: Contributors

Where different, a contributor's position at the time an article was originally published is listed first and then, if known, the author's current post. Unless otherwise noted, faculty positions are at Candler School of Theology, Emory University.

JOHN ERIK ANDURI was a first-year student and Danforth Fellow in the Graduate Division of Religion at Emory. He is currently a student at Iliff School of Theology in Denver.

ROBERTA CHESNUT BONDI is Associate Professor of Church History. She is the author of *Three Monophysite Christologies: Severus of Antioch, Philoxenus of Mabbug, and Jacob of Sarug.*

JOHN LYNN CARR is Associate Professor of Church Ministries and Director of Continuing Education. He is coauthor of *The Power and Light Company.*

ROY C. CLARK was Pastor of West End United Methodist Church in Nashville. In 1980 he was elected to the episcopacy and is currently Bishop of the Columbia, South Carolina, area.

FRED B. CRADDOCK is Franklin N. Parker Professor of Preaching and New Testament. His latest book is *Preaching,* and he is one of the authors of the *Preaching the New Common Lectionary* series.

A. BOB DIXON was Coordinator of Ministries at Peachtree Road United Methodist Church, Atlanta, and is now Diaconal Minister of Education at the First United Methodist Church of Thomasville, Georgia.

DAN W. DUNN was a doctoral student at Candler and Pastor of Stripling Chapel United Methodist Church in Carrollton, Georgia. He is currently Associate Pastor of LaGrange United Methodist Church, LaGrange, Georgia.

JAMES W. FOWLER is Professor of Theology and Human Development and Director of the Center for Faith Development. Among his books are *Becoming Adult, Becoming Christian* and *Faith and Human Development.*

CHARLES V. GERKIN is Professor of Pastoral Psychology. He is the author of *The Living Human Document: Re-visioning Pastoral Counseling in a Hermeneutical Mode* and *Crisis Experience in Modern Life.*

CHARLES D. HACKETT is Assistant Professor of Church Ministries and Director, Episcopal Studies Program. He edited the book *Women of the Word.*

NOLAN B. HARMON, retired Bishop of the United Methodist Church, is Visiting Professor of Practical Theology. Longtime Editor of Abingdon Press, he was on the editorial board for *The Interpreter's Bible* and has written an autobiography entitled *Ninety Years and Counting.*

JOHN H. HAYES is Professor of Old Testament. Editor of the Knox Preaching Guides, he is a coauthor of *A History of Israel and Judah* and of the series *Preaching the New Common Lectionary.*

RICHARD B. HAYS was a graduate student in New Testament at Emory. He is now Assistant Professor of New Testament at Yale Divinity School.

SUSAN HENRY-CROWE served Arrington United Methodist Church in Greenville, South Carolina, and was a Chaplain at Furman University. She is now Pastor of Shady Grove United Methodist Church in Irmo, South Carolina.

MANFRED HOFFMANN is Professor of Church History and Historical Theology. He is editor of the book *Martin Luther and the Modern Mind: Freedom, Conscience, Toleration, Rights.*

E. BROOKS HOLIFIELD is Charles Howard Candler Professor of American Church History. He is author of *A History of Pastoral Care in America: From Salvation to Self-Realization* and *The Gentlemen Theologians: American Theology in Southern Culture, 1795-1860.*

JAMES F. HOPEWELL was Professor of Religion and the Church and was Director of Candler's Rollins Center for Church Ministries at the time of his death in 1984.

RODNEY J. HUNTER is Associate Professor of Pastoral Theology. He is General Editor of the forthcoming *Dictionary of Pastoral Care and Counseling.*

THEODORE W. JENNINGS was Research Associate Professor of Systematic Theology. He is now teaching at Seminario Metodista de Mexico, Mexico City.

JOEL KAILING was a second-year student at Candler. He is currently Overseas Resource Teacher at the Trinity Foundation in Atlanta, serving an apppointment beyond the local church from the North Georgia Annual Conference of the United Methodist Church.

JAMES T. LANEY was Dean of the Candler School of Theology and is now President of Emory University and Professor of Christian Ethics. He is author of *Character and the Moral Life.*

ED LORING was Pastor of Clifton Presbyterian Church and on the faculty of Columbia Theological Seminary in Atlanta. He is a partner in the Open Door Community ministering to Atlanta's homeless.

ROBIN W. LOVIN was Instructor in Christian Ethics at Candler and is now Associate Professor of Ethics and Society at the Divinity School of the University of Chicago.

WALTER LOWE is Associate Professor of Systematic Theology. He is the author of *Evil and the Unconscious*.

WILLIAM MALLARD is Professor of Church History. He is a contributor to the recently published *Encyclopedia of Religion in the South*.

EDWARD JEREMY MILLER was Assistant Professor of Systematic Theology. Currently he is a foreign policy analyst and intelligence officer for the U.S. government.

G. MELTON MOBLEY was Assistant Professor of Sociology and Religion and Director of the Center for Religious Research. He is author of *An Educated Ministry Among Us: United Methodism's Investment in Theological Education*.

GEORGE E. MORRIS is Associate Professor in the Arthur J. Moore Chair of Evangelism and Director of the Institute for World Evangelism. He is editor of *Rethinking Congregational Development*.

ROMNEY M. MOSELEY is Assistant Professor of Theology and Human Development and Associate Director of the Center for Faith Development. He is author of "Faith Development and Conversion in the Catechumenate" in *Conversion and the Catechumenate*.

GEORGE E. OGLE was Professor of World Christianity. He currently serves as Program Director for the Department of Social and Economic Justice of the United Methodist Board of Church and Society in Washington, D.C.

DALE OWEN was a Chaplain for Emory University-affiliated hospitals. She is now Chief of Pastoral Services at the William S. Hall Psychiatric Institute in Columbia, South Carolina, serving in an appointment beyond the local church from the Mississippi Annual Conference of the United Methodist Church.

J. MICHAEL RIPSKI served Grace United Methodist Church in Memphis and now serves Northside United Methodist Church in Jackson, Tennessee.

THEODORE H. RUNYON is Professor of Systematic Theology and Director of Methodist and Ecumenical Studies. He is editor of *Sanctification and Liberation: Liberation Theologies in the Light of the Wesleyan Tradition.*

DON E. SALIERS is Professor of Theology and Worship. Among his publications are *Worship and Spirituality* and *From Hope to Joy: Services of Worship and Additional Resources for the Seasons of Advent and Christmas.*

LUTHER E. SMITH, JR., is Associate Professor of Church and Community. He is author of *Howard Thurman: The Mystic as Prophet.*

BARBARA BROWN TAYLOR (Editor) served as editor of *Ministry & Mission* from 1976 to 1981, during which time she was also Assistant to the Dean. She is now Assistant Rector at All Saints' Episcopal Church in Atlanta.

GORDON G. THOMPSON is Genevieve Sewell Shatford Professor of Homiletics. He is a frequent contributor to the *Wesleyan Christian Advocate.*

ARTHUR WAINWRIGHT is Associate Professor of New Testament. He is author of the book *Beyond Biblical Criticism.*

JIM L. WAITS is Dean and Asa Griggs Candler Professor of Divinity. He is the author of *Free to Believe.*

THEODORE R. WEBER is Professor of Social Ethics. He is the author of *Foreign Policy Is Your Business.*

TONI WHITE was Associate Pastor at Washington Street United Methodist Church in Columbia, South Carolina. She is currently on honorable location from the South Carolina Annual Conference.

REBECCA YOUNGBLOOD was Associate Pastor of St. John's United Methodist Church in Greenwood, Mississippi. Now she serves the Oxford-South Charge in Mississippi.

# Index: Scriptural References